The New Negro

The New Negro
Alain Locke

MINT EDITIONS

The New Negro was first published in 1925.

This edition published by Mint Editions 2021.

ISBN 9781513282398 | E-ISBN 9781513287416

Published by Mint Editions®

MINT
EDITIONS

minteditionbooks.com

Publishing Director: Jennifer Newens
Design & Production: Rachel Lopez Metzger
Project Manager: Micaela Clark
Typesetting: Westchester Publishing Services

This volume
is dedicated
to the
YOUNGER GENERATION

Contents

Foreword

This volume aims to document the New Negro culturally and socially,—to register the transformations of the inner and outer life of the Negro in America that have so significantly taken place in the last few years. There is ample evidence of a New Negro in the latest phases of social change and progress, but still more in the internal world of the Negro mind and spirit. Here in the very heart of the folk-spirit are the essential forces, and folk interpretation is truly vital and representative only in terms of these. Of all the voluminous literature on the Negro, so much is mere external view and commentary that we may warrantably say that nine-tenths of it is *about* the Negro rather than of him, so that it is the Negro problem rather than the Negro that is known and mooted in the general mind. We turn therefore in the other direction to the elements of truest social portraiture, and discover in the artistic self-expression of the Negro to-day a new figure on the national canvas and a new force in the foreground of affairs. Whoever wishes to see the Negro in his essential traits, in the full perspective of his achievement and possibilities, must seek the enlightenment of that self-portraiture which the present developments of Negro culture are offering. In these pages, without ignoring either the fact that there are important interactions between the national and the race life, or that the attitude of America toward the Negro is as important a factor as the attitude of the Negro toward America, we have nevertheless concentrated upon self-expression and the forces and motives of self-determination. So far as he is culturally articulate, we shall let the Negro speak for himself.

Yet the New Negro must be seen in the perspective of a New World, and especially of a New America. Europe seething in a dozen centers with emergent nationalities, Palestine full of a renascent Judaism—these are no more alive with the progressive forces of our era than the quickened centers of the lives of black folk. America seeking a new spiritual expansion and artistic maturity, trying to found an American literature, a national art, and national music implies a Negro-American culture seeking the same satisfactions and objectives. Separate as it may be in color and substance, the culture of the Negro is of a pattern integral with the times and with its cultural setting. The achievements of the present generation have eventually made this apparent. Liberal minds to-day cannot be asked to peer with sympathetic curiosity into the darkened Ghetto of a segregated race life. That was yesterday. Nor must they expect to find a mind and soul bizarre and alien as the mind of a savage, or even as naive and refreshing as the mind of the peasant or the child. That too was yesterday, and the day before. Now that there is cultural adolescence and the approach to maturity,—there has come a development that makes these phases of Negro life only an interesting and significant segment of the general American scene.

Until recently, except for occasional discoveries of isolated talent here and there, the main stream of this development has run in the special channels of "race literature" and "race journalism." Particularly as a literary movement, it has gradually gathered momentum in the effort and output of such progressive race periodicals as the *Crisis* under the editorship of Dr. Du Bois and more lately, through the quickening encouragement of Charles Johnson, in the brilliant pages of *Opportunity*, a Journal of Negro Life. But more and more the creative talents of the race have been taken up into the general journalistic, literary and artistic agencies, as the wide range of the acknowledgments of the material here collected will in itself be sufficient to demonstrate. Recently in a project of *The Survey Graphic*, whose Harlem Number of March, 1925, has been taken by kind permission as the nucleus of this book, the whole movement was presented as it is epitomized in the progressive Negro community of the American metropolis. Enlarging this stage we are now presenting the New Negro in a national and even international scope. Although there are few centers that can be pointed out approximating Harlem's significance, the full significance of that even is a racial awakening on a national and perhaps even a world scale.

That is why our comparison is taken with those nascent movements of folk-expression and self-determination which are playing a creative part in the world to-day. The galvanizing shocks and reactions of the last few years are making by subtle processes of internal reorganization a race out of its own disunited and apathetic elements. A race experience penetrated in this way invariably flowers. As in India, in China, in Egypt, Ireland, Russia, Bohemia, Palestine and Mexico, we are witnessing the resurgence of a people: it has aptly been said,—"For all who read the signs aright, such a dramatic flowering of a new race-spirit is taking place close at home—among American Negroes."

Negro life is not only establishing new contacts and founding new centers, it is finding a new soul. There is a fresh spiritual and cultural

ALAIN LOCKE

focusing. We have, as the heralding sign, an unusual outburst of creative expression. There is a renewed race-spirit that consciously and proudly sets itself apart. Justifiably then, we speak of the offerings of this book embodying these ripening forces as culled from the first fruits of the Negro Renaissance.

Alain Locke.
Washington, D. C.
November, 1925.

PART I
THE NEGRO RENAISSANCE

THE NEW NEGRO

The New Negro

Alain Locke

In the last decade something beyond the watch and guard of statistics has happened in the life of the American Negro and the three norns who have traditionally presided over the Negro problem have a changeling in their laps. The Sociologist, the Philanthropist, the Race-leader are not unaware of the New Negro, but they are at a loss to account for him. He simply cannot be swathed in their formulæ. For the younger generation is vibrant with a new psychology; the new spirit is awake in the masses, and under the very eyes of the professional observers is transforming what has been a perennial problem into the progressive phases of contemporary Negro life.

Could such a metamorphosis have taken place as suddenly as it has appeared to? The answer is no; not because the New Negro is not here, but because the Old Negro had long become more of a myth than a man. The Old Negro, we must remember, was a creature of moral debate and historical controversy. His has been a stock figure perpetuated as an historical fiction partly in innocent sentimentalism, partly in deliberate reactionism. The Negro himself has contributed his share to this through a sort of protective social mimicry forced upon him by the adverse circumstances of dependence. So for generations in the mind of America, the Negro has been more of a formula than a human being—a something to be argued about, condemned or defended, to be "kept down," or "in his place," or "helped up," to be worried with or worried over, harassed or patronized, a social bogey or a social burden. The thinking Negro even has been induced to share this same general attitude, to focus his attention on controversial issues, to see himself in the distorted perspective of a social problem. His shadow, so to speak, has been more real to him than his personality. Through having had to appeal from the unjust stereotypes of his oppressors and traducers to those of his liberators, friends and benefactors he has had to subscribe to the traditional positions from which his case has been viewed. Little true social or self-understanding has or could come from such a situation.

But while the minds of most of us, black and white, have thus burrowed in the trenches of the Civil War and Reconstruction, the actual march of development has simply flanked these positions, necessitating a sudden reorientation of view. We have not been watching in the right direction; set North and South on a sectional axis, we have not noticed the East till the sun has us blinking.

Recall how suddenly the Negro spirituals revealed themselves; suppressed for generations under the stereotypes of Wesleyan hymn harmony, secretive, half-ashamed, until the courage of being natural brought them out—and behold, there was folk-music. Similarly the mind of the Negro seems suddenly to have slipped from under the tyranny of social intimidation and to be shaking off the psychology of imitation and implied inferiority. By shedding the old chrysalis of the Negro problem we are achieving something like a spiritual emancipation. Until recently, lacking self-understanding, we have been almost as much of a problem to ourselves as we still are to others. But the decade that found us with a problem has left us with only a task. The multitude perhaps feels as yet only a strange relief and a new vague urge, but the thinking few know that in the reaction the vital inner grip of prejudice has been broken.

With this renewed self-respect and self-dependence, the life of the Negro community is bound to enter a new dynamic phase, the buoyancy from within compensating for whatever pressure there may be of conditions from without. The migrant masses, shifting from countryside to city, hurdle several generations of experience at a leap, but more important, the same thing happens spiritually in the life-attitudes and self-expression of the Young Negro, in his poetry, his art, his education and his new outlook, with the additional advantage, of course, of the poise and greater certainty of knowing what it is all about. From this comes the promise and warrant of a new leadership. As one of them has discerningly put it:

We have tomorrow
Bright before us
Like a flame.

Yesterday, a night-gone thing
A sun-down name.

And dawn today
Broad arch above the road we came.
We march!

ALAIN LOCKE

This is what, even more than any "most creditable record of fifty years of freedom," requires that the Negro of to-day be seen through other than the dusty spectacles of past controversy. The day of "aunties," "uncles" and "mammies" is equally gone. Uncle Tom and Sambo have passed on, and even the "Colonel" and "George" play barnstorm rôles from which they escape with relief when the public spotlight is off. The popular melodrama has about played itself out, and it is time to scrap the fictions, garret the bogeys and settle down to a realistic facing of facts.

First we must observe some of the changes which since the traditional-lines of opinion were drawn have rendered these quite obsolete. A main change has been, of course, that shifting of the Negro population which has made the Negro problem no longer exclusively or even predominantly Southern. Why should our minds remain sectionalized, when the problem itself no longer is? Then the trend of migration has not only been toward the North and the Central Midwest, but city-ward and to the great centers of industry—the problems of adjustment are new, practical, local and not peculiarly racial. Rather they are an integral part of the large industrial and social problems of our present-day democracy. And finally, with the Negro rapidly in process of class differentiation, if it ever was warrantable to regard and treat the Negro *en masse* it is becoming with every day less possible, more unjust and more ridiculous.

In the very process of being transplanted, the Negro is becoming transformed.

The tide of Negro migration, northward and city-ward, is not to be fully explained as a blind flood started by the demands of war industry coupled with the shutting off of foreign migration, or by the pressure of poor crops coupled with increased social terrorism in certain sections of the South and Southwest. Neither labor demand, the boll-weevil nor the Ku Klux Klan is a basic factor, however contributory any or all of them may have been. The wash and rush of this human tide on the beach line of the northern city centers is to be explained primarily in terms of a new vision of opportunity, of social and economic freedom, of a spirit to seize, even in the face of an extortionate and heavy toll, a chance for the improvement of conditions. With each successive wave of it, the movement of the Negro becomes more and more a mass movement toward the larger and the more democratic chance—in the Negro's case a deliberate flight not only from countryside to city, but from medieval America to modern.

Take Harlem as an instance of this. Here in Manhattan is not merely the largest Negro community in the world, but the first concentration in history of so many diverse elements of Negro life. It has attracted the African, the West Indian, the Negro American; has brought together the Negro of the North and the Negro of the South; the man from the city and the man from the town and village; the peasant, the student, the business man, the professional man, artist, poet, musician, adventurer and worker, preacher and criminal, exploiter and social outcast. Each group has come with its own separate motives and for its own special ends, but their greatest experience has been the finding of one another. Proscription and prejudice have thrown these dissimilar elements into a common area of contact and interaction. Within this area, race sympathy and unity have determined a further fusing of sentiment and experience. So what began in terms of segregation becomes more and more, as its elements mix and react, the laboratory of a great race-welding. Hitherto, it must be admitted that American Negroes have been a race more in name than in fact, or to be exact, more in sentiment than in experience. The chief bond between them has been that of a common condition rather than a common consciousness; a problem in common rather than a life in common. In Harlem, Negro life is seizing upon its first chances for group expression and self-determination. It is—or promises at least to be—a race capital. That is why our comparison is taken with those nascent centers of folk-expression and self-determination which are playing a creative part in the world to-day. Without pretense to their political significance. Harlem has the same rôle to play for the New Negro as Dublin has had for the New Ireland or Prague for the New Czechoslovakia.

Harlem, I grant you, isn't typical—but it is significant, it is prophetic. No sane observer, however sympathetic to the new trend, would contend that the great masses are articulate as yet, but they stir, they move, they are more than physically restless. The challenge of the new intellectuals among them is clear enough—the "race radicals" and realists who have broken with the old epoch of philanthropic guidance, sentimental appeal and protest. But are we after all only reading into the stirrings of a sleeping giant the dreams of an agitator? The answer is in the migrating peasant. It is the "man farthest down" who is most active in getting up. One of the most characteristic symptoms of this is the professional man himself migrating to recapture his constituency after a vain effort to maintain in some Southern corner what for years back seemed an established living and clientele. The clergyman following his errant flock, the physician or lawyer trailing his clients, supply the true clues. In a real sense it is the rank and file who are leading, and the leaders who are following. A transformed and transforming psychology permeates the masses.

When the racial leaders of twenty years ago spoke of developing race-pride and stimulating race-consciousness, and of the desirability of race solidarity, they could not in any accurate degree have anticipated the abrupt feeling that has surged up and now pervades the awakened centers. Some of the recognized Negro leaders and a powerful section of white opinion identified with "race work" of the older order have indeed attempted to discount this feeling as a "passing phase," an attack of "race nerves" so to speak, an "aftermath of the war," and the like. It has not abated, however, if we are to gauge by the present tone and temper of the Negro press, or by the shift in popular support from the officially recognized and orthodox spokesmen to those of the independent, popular, and often radical type who are unmistakable symptoms of a new order. It is a social disservice to blunt the fact that the Negro of the Northern centers has reached a stage where tutelage, even of the most interested and well-intentioned sort, must give place to new relationships, where positive self-direction must be reckoned with in ever increasing measure. The American mind must reckon with a fundamentally changed Negro.

The Negro too, for his part, has idols of the tribe to smash. If on the one hand the white man has erred in making the Negro appear to be that which would excuse or extenuate his treatment of him, the Negro, in turn, has too often unnecessarily excused himself because of the way he has been treated. The intelligent Negro of to-day is resolved not to make discrimination an extenuation for his shortcomings in performance, individual or collective; he is trying to hold himself at par, neither inflated by sentimental allowances nor depreciated by current social discounts. For this he must know himself and be known for precisely what he is, and for that reason he welcomes the new scientific rather than the old sentimental interest. Sentimental interest in the Negro has ebbed. We used to lament this as the falling off of our friends; now we rejoice and pray to be delivered both from self-pity and condescension. The mind of each racial group has had a bitter weaning, apathy or hatred on one side matching disillusionment or resentment on the other; but they face each other to-day with the possibility at least of entirely new mutual attitudes.

It does not follow that if the Negro were better known, he would be better liked or better treated. But mutual understanding is basic for any subsequent coöperation and adjustment. The effort toward this will at least have the effect of remedying in large part what has been the most unsatisfactory feature of our present stage of race relationships in America, namely the fact that the more intelligent and representative elements of the two race groups have at so many points got quite out of vital touch with one another.

The fiction is that the life of the races is separate, and increasingly so. The fact is that they have touched too closely at the unfavorable and too lightly at the favorable levels.

While inter-racial councils have sprung up in the South, drawing on forward elements of both races, in the Northern cities manual laborers may brush elbows in their everyday work, but the community and business leaders have experienced no such interplay or far too little of it. These segments must achieve contact or the race situation in America becomes desperate. Fortunately this is happening. There is a growing realization that in social effort the co-operative basis must supplant long-distance philanthropy, and that the only safeguard for mass relations in the future must be provided in the carefully maintained contacts of the enlightened minorities of both race groups. In the intellectual realm a renewed and keen curiosity is replacing the recent apathy; the Negro is being carefully studied, not just talked about and discussed. In art and letters, instead of being wholly caricatured, he is being seriously portrayed and painted.

To all of this the New Negro is keenly responsive as an augury of a new democracy in American culture. He is contributing his share to the new social understanding. But the desire to be understood would never in itself have been sufficient to have opened so completely the protectively closed portals of the thinking Negro's mind. There is still too much possibility of being snubbed or patronized for that. It was rather the necessity for fuller, truer self-expression, the realization of the unwisdom of allowing social discrimination to segregate him mentally, and a counter-attitude to cramp and fetter his own living—and so the "spite-wall" that the intellectuals built over the "color-line" has happily been taken down. Much of this reopening of intellectual contacts has centered in New York and has been richly fruitful not merely in the enlarging of personal experience, but in the definite enrichment of American art and letters and in the clarifying of our common vision of the social tasks ahead.

ALAIN LOCKE

The particular significance in the re-establishment of contact between the more advanced and representative classes is that it promises to offset some of the unfavorable reactions of the past, or at least to re-surface race contacts somewhat for the future. Subtly the conditions that are molding a New Negro are molding a new American attitude.

However, this new phase of things is delicate; it will call for less charity but more justice; less help, but infinitely closer understanding. This is indeed a critical stage of race relationships because of the likelihood, if the new temper is not understood, of engendering sharp group antagonism and a second crop of more calculated prejudice. In some quarters, it has already done so. Having weaned the Negro, public opinion cannot continue to paternalize. The Negro to-day is inevitably moving forward under the control largely of his own objectives. What are these objectives? Those of his outer life are happily already well and finally formulated, for they are none other than the ideals of American institutions and democracy. Those of his inner life are yet in process of formation, for the new psychology at present is more of a consensus of feeling than of opinion, of attitude rather than of program. Still some points seem to have crystallized.

Up to the present one may adequately describe the Negro's "inner objectives" as an attempt to repair a damaged group psychology and reshape a warped social perspective. Their realization has required a new mentality for the American Negro. And as it matures we begin to see its effects; at first, negative, iconoclastic, and then positive and constructive. In this new group psychology we note the lapse of sentimental appeal, then the development of a more positive self-respect and self-reliance; the repudiation of social dependence, and then the gradual recovery from hyper-sensitiveness and "touchy" nerves, the repudiation of the double standard of judgment with its special philanthropic allowances and then the sturdier desire for objective and scientific appraisal; and finally the rise from social disillusionment to race pride, from the sense of social debt to the responsibilities of social contribution and offsetting the necessary working and commonsense acceptance of restricted conditions, the belief in ultimate esteem and recognition. Therefore the Negro to-day wishes to be known for what he is, even in his faults and shortcomings, and scorns a craven and precarious survival at the price of seeming to be what he is not. He resents being spoken of as a social ward or minor, even by his own, and to being regarded a chronic patient for the sociological clinic, the sick man of American Democracy. For the same reasons, he himself is through with those social nostrums and panaceas, the so-called "solutions" of his "problem," with which he and the country have been so liberally dosed in the past. Religion freedom, education, money—in turn, he has ardently hoped for and peculiarly trusted these things; he still believes in them, but not in blind trust that they alone will solve his life-problem.

Each generation, however, will have its creed, and that of the present is the belief in the efficacy of collective effort, in race co-operation. This deep feeling of race is at present the mainspring of Negro life. It seems to be the outcome of the reaction to proscription and prejudice; an attempt, fairly successful on the whole, to convert a defensive into an offensive position, a handicap into an incentive. It is radical in tone, but not in purpose and only the most stupid forms of opposition, misunderstanding or persecution could make it otherwise. Of course, the thinking Negro has shifted a little toward the left with the world-trend, and there is an increasing group who affiliate with radical and liberal movements. But fundamentally for the present the Negro is radical on race matters, conservative on others, in other words, a "forced radical," a social protestant rather than a genuine radical. Yet under further pressure and injustice iconoclastic thought and motives will inevitably increase. Harlem's quixotic radicalisms call for their ounce of democracy to-day lest to-morrow they be beyond cure.

The Negro mind reaches out as yet to nothing but American wants, American ideas. But this forced attempt to build his Americanism on race values is a unique social experiment, and its ultimate success is impossible except through the fullest sharing of American culture and institutions. There should be no delusion about this. American nerves in sections unstrung with race hysteria are often fed the opiate that the trend of Negro advance is wholly separatist, and that the effect of its operation will be to encyst the Negro as a benign foreign body in the body politic. This cannot be—even if it were desirable. The racialism of the Negro is no limitation or reservation with respect to American life; it is only a constructive effort to build the obstructions in the stream of his progress into an efficient dam of social energy and power. Democracy itself is obstructed and stagnated to the extent that any of its channels are closed. Indeed they cannot be selectively closed. So the choice is not between one way for the Negro and another way for the rest, but between American institutions frustrated on the one hand and American ideals progressively fulfilled and realized on the other.

There is, of course, a warrantably comfortable feeling in being on the right side of the country's professed ideals. We realize that we cannot be undone without America's undoing. It is within the gamut of this attitude that the thinking Negro faces America, but with variations of mood that are if anything more significant than the attitude itself. Sometimes we have it taken with the defiant ironic challenge of McKay:

> *Mine is the future grinding down to-day*
> *Like a great landslip moving to the sea,*
> *Bearing its freight of debris far away*
> *Where the green hungry waters restlessly*
> *Heave mammoth pyramids, and break and roar*
> *Their eerie challenge to the crumbling shore.*

Sometimes, perhaps more frequently as yet, it is taken in the fervent and almost filial appeal and counsel of Weldon Johnson's:

> *O Southland, dear Southland!*
> *Then why do you still cling*
> *To an idle age and a musty page,*
> *To a dead and useless thing?*

But between defiance and appeal, midway almost between cynicism and hope, the prevailing mind stands in the mood of the same author's *To America*, an attitude of sober query and stoical challenge:

> *How would you have us, as we are?*
> *Or sinking 'neath the load we bear,*
> *Our eyes fixed forward on a star,*
> *Or gazing empty at despair?*
>
> *Rising or falling? Men or things?*
> *With dragging pace or footsteps fleet?*
> *Strong, willing sinews in your wings,*
> *Or tightening chains about your feet?*

More and more, however, an intelligent realization of the great discrepancy between the American social creed and the American social practice forces upon the Negro the taking of the moral advantage that is his. Only the steadying and sobering effect of a truly characteristic gentleness of spirit prevents the rapid rise of a definite cynicism and counter-hate and a defiant superiority feeling. Human as this reaction would be, the majority still deprecate its advent, and would gladly see it forestalled by the speedy amelioration of its causes. We wish our race pride to be a healthier, more positive achievement than a feeling based upon a realization of the shortcomings of others. But all paths toward the attainment of a sound social attitude have been difficult; only a relatively few enlightened minds have been able as the phrase puts it "to rise above" prejudice. The ordinary man has had until recently only a hard choice between the alternatives of supine and humiliating submission and stimulating but hurtful counter-prejudice. Fortunately from some inner, desperate resourcefulness has recently sprung up the simple expedient of fighting prejudice by mental passive resistance, in other words by trying to ignore it. For the few, this manna may perhaps be effective, but the masses cannot thrive upon it.

Fortunately there are constructive channels opening out into which the balked social feelings of the American Negro can flow freely.

Without them there would be much more pressure and danger than there is. These compensating interests are racial but in a new and enlarged way. One is the consciousness of acting as the advance-guard of the African peoples in their contact with Twentieth Century civilization; the other, the sense of a mission of rehabilitating the race in world esteem from that loss of prestige for which the fate and conditions of slavery have so largely been responsible. Harlem, as we shall see, is the center of both these movements; she is the home of the Negro's "Zionism." The pulse of the Negro world has begun to beat in Harlem. A Negro newspaper carrying news material in English, French and Spanish, gathered from all quarters of America, the West Indies and Africa has maintained itself in Harlem for over five years. Two important magazines, both edited from New York, maintain their news and circulation consistently on a cosmopolitan scale. Under American auspices and backing, three pan-African congresses have been held abroad for the discussion of common interests, colonial questions and the future co-operative development of Africa. In terms of the race question as a world problem, the Negro mind has leapt, so to speak, upon the parapets of prejudice and extended its cramped horizons. In so doing it has linked up with the growing group consciousness of the dark-peoples and is gradually learning their common interests. As one of our writers has recently put it: "It is imperative that we understand the white world in its relations to the non-white world." As with the Jew, persecution is making the Negro international.

As a world phenomenon this wider race consciousness is a different thing from the much asserted rising tide of color. Its inevitable causes are not of our making. The consequences are not necessarily damaging to the best interests of civilization. Whether it actually brings into being new Armadas of conflict or argosies of cultural exchange and enlightenment can only be decided by the attitude of the dominant races in an era of critical change. With the American Negro, his new internationalism is primarily an effort to recapture contact with the scattered peoples of African derivation. Garveyism may be a transient, if spectacular, phenomenon, but the possible rôle of the American Negro in the future development of Africa is one of the most constructive and universally helpful missions that any modern people can lay claim to.

Constructive participation in such causes cannot help giving the Negro valuable group incentives, as well as increased prestigé at home and abroad. Our greatest rehabilitation may possibly come through such channels, but for the present, more immediate hope rests in the revaluation by white and black alike of the Negro in terms of his artistic endowments and cultural contributions, past and prospective. It must be increasingly recognized that the Negro has already made very substantial contributions, not only in his folk-art, music especially, which has always found appreciation, but in larger, though humbler and less acknowledged ways. For generations the Negro has been the peasant matrix of that section of America which has most undervalued him, and here he has contributed not only materially in labor and in social patience, but spiritually as well. The South has unconsciously absorbed the gift of his folk-temperament. In less than half a generation it will be easier to recognize this, but the fact remains that a leaven of humor, sentiment, imagination and tropic nonchalance has gone into the making of the South from a humble, unacknowledged source. A second crop of the Negro's gifts promises still more largely. He now becomes a conscious contributor and lays aside the status of a beneficiary and ward for that of a collaborator and participant in American civilization. The great social gain in this is the releasing of our talented group from the arid fields of controversy and debate to the productive fields of creative expression. The especially cultural recognition they win should in turn prove the key to that revaluation of the Negro which must precede or accompany any considerable further betterment of race relationships. But whatever the general effect, the present generation will have added the motives of self-expression and spiritual development to the old and still unfinished task of making material headway and progress. No one who understandingly faces the situation with its substantial accomplishment or views the new scene with its still more abundant promise can be entirely without hope. And certainly, if in our lifetime the Negro should not be able to celebrate his full initiation into American democracy, he can at least, on the warrant of these things, celebrate the attainment of a significant and satisfying new phase of group development, and with it a spiritual Coming of Age.

NEGRO ART AND AMERICA

Negro Art and America

Albert C. Barnes

That there should have developed a distinctively Negro art in America was natural and inevitable. A primitive race, transported into an Anglo-Saxon environment and held in subjection to that fundamentally alien influence, was bound to undergo the soul-stirring experiences which always find their expression in great art. The contributions of the American Negro to art are representative because they come from the hearts of the masses of a people held together by like yearnings and stirred by the same causes. It is a sound art because it comes from a primitive nature upon which a white man's education has never been harnessed. It is a great art because it embodies the Negroes' individual traits and reflects their suffering, aspirations and joys during a long period of acute oppression and distress.

The most important element to be considered is the psychological complexion of the Negro as he inherited it from his primitive ancestors and which he maintains to this day. The outstanding characteristics are his tremendous emotional endowment, his luxuriant and free imagination and a truly great power of individual expression. He has in superlative measure that fire and light which, coming from within, bathes his whole world, colors his images and impels him to expression. The Negro is a poet by birth. In the masses, that poetry expresses itself in religion which acquires a distinction by extraordinary fervor, by simple and picturesque rituals and by a surrender to emotion so complete that ecstasy, amounting to automatisms, is the rule when he worships in groups. The outburst may be started by any unlettered person provided with the average Negro's normal endowment of eloquence and vivid imagery. It begins with a song or a wail which spreads like fire and soon becomes a spectacle of a harmony of rhythmic movement and rhythmic sound unequalled in the ceremonies of any other race. Poetry is religion brought down to earth and it is of the essence of the Negro soul. He carries it with him always and everywhere; he lives it in the field, the shop, the factory. His daily habits of thought, speech and movement are flavored with the picturesque, the rhythmic, the euphonious.

The white man in the mass cannot compete with the Negro in spiritual endowment. Many centuries of civilization have attenuated his original gifts and have made his mind dominate his spirit. He has wandered too far from the elementary human needs and their easy means of natural satisfaction. The deep and satisfying harmony which the soul requires no longer arises from the incidents of daily life. The requirements for practical efficiency in a world alien to his spirit have worn thin his religion and devitalized his art. His art and his life are no longer one and the same as they were in primitive man. Art has become exotic, a thing apart, an indulgence, a something to be possessed. When art is real and vital it effects the harmony between ourselves and nature which means happiness. Modern life has forced art into being a mere adherent upon the practical affairs of life which offer it no sustenance. The result has been that hopeless confusion of values which mistakes sentimentalism and irrational day-dreaming for art.

The Negro has kept nearer to the ideal of man's harmony with nature and that, his blessing, has made him a vagrant in our arid, practical American life. But his art is so deeply rooted in his nature that it has thrived in a foreign soil where the traditions and practices tend to stamp out and starve out both the plant and its flowers. It has lived because it was an achievement, not an indulgence. It has been his happiness through that mere self-expression which is its own immediate and rich reward. Its power converted adverse material conditions into nutriment for his soul and it made a new world in which his soul has been free. Adversity has always been his lot but he converted it into a thing of beauty in his songs. When he was the abject, down-trodden slave, he burst forth into songs which constitute America's only great music—the spirituals. These wild chants are the natural, naive, untutored, spontaneous utterance of the suffering, yearning, prayerful human soul. In their mighty roll there is a nobility truly superb. Idea and emotion are fused in an art which ranks with the Psalms and the songs of Zion in their compelling, universal appearl.

The emancipation of the Negro slave in America gave him only a nominal freedom. Like all other human beings he is a creature of habits which tie him to his past; equally set are his white brothers' habits toward him. The relationship of master and slave has changed but little in the sixty years of freedom. He is still a slave to the ignorance, the prejudice, the cruelty which were the fate of his forefathers. To-day he has not yet found a place of equality in the social, educational or industrial world of the white man. But he has the same singing soul as the ancestors who created the single form of great art which America can claim as her own.

ALAIN LOCKE

Of the tremendous growth and prosperity achieved by America since emancipation day, the Negro has had scarcely a pittance. The changed times did, however, give him an opportunity to develop and strengthen the native, indomitable courage and the keen powers of mind which were not suspected during the days of slavery. The character of his song changed under the new civilization and his mental and moral stature now stands measurement with those of the white man of equal educational and civilizing opportunities. That growth he owes chiefly to his own efforts; the attendant strife has left unspoiled his native gift of song. We have in his poetry and music a true, infallible record of what the struggle has meant to his inner life. It is art of which America can well be proud.

The renascence of Negro art is one of the events of our age which no seeker for beauty can afford to overlook. It is as characteristically Negro as are the primitive African sculptures. As art forms, each bears comparison with the great art expressions of any race or civilization. In both ancient and modern Negro art we find a faithful expression of a people and of an epoch in the world's evolution.

The Negro renascence dates from about 1895 when two men, Paul Laurence Dunbar and Booker T. Washington, began to attract the world's attention. Dunbar was a poet, Washington an educator in the practical business of life. They lived in widely-distant parts of America, each working independently of the other. The leavening power of each upon the Negro spirit was tremendous; each fitted into and reinforced the other; their combined influences brought to birth a new epoch for the American Negro. Washington showed that by a new kind of education the Negro could attain to an economic condition that enables him to preserve his identity, free his soul and make himself an important factor in American life. Dunbar revealed the virgin field which the Negro's own talents and conditions of life offered for creating new forms of beauty. The race became self-conscious and pride of race supplanted the bitter wail of unjust persecution. The Negro saw and followed the path that was to lead him out of the wilderness and back to his own heritage through the means of his own endowments. Many new poets were discovered, while education had a tremendous quickening. The yield to art was a new expression of Negro genius in a form of poetry which connoisseurs place in the class reserved for the disciplined art of all races. Intellect and culture of a high order became the goals for which they fought, and with a marked degree of success.

Only through bitter and long travail has Negro poetry attained to its present high level as an art form and the struggle has produced much writing which, while less perfect in form, is no less important as poetry. We find nursery rhymes, dances, love-songs, pæans of joy, lamentations, all revealing unerringly the spirit of the race in its varied contacts with life. There has grown a fine tradition which is fundamentally Negro in character. Every phase of that growth in alien surroundings is marked with reflections of the multitudinous vicissitudes that cumbered the path from slavery to culture. Each record is loaded with feeling, powerfully expressed in uniquely Negro forms. The old chants, known as spirituals, were pure soul, their sadness untouched by vindictiveness. After the release from slavery, bitterness crept into their songs. Later, as times changed, we find self-assertion, lofty aspirations and only a scattered cry for vengeance. As he grew in culture, there came expressions of the deep consolation of resignation which is born of the wisdom that the Negro race is its own, all-sufficient justification. Naturally, sadness is the note most often struck; but the frequently-expressed joy, blithesome, carefree, overflowing joy, reveals what an enviable creature the Negro is in his happy moods. No less evident is that native understanding and wisdom which—from the homely and crude expressions of their slaves, to the scholarly and cultured contributions of to-day—we know go with the Negro's endowment. The black scholar, seer, sage, prophet sings his message; that explains why the Negro tradition is so rich and is so firmly implanted in the soul of the race.

The Negro tradition has been slow in forming but it rests upon the firmest of foundations. Their great men and women of the past—Wheatley, Sojourner Truth, Douglass, Dunbar, Washington—have each laid a personal and imperishable stone in that foundation. A host of living Negroes, better educated and unalterably faithful to their race, are still building, and each with some human value which is an added guarantee that the tradition will be strengthened and made serviceable for the new era that is sure to come when more of the principles of humanity and rationality become the white man's guides. Many living Negroes—Du Bois, Cotter, Grimke, Braithwaite, Burleigh, the Johnsons, McKay, Dett, Locke, Hayes, and many others—know the Negro soul and lead it to richer fields by their own ideals of culture, art and citizenship. It is a healthy development, free from that pseudo-culture which stifles the soul and misses rational happiness as the goal of human life. Through the compelling powers of his poetry and music the American Negro is revealing to the rest of the world the essential oneness of all human beings.

The cultured white race owes to the soul-expressions of its black brother too many moments of happiness not to acknowledge ungrudgingly the significant fact that what the Negro has achieved is of tremendous civilizing value. We see that in certain qualities of soul essential to happiness our own endowment is comparatively deficient. We have to acknowledge not only that our civilization has done practically nothing to help the Negro create his art but that our unjust oppression has been powerless to prevent the black man from realizing in a rich measure the expressions of his own rare gifts. We have begun to imagine that a better education and a greater social and economic equality for the Negro might produce something of true importance for a richer and fuller American life. The unlettered black singers have taught us to live music that rakes our souls and gives us moments of exquisite joy. The later Negro has made us feel the majesty of Nature, the ineffable peace of the woods and the great open spaces. He has shown us that the events of our every-day American life contain for him a poetry, rhythm and charm which we ourselves had never discovered. Through him we have seen the pathos, comedy, affection, joy of his own daily life, unified into humorous dialect verse or perfected sonnet that is a work of exquisite art. He has taught us to respect the sheer manly greatness of the fiber which has kept his inward light burning with an effulgence that shines through the darkness in which we have tried to keep him. All these visions, and more, he has revealed to us. His insight into realities has been given to us in vivid images loaded with poignancy and passion. His message has been lyrical, rhythmic, colorful. In short, the elements of beauty he has controlled to the ends of art.

This mystic whom we have treated as a vagrant has proved his possession of a power to create out of his own soul and our own America, moving beauty of an individual character whose existence we never knew. We are beginning to recognize that what the Negro singers and sages have said is only what the ordinary Negro feels and thinks, in his own measure, every day of his life. We have paid more attention to that everyday Negro and have been surprised to learn that nearly all of his activities are shot through and through with music and poetry. When we take to heart the obvious fact that what our prosaic civilization needs most is precisely the poetry which the average Negro actually lives, it is incredible that we should not offer the consideration which we have consistently denied to him. If at that time, he is the simple, ingenuous, forgiving, good-natured, wise and obliging person that he has been in the past, he may consent to form a working alliance with us for the development of a richer American civilization to which he will contribute his full share.

THE NEGRO IN AMERICAN LITERATURE

The Negro in American Literature

William Stanley Braithwaite

True to his origin on this continent, the Negro was projected into literature by an over-mastering and exploiting hand. In the generations that he has been so voluminously written and talked about he has been accorded as little artistic justice as social justice. Ante-bellum literature imposed the distortions of moralistic controversy and made the Negro a wax-figure of the market place: post-bellum literature retaliated with the condescending reactions of sentiment and caricature, and made the Negro a *genre* stereotype. Sustained, serious or deep study of Negro life and character has thus been entirely below the horizons of our national art. Only gradually through the dull purgatory of the Age of Discussion, has Negro life eventually issued forth to an Age of Expression.

Perhaps I ought to qualify this last statement that the Negro was *in* American literature generations before he was part of it as a creator. From his very beginning in this country the Negro has been, without the formal recognition of literature and art, creative. During more than two centuries of an enslaved peasantry, the race has been giving evidence, in song and story lore, of an artistic temperament and psychology precious for itself as well as for its potential use and promise in the sophisticated forms of cultural expression. Expressing itself with poignancy and a symbolic imagery unsurpassed, indeed, often unmatched, by any folk-group, the race in servitude was at the same time the finest national expression of emotion and imagination and the most precious mass of raw material for literature America was producing. Quoting these stanzas of James Weldon Johnson's *O Black and Unknown Bards*, I want you to catch the real point of its assertion of the Negro's way into domain of art:

> *O black and unknown bards of long ago,*
> *How came your lips to touch the sacred fire?*
> *How, in your darkness, did you come to know*
> *The power and beauty of the minstrel's lyre?*
> *Who first from midst his bonds lifted his eyes?*
> *Who first from out the still watch, lone and long,*

Feeling the ancient faith of prophets rise
Within his dark-kept soul, burst into song?

There is a wide, wide wonder in it all,
That from degraded rest and servile toil
The fiery spirit of the seer should call
These simple children of the sun and soil.
O black slave singers, gone, forgot, unfamed,
You—you, alone, of all the long, long line
Of those who've sung untaught, unknown, unnamed,
Have stretched out upward, seeking the divine.

How misdirected was the American imagination, how blinded by the dust of controversy and the pall of social hatred and oppression, not to have found it irresistibly urgent to make literary use of the imagination and emotion it possessed in such abundance.

CONTROVERSY AND MORAL APPEAL GAVE us *Uncle Tom's Cabin*,—the first conspicuous example of the Negro as a subject for literary treatment. Published in 1852, it dominated in mood and attitude the American literature of a whole generation; until the body of Reconstruction literature with its quite different attitude came into vogue. Here was sentimentalized sympathy for a down-trodden race, but one in which was projected a character, in Uncle Tom himself, which has been unequalled in its hold upon the popular imagination to this day. But the moral gain and historical effect of Uncle Tom have been an artistic loss and setback. The treatment of Negro life and character, overlaid with these forceful stereotypes, could not develop into artistically satisfactory portraiture.

Just as in the anti-slavery period, it had been impaled upon the dilemmas of controversy, Negro life with the Reconstruction, became involved in the paradoxes of social prejudice. Between the Civil War and the end of the century the subject of the Negro in literature is one that will some day inspire the literary historian with a magnificent theme. It will be magnificent not because there is any sharp emergence of character or incidents, but because of the immense paradox of racial life which came up thunderingly against the principles and doctrines of democracy, and put them to the severest test that they had known. It was a period when, in literature, Negro life was a shuttlecock between the two extremes of humor and pathos. The Negro was free, and was not free. The writers who dealt with him for the most part refused to see more than skin-deep,—the grin, the grimaces and the picturesque externalities. Occasionally there was some penetration into the heart and flesh of Negro characters, but to see more than the humble happy peasant would have been to flout the fixed ideas and conventions of an entire generation. For more than artistic reasons, indeed against them, these writers refused to see the tragedy of the Negro and capitalized his comedy. The social conscience had as much need for this comic mask as the Negro. However, if any of the writers of the period had possessed gifts of genius of the first caliber, they would have penetrated this deceptive exterior of Negro life, sounded the depths of tragedy in it, and produced a masterpiece.

American literature still feels the hold of this tradition and its indulgent sentimentalities. Irwin Russell was the first to discover the happy, care-free, humorous Negro. He became a fad. It must be sharply called to attention that the tradition of the ante-bellum Negro is a post-bellum product, stranger in truth than in fiction. Contemporary realism in American fiction has not only recorded his passing, but has thrown serious doubts upon his ever having been a very genuine and representative view of Negro life and character. At best this school of Reconstruction fiction represents the romanticized high-lights of a régime that as a whole was a dark, tragic canvas. At most, it presents a Negro true to type for less than two generations. Thomas Nelson Page, kindly perhaps, but with a distant view and a purely local imagination did little more than paint the conditions and attitudes of the period contemporary with his own manhood, the restitution of the over-lordship of the defeated slave owners in the Eighties. George W. Cable did little more than idealize the aristocratic tradition of the Old South with the Negro as a literary foil. The effects, though not the motives of their work, have been sinister. The "Uncle" and the "Mammy" traditions, unobjectionable as they are in the setting of their day and generation, and in the atmosphere of sentimental humor, can never stand as the great fiction of their theme and subject: the great period novel of the South has yet to be written. Moreover, these type pictures have degenerated into reactionary social fetishes, and from that descended into libelous artistic caricature of the Negro; which has hampered art quite as much as it has embarrassed the Negro.

Of all of the American writers of this period, Joel Chandler Harris has made the most permanent contribution in dealing with the Negro. There is in his work both a deepening of interest and technique. Here at least we have something approaching true portraiture. But much as we admire this lovable personality, we are forced to say that in the Uncle Remus stories the race was its own artist, lacking only in its illiteracy the power to record its speech. In the perspective of time and fair judgment the credit will be divided, and Joel Chandler Harris regarded as a sort of providentially provided amanuensis for preserving the folk tales and legends of a race. The three writers I have mentioned do not by any means exhaust the list of writers who put the Negro into literature during the last half of the nineteenth century. Mr. Howells added a shadowy note to his social record of American life with *An Imperative Duty* and prophesied the Fiction of the Color Line." But his moral scruples—the persistent artistic vice in all his novels—prevented him from consummating a just union between his heroine with a touch of Negro blood and his hero. It is useless to consider any others, because there were none who succeeded in creating either a great story or a great character out of Negro life. Two writers of importance I am reserving for discussion in the group of Negro writers I shall consider presently. One ought perhaps to say in justice to the writers I have mentioned that their nonsuccess was more largely due to the limitations of their social view than of their technical resources. As white Americans of their day, it was incompatible with their conception of the inequalities between the races to glorify the Negro into the serious and leading position of hero or heroine in fiction. Only one man that I recall, had the moral and artistic courage to do this, and he was Stephen Crane in a short story called *The Monster*. But Stephen Crane was a genius, and therefore could not besmirch the integrity of an artist.

With Thomas Dixon, of *The Leopard's Spots*, we reach a distinct stage in the treatment of the Negro in fiction. The portraiture here descends from caricature to libel. A little later with the vogue of the "darkey-story," and its devotees from Kemble and McAllister to Octavus Roy Cohen, sentimental comedy in the portrayal of the Negro similarly degenerated to blatant but diverting farce. Before the rise of a new attitude, these represented the bottom reaction, both in artistic and social attitude. Reconstruction fiction was passing out in a flood of propagandist melodrama and ridicule. One hesitates to lift this material up to the plane of literature even for the purposes of comparison. But the gradual climb of the new literature of the Negro must be traced and measured from these two nadir points. Following *The Leopard's Spots*, it was only occasionally during the next twenty years that the Negro was sincerely treated in fiction by white authors. There were two or three tentative efforts to dramatize him. Sheldon's *The Nigger*, was the one notable early effort. And in fiction Paul Kester's *His Own Country* is, from a purely literary point of view, its outstanding performance. This type of novel failed, however, to awaken any general interest. This failure was due to the illogical treatment of the human situations presented. However indifferent and negative it may seem, there is the latent desire in most readers to have honesty of purpose and a full vision in the artist: and especially in fiction, a situation handled with gloves can never be effectively handled.

The first hint that the American artist was looking at this subject with full vision was in Torrence's *Granny Maumee*. It was drama, conceived and executed for performance on the stage, and therefore had a restricted appeal. But even here the artist was concerned with the primitive instincts of the Race, and, though faithful and honest in his portrayal, the note was still low in the scale of racial life. It was only a short time, however, before a distinctly new development took place in the treatment of Negro life by white authors. This new class of work honestly strove to endow the Negro life with purely æsthetic vision and values, but with one or two exceptions, still stuck to the peasant level of race experience, and gave, unwittingly, greater currency to the popular notion of the Negro as an inferior, superstitious, half-ignorant and servile class of folk. Where they did in a few isolated instances recognize an ambitious impulse, it was generally defeated in the course of the story.

Perhaps this is inevitable with an alien approach, however well-intentioned. The folk lore attitude discovers only the lowly and the naïve: the sociological attitude finds the problem first and the human beings after, if at all. But American art in a reawakened seriousness, and using the technique of the new realism, is gradually penetrating Negro life to the core. George Madden Martin, with her pretentious foreword to a group of short stories, *The Children in the Mist*,—and this is an extraordinary volume in many ways—quite seriously tried, as a Southern woman, to elevate the Negro to a higher plane of fictional treatment and interest. In succession, followed Mary White Ovington's *The Shadow*, in which Miss Ovington daringly created the kinship of brother and sister between a black boy and white girl, had it brought to disaster by prejudice, out of which the white girl rose to a sacrifice no white girl in a novel had hitherto accepted and endured; then Shands' *White and Black,* as honest a piece of fiction with the Negro as a subject as was ever produced by a Southern pen—and in this story, also, the hero, Robinson, making an equally glorious sacrifice for truth and justice, as Miss Ovington's heroine; Clement Wood's *Nigger,* with defects of treatment, but admirable in purpose, wasted though, I think, in the effort to prove its thesis on wholly illogical material; and lastly, T. S. Stribling's *Birthright,* more significant than any of these other books, in fact, the most significant novel on the Negro written by a white American, and this in spite of its totally false conception of the character of Peter Siner.

Mr. Stribling's book broke ground for a white author in giving us a Negro hero and heroine. There is an obvious attempt to see objectively. But the formula of the Nineties,—atavistic race-heredity, still survives and protrudes through the flesh and blood of the characters. Using Peter as a symbol of the man tragically linked by blood to one world and by training and thought to another, Stribling portrays a tragic struggle against the pull of lowly origins and sordid environment. We do not deny this element of tragedy in Negro life—and Mr. Stribling, it must also be remembered, presents, too, a severe indictment in his painting of the Southern conditions which brought about the disintegration of his hero's dreams and ideals. But the preoccupation, almost obsession of otherwise strong and artistic work like O'Neill's *Emperor Jones, All God's Chillum Got Wings,* and Culbertson's *Goat Alley* with this same theme and doubtful formula of hereditary cultural reversion suggests that, in spite of all good intentions, the true presental of the real tragedy of Negro life is a task still left for Negro writers to perform. This is especially true for those phases of culturally representative race life that as yet have scarcely at all found treatment by white American authors. In corroborating this, let me quote a passage from a recent number of the *Independent,* on the Negro novelist which reads:

"During the past few years stories about Negroes have been extremely popular. A magazine without a Negro story is hardly living up to its opportunities. But almost every one of these stories is written in a tone of condescension. The artists have caught the contagion from the writers, and the illustrations are ninety-nine times out of a hundred purely slapstick stuff. Stories and pictures make a Roman holiday for the millions who are convinced that the most important fact about the Negro is that his skin is black. Many of these writers live in the South or are from the South. Presumably they are well acquainted with the Negro, but it is a remarkable fact that they almost never tell us anything vital about him, about the real human being in the black man's skin. Their most frequent method is to laugh at the colored man and woman, to catalogue their idiosyncrasies, their departure from the norm, that is, from the ways of the whites. There seems to be no suspicion in the minds of the writers that there may be a fascinating thought life in the minds of the Negroes, whether of the cultivated or of the most ignorant type. Always the Negro is interpreted in the terms of the white man. White-man psychology is applied and it is no wonder that the result often shows the Negro in a ludicrous light."

I shall have to run back over the years to where I began to survey the achievement of Negro authorship. The Negro as a creator in American literature is of comparatively recent importance. All that was accomplished between Phyllis Wheatley and Paul Laurence Dunbar, considered by critical standards, is negligible, and of historical interest only. Historically it is a great tribute to the race to have produced in Phyllis Wheatley not only the slave poetess in eighteenth century Colonial America, but to know she was as good, if not a better, poetess than Ann Bradstreet whom literary historians give the honor of being the first person of her sex to win fame as a poet in America.

Negro authorship may, for clearer statement, be classified into three main activities: Poetry, Fiction, and the Essay, with an occasional excursion into other branches. In the drama, until very recently, practically nothing worth while has been achieved, with the exception of Angelina Grimke's *Rachel*, notable for its sombre craftsmanship. Biography has given us a notable life story, told by himself, of Booker T. Washington. Frederick Douglass's story of his life is eloquent as a human document, but not in the graces of narration and psychologic portraiture, which has definitely put this form of literature in the domain of the fine arts. Indeed, we may well believe that the efforts of controversy, of the huge amount of discursive and polemical articles dealing chiefly with the race problem, that have been necessary in breaking and clearing the impeded pathway of racial progress, have absorbed and in a way dissipated the literary energy of many able Negro writers.

Let us survey briefly the advance of the Negro in poetry. Behind Dunbar, there is nothing that can stand the critical test. We shall always have a sentimental and historical interest in those forlorn and pathetic figures who cried in the wilderness of their ignorance and oppression. With Dunbar we have our first authentic lyric utterance, an utterance more authentic, I should say, for its faithful rendition of Negro life and character than for any rare or subtle artistry of expression. When Mr. Howells, in his famous introduction to the *Lyrics of Lowly Life,* remarked that Dunbar was the first black man to express the life of his people lyrically, he summed up Dunbar's achievement and transported him to a place beside the peasant poet of Scotland, not for his art, but precisely because he made a people articulate in verse.

The two chief qualities in Dunbar's work are, however, pathos and humor, and in these he expresses that dilemma of soul that characterized the race between the Civil War and the end of the nineteenth century. The poetry of Dunbar is true to the life of the Negro and expresses characteristically what he felt and knew to be the temper and condition of his people. But its moods reflect chiefly those of the era of Reconstruction and just a little beyond,—the limited experience of a transitional period, the rather helpless and subservient era of testing freedom and reaching out through the difficulties of life to the emotional compensations of laughter and tears. It is the poetry of the happy peasant and the plaintive minstrel. Occasionally, as in the sonnet to *Robert Gould Shaw* and the *Ode to Ethiopia* there broke through Dunbar, as through the crevices of his spirit, a burning and brooding aspiration, an awakening and virile consciousness of race. But for the most part, his dreams were anchored to the minor whimsies; his deepest poetic inspiration was sentiment. He expressed a folk temperament, but not a race soul. Dunbar was the end of a régime, and not the beginning of a tradition, as so many careless critics, both white and colored, seem to think.

After Dunbar many versifiers appeared,—all largely dominated by his successful dialect work. I cannot parade them here for tag or comment, except to say that few have equalled Dunbar in this vein of expression, and none have deepened it as an expression of Negro life. Dunbar himself had clear notions of its limitations;—to a friend in a letter from London, March 15, 1897, he says: "I see now very clearly that Mr. Howells has done me irrevocable harm in the dictum he laid down regarding my dialect verse." Not until James W. Johnson published his *Fiftieth Anniversary Ode* on the emancipation in 1913, did a poet of the race disengage himself from the background of mediocrity into which the imitation of Dunbar snared Negro poetry. Mr. Johnson's work is based upon a broader contemplation of life, life that is not wholly confined within any racial experience, but through the racial he made articulate that universality of the emotions felt by all mankind. His verse possesses a vigor which definitely breaks away from the brooding minor undercurrents of feeling which have previously characterized the verse of Negro poets. Mr. Johnson brought, indeed, the first intellectual substance to the content of our poetry, and a craftsmanship which, less spontaneous than that of Dunbar's, was more balanced and precise.

Here a new literary generation begins; poetry that is racial in substance, but with the universal note, and consciously the background of the full heritage of English poetry. With each new figure somehow the gamut broadens and the technical control improves. The brilliant succession and maturing powers of Fenton Johnson, Leslie Pinckney Hill, Everett Hawkins, Lucien Watkins, Charles Bertram Johnson, Joseph Cotter, Georgia Douglas Johnson, Roscoe Jameson and Anne Spencer bring us at last to Claude McKay and the poets of the younger generation and a poetry of the masterful accent and high distinction. Too significantly for mere coincidence, it was the stirring year of 1917 that heard the first real masterful accent in Negro poetry. In the September *Crisis* of that year, Roscoe Jameson's *Negro Soldiers* appeared:

> *These truly are the Brave,*
> *These men who cast aside*
> *Old memories to walk the blood-stained pave*
> *Of Sacrifice, joining the solemn tide*
> *That moves away, to suffer and to die*
> *For Freedom—when their own is yet denied!*
> *O Pride! A Prejudice! When they pass by*
> *Hail them, the Brave, for you now crucified.*

The very next month, under the pen name of Eli Edwards, Claude McKay printed in *The Seven Arts*,

The Harlem Dancer

Applauding youths laughed with young prostitutes
And watched her perfect, half-clothed body sway;
Her voice was like the sound of blended flutes
Blown by black players upon a picnic day.
She sang and danced on gracefully and calm,
The light gauze hanging loose about her form;
To me she seemed a proudly-swaying palm
Grown lovelier for passing through a storm.

Upon her swarthy neck black, shiny curls
Profusely fell; and, tossing coins in praise
The wine-flushed, bold-eyed boys, and even the girls
Devoured her with their eager, passionate gaze;
But, looking at her falsely-smiling face
I knew her self was not in that strange place.

With Georgia Johnson, Anne Spencer and Angelina Grimke, the Negro woman poet significantly appears. Mrs. Johnson especially has voiced in true poetic spirit the lyric cry of Negro womanhood. In spite of lapses into the sentimental and the platitudinous, she has an authentic gift. Anne Spencer, more sophisticated, more cryptic but also more universal, reveals quite another aspect of poetic genius. Indeed, it is interesting to notice how to-day Negro poets waver between the racial and the universal notes.

Claude McKay, the poet who leads his generation, is a genius meshed in this dilemma. His work is caught between the currents of the poetry of protest and the poetry of expression; he is in turn the violent and strident propagandist, using his poetic gifts to clothe arrogant and defiant thoughts, and then the pure lyric dreamer, contemplating life and nature with a wistful sympathetic passion. When the mood of *Spring* in *New Hampshire* or the sonnet *The Harlem Dancer* possesses him, he is full of that spirit and power of beauty that flowers above any and all men's harming. How different in spite of the admirable spirit of courage and defiance, are his poems of which the sonnet *If We Must Die* is a typical example. Negro poetic expression hovers for the moment, pardonably perhaps, over the race problem, but its highest allegiance is to Poetry—it must soar.

LET ME REFER BRIEFLY TO a type of literature in which there have been many pens, but a single mind. Dr. Du Bois is the most variously gifted writer which the race has produced. Poet, novelist, sociologist, historian and essayist, he has produced books in all these fields with the exception, I believe, of a formal book of poems, and has given to each the distinction of his clear and exact thinking, and of his sensitive imagination and passionate vision. *The Souls of Black Folk* was the book of an era; it was a painful book, a book of tortured dreams woven into the fabric of the sociologist's document. This book has more profoundly influenced the spiritual temper of the race than any other written in its generation. It is only through the intense, passionate idealism of such substance as makes *The Souls of Black Folk* such a quivering rhapsody of wrongs endured and hopes to be fulfilled that the poets of the race with compelling artistry can lift the Negro into the only full and complete nationalism he knows—that of the American democracy. No other book has more clearly revealed to the nation at large the true idealism and high aspiration of the American Negro.

In this book, as well as in many of Dr. Du Bois's essays, it is often my personal feeling that I am witnessing the birth of a poet, phoenix-like, out of a scholar. Between *The Souls of Black Folk* and *Darkwater*, published four years ago, Dr. Du Bois has written a number of books, none more notable, in my opinion, than his novel *The Quest of the Silver Fleece*, in which he made Cotton the great protagonist of fate in the lives of the Southern people, both white and black. I only know of one other such attempt and accomplishment in American fiction—that of Frank Norris—and I am somehow of the opinion that when the great epic novel of the South is written this book will prove to have been its forerunner. Indeed, the Negro novel is one of the great potentialities of American literature. Must it be written by a Negro? To recur to the article from which I have already quoted:

"The white writer seems to stand baffled before the enigma and so he expends all his energies on dialect and in general on the Negro's minstrel characteristics. . . We shall have to look to the Negro himself to go all the way. It is quite likely that no white man can do it. It is reasonable to suppose that his white psychology will always be in his way. I am not thinking at all about a Negro novelist who shall arouse the world to the horror of the deliberate killings by white mobs, to the wrongs that condemn a free people to political serfdom. I am not thinking at all of the propaganda novel, although there is enough horror and enough drama in the bald statistics of each one of the annual Moton letters to keep the whole army of writers busy. But the Negro novelist, if he ever comes, must reveal to us much more than what a Negro thinks about when he is being tied to a stake and the torch is being applied to his living flesh; much more than what he feels when he is being crowded off the sidewalk by a drunken rowdy who may be his intellectual inferior by a thousand leagues. Such a writer, to succeed in a big sense, would have to forget that there are white readers; he would have to lose self-consciousness and forget that his work would be placed before a white jury. He would have to be careless as to what the white critic might think of it; he would need the self-assurance to be his own critic. He would have to forget for the time being, at least, that any white man ever attempted to dissect the soul of a Negro."

What I here quote is both an inquiry and a challenge! Well informed as the writer is, he does not seem to detect the forces which are surely gathering to produce what he longs for.

The development of fiction among Negro authors has been, I might almost say, one of the repressed activities of our literary life. A fair start was made the last decade of the nineteenth century when Chestnutt and Dunbar were turning out both short stories and novels. In Dunbar's case, had he lived, I think his literary growth would have been in the evolution of the Race novel as indicated in *The Uncalled* and the *Sport of the Gods*. The former was, I think, the most ambitious literary effort of Dunbar; the latter was his most significant; significant because, thrown against the background of New York City, it displayed the life of the race as a unit, swayed by currents of existence, of which it was and was not a part. The story was touched with that shadow of destiny which gave to it a purpose more important than the mere racial machinery of its plot. But Dunbar in his fiction dealt only successfully with the same world that gave him the inspiration for his dialect poems; though his ambition was to "write a novel that will deal with the educated class of my own people." Later he writes of *The Fanatics*: "You do not know how my hopes were planted in that book, but it has utterly disappointed me." His contemporary, Charles W. Chestnutt, was concerned more primarily with the fiction of the Color Line and the contacts and conflicts of its two worlds. He was in a way more successful. In the five volumes to his credit, he has revealed himself as a fiction writer of a very high order. But after all Mr. Chestnutt is a story-teller of genius transformed by racial earnestness into the novelist of talent. His natural gift would have found freer vent in a flow of short stories like Bret Harte's, to judge from the facility and power of his two volumes of short stories, *The Wife of His Youth* and *Other Stories* and *The Conjure Woman*. But Mr. Chestnutt's serious effort was in the field of the novel, where he made a brave and partially successful effort to correct the distortions of Reconstruction fiction and offset the school of Page and Cable. Two of these novels, *The Marrow of Tradition* and *The House Behind the Cedars*, must be reckoned among the representative period novels of their time. But the situation was not ripe for the great Negro novelist. The American public preferred spurious values to the genuine; the coinage of the Confederacy was at literary par. Where Dunbar, the sentimentalist, was welcome, Chestnutt, the realist, was barred. In 1905 Mr. Chestnutt wrote *The Colonel's Dream*, and thereafter silence fell upon him.

From this date until the past year, with the exception of *The Quest of the Silver Fleece*, which was published in 1911, there has been no fiction of importance by Negro authors. But then suddenly there comes a series of books, which seems to promise at least a new phase of race fiction, and possibly the era of the major novelists. Mr. Walter White's novel *The Fire in the Flint* is a swift moving straightforward story of the contemporary conflicts of black manhood in the South. Coming from the experienced observation of the author, himself an investigator of many lynchings and riots, it is a social document story of first-hand significance and importance; too vital to be labelled and dismissed as propaganda, yet for the same reason too unvarnished and realistic a story to be great art. Nearer to the requirements of art comes Miss Jessie Fauset's novel *There is Confusion*. Its distinction is to have created an entirely new milieu in the treatment of the race in fiction. She has taken a class within the race of established social standing, tradition and culture, and given in the rather complex family story of *The Marshalls* a social document of unique and refreshing value. In such a story, race fiction, detaching itself from the limitations of propaganda on the one hand and genre fiction on the other, emerges from the color line and is incorporated into the body of general and universal art.

Finally in Jean Toomer, the author of *Cane*, we come upon the very first artist of the race, who with all an artist's passion and sympathy for life, its hurts, its sympathies, its desires, its joys, its defeats and strange yearnings, can write about the Negro without the surrender or compromise of the artist's vision. So objective is it, that we feel that it is a mere accident that birth or association has thrown him into contact with the life he has written about. He would write just as well, just as poignantly, just as transmutingly, about the peasants of Russia, or the peasants of Ireland, had experience brought him in touch with their existence. *Cane* is a book of gold and bronze, of dusk and flame, of ecstasy and pain, and Jean Toomer is a bright morning star of a new day of the race in literature.

NEGRO YOUTH SPEAKS

Negro Youth Speaks

Alain Locke

The Younger Generation comes, bringing its gifts. They are the first fruits of the Negro Renaissance. Youth speaks, and the voice of the New Negro is heard. What stirs inarticulately in the masses is already vocal upon the lips of the talented few, and the future listens, however the present may shut its ears. Here we have Negro youth, with arresting visions and vibrant prophecies; forecasting in the mirror of art what we must see and recognize in the streets of reality tomorrow, foretelling in new notes and accents the maturing speech of full racial utterance.

Primarily, of course, it is youth that speaks in the voice of Negro youth, but the overtones are distinctive; Negro youth speaks out of an unique experience and with a particular representativeness. All classes of a people under social pressure are permeated with a common experience; they are emotionally welded as others cannot be. With them, even ordinary living has epic depth and lyric intensity, and this, their material handicap, is their spiritual advantage. So, in a day when art has run to classes, cliques and coteries, and life lacks more and more a vital common background, the Negro artist, out of the depths of his group and personal experience, has to his hand almost the conditions of a classical art.

Negro genius to-day relies upon the race-gift as a vast spiritual endowment from which our best developments have come and must come. Racial expression as a conscious motive, it is true, is fading out of our latest art, but just as surely the age of truer, finer group expression is coming in—for race expression does not need to be deliberate to be vital. Indeed at its best it never is. This was the case with our instinctive and quite matchless folk-art, and begins to be the same again as we approach cultural maturity in a phase of art that promises now to be fully representative. The interval between has been an awkward age, where from the anxious desire and attempt to be representative much that was really unrepresentative has come; we have lately had an art that was stiltedly self-conscious, and racially rhetorical rather than racially expressive. Our poets have now stopped speaking for the Negro—they speak as Negroes. Where formerly they spoke to others and tried to interpret, they now speak to their own and try to express. They have stopped posing, being nearer the attainment of poise.

The younger generation has thus achieved an objective attitude toward life. Race for them is but an idiom of experience, a sort of added enriching adventure and discipline, giving subtler overtones to life, making it more beautiful and interesting, even if more poignantly so. So experienced, it affords a deepening rather than a narrowing of social vision. The artistic problem of the Young Negro has not been so much that of acquiring the outer mastery of form and technique as that of achieving an inner mastery of mood and spirit. That accomplished, there has come the happy release from self-consciousness, rhetoric, bombast, and the hampering habit of setting artistic values with primary regard for moral effect—all those pathetic over-compensations of a group inferiority complex which our social dilemmas inflicted upon several unhappy generations. Our poets no longer have the hard choice between an over-assertive and an appealing attitude. By the same effort they have shaken themselves free from the minstrel tradition and the fowling-nets of dialect, and through acquiring ease and simplicity in serious expression, have carried the folk-gift to the altitudes of art. There they seek and find art's intrinsic values and satisfactions—and if America were deaf, they would still sing.

But America listens—perhaps in curiosity at first; later, we may be sure, in understanding. But—a moment of patience. The generation now in the artistic vanguard inherits the fine and dearly bought achievement of another generation of creative workmen who have been pioneers and path-breakers in the cultural development and recognition of the Negro in the arts. Though still in their prime, as veterans of a hard struggle, they must have the praise and gratitude that is due them. We have had, in fiction, Chestnutt and Burghardt Du Bois; in drama, Du Bois again and Angelina Grimke; in poetry Dunbar, James Weldon Johnson, Fenton and Charles Bertram Johnson, Everett Hawkins, Lucien Watkins, Cotter, Jameson; and in another file of poets, Miss Grimke, Anne Spencer, and Georgia Douglas Johnson; in criticism and *belles lettres*, Braithwaite and Dr. Du Bois; in painting, Tanner and Scott; in sculpture, Meta Warrick and May Jackson; in acting, Gilpin and Robeson; in music, Burleigh. Nor must the fine collaboration of white American artists be omitted; the work of Ridgeley Torrence and Eugene O'Neill in drama, of Stribling, and Shands and Clement Wood in fiction, all of which has helped in the bringing of the materials of Negro life out of the shambles of conventional polemics, cheap romance and journalism into the domain of pure and unbiassed art. Then, rich in this legacy, but richer still, I think, in their own endowment of talent, comes the youngest generation of our Afro-American culture: in music Diton, Dett, Grant Still, and Roland Hayes; in fiction, Jessie Fauset, Walter White, Claude McKay (a forthcoming book); in drama, Willis Richardson; in the field of the short story, Jean Toomer, Eric Walrond, Rudolph Fisher; and finally a vivid galaxy of young Negro poets, McKay, Jean Toomer, Langston Hughes and Countée Cullen.

These constitute a new generation not because of years only, but because of a new æsthetic and a new philosophy of life. They have all swung above the horizon in the last three years, and we can say without disparagement of the past that in that short space of time they have gained collectively from publishers, editors, critics and the general public more recognition than has ever before come to Negro creative artists in an entire working lifetime. First novels of unquestioned distinction, first acceptances by premier journals whose pages are the ambition of veteran craftsmen, international acclaim, the conquest for us of new provinces of art, the development for the first time among us of literary coteries and channels for the contact of creative minds, and most important of all, a spiritual quickening and racial leavening such as no generation has yet felt and known. It has been their achievement also to bring the artistic advance of the Negro sharply into stepping alignment with contemporary artistic thought, mood and style. They are thoroughly modern, some of them ultra-modern, and Negro thoughts now wear the uniform of the age.

Through their work, these younger artists have declared for a lusty vigorous realism; the same that is molding contemporary American letters, but their achievement of it, as it has been doubly difficult, is doubly significant. The elder generation of Negro writers expressed itself in cautious moralism and guarded idealizations; the trammels of Puritanism were on its mind because the repressions of prejudice were heavy on its heart. They felt art must fight social battles and compensate social wrongs; "Be representative": put the better foot foremost, was the underlying mood. Just as with the Irish Renaissance, there were the riots and controversies over Synge's folk plays and other frank realisms of the younger school, so we are having and will have turbulent discussion and dissatisfaction with the stories, plays and poems of the younger Negro group. But writers like Rudolph Fisher, Zora Hurston, Jean Toomer, Eric Walrond, Willis Richardson, and Langston Hughes take their material objectively with detached artistic vision; they have no thought of their racy folk types as typical of anything but themselves or of their being taken or mistaken as racially representative. Contrast Ellen Glasgow's *Barren Ground* with Thomas Nelson Page, or Waldo Frank's *Holiday* with anything of Mr. Cable's, and you will get the true clue for this contrast between the younger and the elder generations of Negro literature; Realism in "crossing the Potomac" had also to cross the color line. Indeed it was the other way round; the pioneer writing of the fiction of the New South was the realistic fiction of Negro life. Fortunately just at the time the younger generation was precipitating out, *Batouala* came to attention through the award of the Prix Goncourt to René Maran, its author, in 1923. Though *Batouala* is not of the American Negro either in substance or authorship, the influence of its daring realism and Latin frankness was educative and emancipating. And so not merely for modernity of style, but for vital originality of substance, the young Negro writers dig deep into the racy peasant undersoil of the race life. Jean Toomer writes:

"Georgia opened me. And it may well be said that I received my initial impulse to an individual art from my experience there. For no other section of the country has so stirred me. There one finds soil, soil in the sense the Russians know it,—the soil every art and literature that is to live must be imbedded in."

The newer motive, then, in being racial is to be so purely for the sake of art. Nowhere is this more apparent, or more justified than in the increasing tendency to evolve from the racial substance something technically distinctive, something that as an idiom of style may become a contribution to the general resources of art. In flavor of language, flow of phrase, accent of rhythm in prose, verse and music, color and tone of imagery, idiom and timbre of emotion and symbolism, it is the ambition and promise of Negro artists to make a distinctive contribution. Much of this is already discernible. The interesting experiment of Weldon Johnson in *Creation: A Negro Sermon*, to transpose the dialect motive and carry it through in the idioms of imagery rather than the broken phonetics of speech, is a case in point. In music such transfusions of racial idioms with the modernistic styles of expression has already taken place; in the other arts it is just as possible and likely. Thus under the sophistications of modern style may be detected in almost all our artists a fresh distinctive note that the majority of them admit as the instinctive gift of the folk-spirit. Toomer gives a musical folk-lilt and a glamorous sensuous ecstasy to the style of the American prose modernists. McKay adds Aesop and peasant irony to the social novel and folk clarity and naïveté to lyric thought. Fisher adds the terseness and emotional raciness of Uncle Remus to the art of Maupassant and O. Henry. Walrond has a tropical color and almost volcanic gush that are unique even after more than a generation of exotic word painting by master artists. Langston Hughes has a distinctive fervency of color and rhythm, and a Biblical simplicity of speech that is colloquial in derivation, but full of artistry. Roland Hayes carries the rhapsodic gush and depth of folk-song to the old masters. Countée Cullen blends the simple with the sophisticated so originally as almost to put the vineyards themselves into his crystal goblets.

There is in all the marriage of a fresh emotional endowment with the finest niceties of art. Here for the enrichment of American and modern art, among our contemporaries, in a people who still have the ancient key, are some of the things we thought culture had forever lost. Art cannot disdain the gift of a natural irony, of a transfiguring imagination, of rhapsodic Biblical speech, of dynamic musical swing, of cosmic emotion such as only the gifted pagans knew, of a return to nature, not by way of the forced and worn formula of Romanticism, but through the closeness of an imagination that has never broken kinship with nature. Art must accept such gifts, and revaluate the giver.

Not all the new art is in the field of pure art values. There is poetry of sturdy social protest, and fiction of calm, dispassionate social analysis. But reason and realism have cured us of sentimentality: instead of the wail and appeal, there is challenge and indictment. Satire is just beneath the surface of our latest prose, and tonic irony has come into our poetic wells. These are good medicines for the common mind, for us they are necessary antidotes against social poison. Their influence means that at least for us the worst symptoms of the social distemper are passing. And so the social promise of our recent art is as great as the artistic. It has brought with it, first of all, that wholesome, welcome virtue of finding beauty in oneself; the younger generation can no longer be twitted as "cultural nondescripts" or accused of "being out of love with their own nativity." They have instinctive love and pride of race, and, spiritually compensating for the present lacks of America, ardent respect and love for Africa, the motherland. Gradually too, under some spiritualizing reaction, the brands and wounds of social persecution are becoming the proud stigmata of spiritual immunity and moral victory. Already enough progress has been made in this direction so that it is no longer true that the Negro mind is too engulfed in its own social dilemmas for control of the necessary perspective of art, or too depressed to attain the full horizons of self and social criticism. Indeed, by the evidence and promise of the cultured few, we are at last spiritually free, and offer through art an emancipating vision to America. But it is a presumption to speak further for those who in the selections of their work in the succeeding sections speak so adequately for themselves.

FICTION

The City of Refuge

Rudolph Fisher

I

Confronted suddenly by daylight, King Solomon Gillis stood dazed and blinking. The railroad station, the long, white-walled corridor, the impassible slot-machine, the terrifying subway train—he felt as if he had been caught up in the jaws of a steam-shovel, jammed together with other helpless lumps of dirt, swept blindly along for a time, and at last abruptly dumped.

There had been strange and terrible sounds: "New York! Penn Terminal—all change!" "Pohter, hyer, pohter, suh?" Shuffle of a thousand soles, clatter of a thousand heels, innumerable echoes. Cracking rifle-shots—no, snapping turnstiles. "Put a nickel in!" "Harlem? Sure. This side—next train." Distant thunder, nearing. The screeching onslaught of the fiery hosts of hell, headlong, breath-taking. Car doors rattling, sliding, banging open. "Say, wha' d'ye think this is, a baggage car?" Heat, oppression, suffocation—eternity—"Hundred 'n turdy-fif' next!" More turnstiles. Jonah emerging from the whale.

Clean air, blue sky, bright sunlight.

Gillis set down his tan-cardboard extension-case and wiped his black, shining brow. Then slowly, spreadingly, he grinned at what he saw: Negroes at every turn; up and down Lenox Avenue, up and down One Hundred and Thirty-fifth Street; big, lanky Negroes, short, squat Negroes; black ones, brown ones, yellow ones; men standing idle on the curb, women, bundle-laden, trudging reluctantly homeward, children rattle-trapping about the sidewalks; here and there a white face drifting along, but Negroes predominantly, overwhelmingly everywhere. There was assuredly no doubt of his whereabouts. This was Negro Harlem.

Back in North Carolina Gillis had shot a white man and, with the aid of prayer and an automobile, probably escaped a lynching. Carefully avoiding the railroads, he had reached Washington in safety. For his car a Southwest bootlegger had given him a hundred dollars and directions to Harlem; and so he had come to Harlem.

Ever since a travelling preacher had first told him of the place, King Solomon Gillis had longed to come to Harlem. The Uggams were always talking about it; one of their boys had gone to France in the draft and, returning, had never got any nearer home than Harlem. And there were occasional "colored" newspapers from New York: newspapers that mentioned Negroes without comment, but always spoke of a white person as "So-and-so, white." That was the point. In Harlem, black was white. You had rights that could not be denied you; you had privileges, protected by law. And you had money. Everybody in Harlem had money. It was a land of plenty. Why, had not Mouse Uggam sent back as much as fifty dollars at a time to his people in Waxhaw?

The shooting, therefore, simply catalyzed whatever sluggish mental reaction had been already directing King Solomon's fortunes toward Harlem. The land of plenty was more than that now: it was also the city of refuge.

Casting about for direction, the tall newcomer's glance caught inevitably on the most conspicuous thing in sight, a magnificent figure in blue that stood in the middle of the crossing and blew a whistle and waved great white-gloved hands. The Southern Negro's eyes opened wide; his mouth opened wider. If the inside of New York had mystified him, the outside was amazing him. For there stood a handsome, brass-buttoned giant directing the heaviest traffic Gillis had ever seen; halting unnumbered tons of automobiles and trucks and wagons and pushcarts and street-cars; holding them at bay with one hand while he swept similar tons peremptorily on with the other; ruling the wide crossing with supreme self-assurance; and he, too, was a Negro!

Yet most of the vehicles that leaped or crouched at his bidding carried white passengers. One of these overdrove bounds a few feet and Gillis heard the officer's shrill whistle and gruff reproof, saw the driver's face turn red and his car draw back like a threatened pup. It was beyond belief—impossible. Black might be white, but it couldn't be that white!

"Done died an' woke up in Heaven," thought King Solomon, watching, fascinated; and after a while, as if the wonder of it were too great to believe simply by seeing, "Cullud policemans!" he said, half aloud; then repeated over and over, with greater and greater conviction, "Even got cullud policemans—even got cullud—"

"Where y' want to go, big boy?"

Gillis turned. A little, sharp-faced yellow man was addressing him.

"Saw you was a stranger. Thought maybe I could help y' out."

King Solomon located and gratefully extended a slip of paper. "Wha' dis hyeh at, please, suh?"

The other studied it a moment, pushing back his hat and scratching his head. The hat was a tall-crowned, unindented brown felt; the head was brown patent-leather, its glistening brush-back flawless save for a suspicious crimpiness near the clean-grazed edges.

"See that second corner? Turn to the left when you get there. Number forty-five's about halfway the block."

"Thank y', suh."

"You from—Massachusetts?"

"No, suh, Nawth Ca'lina."

"Is 'at so? You look like a Northerner. Be with us long?"

"Till I die," grinned the flattered King Solomon.

"Stoppin' there?"

"Reckon I is. Man in Washin'ton 'lowed I'd find lodgin' at dis ad-dress."

"Good enough. If y' don't, maybe I can fix y' up. Harlem's pretty crowded. This is me," He proffered a card.

"Thank y', suh," said Gillis, and put the card in his pocket.

The little yellow man watched him plod flat-footedly on down the street, long awkward legs never quite straightened, shouldered extension-case bending him sidewise, wonder upon wonder halting or turning him about. Presently, as he proceeded, a pair of bright-green stockings caught and held his attention. Tony, the storekeeper, was crossing the sidewalk with a bushel basket of apples. There was a collision; the apples rolled; Tony exploded; King Solomon apologized. The little yellow man laughed shortly, took out a notebook, and put down the address he had seen on King Solomon's slip of paper.

"Guess you're the shine I been waitin' for," he surmised.

As Gillis, approaching his destination, stopped to rest, a haunting notion grew into an insistent idea. "Dat li'l yaller nigger was a sho' 'nuff gen'man to show me de road. Seem lak I knowed him befo'—" He pondered. That receding brow, that sharp-ridged, spreading nose, that tight upper lip over the two big front teeth, that chinless jaw—He fumbled hurriedly for the card he had not looked at and eagerly made out the name.

"Mouse Uggam, sho' 'nuff! Well, dog-gone!"

II

Uggam sought out Tom Edwards, once a Pullman porter, now prosperous proprietor of a cabaret, and told him:

"Chief, I got him: a baby jess in from the land o' cotton and so dumb he thinks ante-bellum's an old woman."

"Wher'd you find him?"

"Where you find all the jay birds when they first hit Harlem—at the subway entrance. This one come up the stairs, batted his eyes once or twice, an' froze to the spot—with his mouth open. Sure sign he's from 'way down behind the sun an' ripe f' the pluckin'."

Edwards grinned a gold-studded, fat-jowled grin. "Gave him the usual line, I suppose?"

"Didn't miss. An' he fell like a ton o' bricks. 'Course I've got him spotted, but damn' if I know jess how to switch 'em on to him."

"Get him a job around a store somewhere. Make out you're befriendin' him. Get his confidence."

"Sounds good. Ought to be easy. He's from my state. Maybe I know him or some of his people."

"Make out you do, anyhow. Then tell him some fairy tale that'll switch your trade to him. The cops'll follow the trade. We could even let Froggy flop into some dumb white cop's hands and 'confess' where he got it. See?"

"Chief, you got a head, no lie."

"Don't lose no time. And remember, hereafter, it's better to sacrifice a little than to get squealed on. Never refuse a customer. Give him a little credit. Humor him along till you can get rid of him safe. You don't know what that guy that died may have said; you don't know who's on to you now. And if they get you—I don't know you."

"They won't get *me*," said Uggam.

KING SOLOMON GILLIS SAT MEDITATING in a room half the size of his hencoop back home, with a single window opening into an airshaft.

An airshaft: cabbage and chitterlings cooking; liver and onions sizzling, sputtering; three player-pianos out-plunking each other; a man and woman calling each other vile things; a sick, neglected baby wailing; a phonograph broadcasting blues; dishes clacking; a girl crying heartbrokenly; waste noises, waste odors of a score of families, seeking issue through a common channel; pollution from bottom to top—a sewer of sounds and smells.

Contemplating this, King Solomon grinned and breathed, "Dog-gone!" A little later, still gazing into the sewer, he grinned again. "Green stockin's," he said; "loud green!" The sewer gradually grew darker. A window lighted up opposite, revealing a woman in camisole and petticoat, arranging her hair. King Solomon, staring vacantly, shook his head and grinned yet again. "Even got cullud policemans!" he mumbled softly.

III

UGGAM LEANED OUT OF THE room's one window and spat maliciously into the dinginess of the airshaft. "Damn glad you got him," he commented, as Gillis finished his story. "They's a thousand shines in Harlem would change places with you in a minute jess f' the honor of killin' a cracker."

"But I didn't go to do it. 'Twas a accident."

"That's the only part to keep secret."

"Know whut dey done? Dey killed five o' Mose Joplin's hawses 'fo he lef'. Put groun' glass in de feed-trough. Sam Cheevers come up on three of 'em one night pizenin' his well. Bleesom beat Crinshaw out o' sixty acres o' lan' an' a year's crops. Dass jess how 'tis. Soon's a nigger make a li'l sump'n he better git to leavin'. An' 'fo long ev'ybody's goin' be lef'!"

"Hope to hell they don't all come here."

The doorbell of the apartment rang. A crescendo of footfalls in the hallway culminated in a sharp rap on Gillis's door. Gillis jumped. Nobody but a policeman would rap like that. Maybe the landlady had been listening and had called in the law. It came again, loud, quick, angry. King Solomon prayed that the policeman would be a Negro.

Uggam stepped over and opened the door. King Solomon's apprehensive eyes saw framed therein, instead of a gigantic officer, calling for him, a little blot of a creature, quite black against even the darkness of the hallway, except for a dirty, wide-striped silk shirt, collarless, with the sleeves rolled up.

"Ah hahve bill fo' Mr. Gillis." A high, strongly accented Jamaican voice, with its characteristic singsong intonation, interrupted King Solomon's sigh of relief.

"Bill? Bill fo' me? What kin' o' bill?"

"Wan bushel appels. T'ree seventy-fife."

"Apples? I ain' bought no apples." He took the paper and read aloud, laboriously, "Antonio Gabrielli to K. S. Gillis, Debtor—"

"Mr. Gabrielli say, you not pays him, he send policemon."

"What I had to do wid 'is apples?"

"You bumps into him yesterday, no? Scatter appels everywhere—on de sidewalk, in de gutter. Kids pick up an' run away. Others all spoil. So you pays."

Gillis appealed to Uggam. "How 'bout it, Mouse?"

"He's a damn liar. Tony picked up most of 'em; I seen him. Lemme look at that bill—Tony never wrote this thing. This baby's jess playin' you for a sucker."

"Ain' had no apples, ain' payin' fo' none," announced King Solomon, thus prompted. "Didn't have to come to Harlem to git cheated. Plenty o' dat right wha' I come fum."

But the West Indian warmly insisted. "You cahn't do daht, mon. Whaht you t'ink, 'ey? Dis mon loose 'is appels an' 'is money too?"

"What diff'ence it make to you, nigger?"

"Who you call nigger, mon? Ah hahve you understahn'—"

"Oh, well, white folks, den. What all you got t' do wid dis hyeh, anyhow?"

"Mr. Gabrielli send me to collect bill!"

"How I know dat?"

"Do Ah not bring bill? You t'ink Ah steal t'ree dollar, 'ey?"

"Three dollars an' sebenty-fi' cent," corrected Gillis. "'Nuther thing: wha' you ever see me befo'? How you know dis is me?"

"Ah see you, sure. Ah help Mr. Gabrielli in de store. When you knocks down de baskette appels, Ah see. Ah follow you. Ah know you comes in dis house."

"Oh, you does? An' how come you know my name an' flat an' room so good? How come dat?"

"Ah fin' out. Sometime Ah brings up here vegetables from de store."

"Humph! Mus' be workin' on shares."

"You pays, 'ey? You pays me or de policemon?"

"Wait a minute," broke in Uggam, who had been thoughtfully contemplating the bill. "Now listen, big shorty. You haul hips on back to Tony. We got your menu all right"—he waved the bill—"but we don't eat your kind o' cookin', see?"

The West Indian flared. "Whaht it is to you, 'ey? You can not mind your own business? Ah hahve not spik to you!"

"No, brother. But this is my friend, an' I'll be john-browned if there's a monkey-chaser in Harlem can gyp him if I know it, see? Bes' thing f' you to do is catch air, toot sweet."

Sensing frustration, the little islander demanded the bill back.

Uggam figured he could use the bill himself, maybe. The West Indian hotly persisted; he even menaced. Uggam pocketed the paper and invited him to take it. Wisely enough, the caller preferred to catch air.

When he had gone, King Solomon sought words of thanks.

"Bottle it," said Uggam. "The point is this: I figger you got a job."

"Job? No I ain't! Wha'at?"

"When you show Tony this bill, he'll hit the roof and fire that monk."

"What ef he do?"

"Then you up 'n ask f' the job. He'll be too grateful to refuse. I know Tony some, an' I'll be there to put in a good word. See?"

King Solomon considered this. "Sho' needs a job, but ain' after stealin' none."

"Stealin'? 'Twouldn't be stealin'. Stealin's what that damn monkey-chaser tried to do from you. This would be doin' Tony a favor, an' gettin' y'self out o' the barrel. What's the hold-back?"

"What make you keep callin' him monkey-chaser?"

"West Indian. That's another thing. Any time y' can knife a monk, do it. They's too damn many of 'em here. They're an achin' pain."

"Jess de way white folks feels 'bout niggers."

"Damn that. How 'bout it? Y' want the job?"

"Hm—well—I'd ruther be a policeman."

"Policeman?" Uggam gasped.

"M-hm. Dass all I wants to be, a policeman, so I kin police all de white folks right plumb in jail!"

Uggam said seriously, "Well, y' might work up to that. But it takes time. An' y've got to eat while y're waitin'." He paused to let this penetrate. "Now, how 'bout this job at Tony's in the meantime? I should think y'd jump at it."

King Solomon was persuaded.

"Hm—well—reckon I does," he said slowly.

"Now y're tootin'!" Uggam's two big front teeth popped out in a grin of genuine pleasure. "Come on. Let's go."

IV

SPITTING BLOOD AND CRYING WITH rage, the West Indian scrambled to his feet. For a moment he stood in front of the store gesticulating furiously and jabbering shrill threats and unintelligible curses. Then abruptly he stopped and took himself off.

King Solomon Gillis, mildly puzzled, watched him from Tony's doorway. "I jess give him a li'l shove," he said to himself, "an' he roll' clean 'cross de sidewalk." And a little later, disgustedly, "Monkey-chaser!" he grunted, and went back to his sweeping.

"Well, big boy, how y' comin' on?"

Gillis dropped his broom. "Hay-o, Mouse. Wha' you been las' two-three days?"

"Oh, around. Gettin' on all right here? Had any trouble?"

"Deed I ain't—'ceptin' jess now I had to throw 'at li'l jigger out."

"Who? The monk?"

"M-hm. He sho' Lawd doan like me in his job. Look like he think I stole it from him, stiddy him tryin' to steal from me. Had to push him down sho' 'nuff 'fo I could git rid of 'im. Den he run off talkin' Wes' Indi'man an' shakin' his fis' at me."

"Ferget it." Uggam glanced about. "Where's Tony?"

"Boss man? He be back direckly."

"Listen—like to make two or three bucks a day extra?"

"Huh?"

"Two or three dollars a day more'n what you're gettin' already?"

"Ain' I near 'nuff in jail now?"

"Listen." King Solomon listened. Uggam hadn't been in France for nothing. Fact was, in France he'd learned about some valuable French medicine. He'd brought some back with him,—little white pills,—and while in Harlem had found a certain druggist who knew what they were and could supply all he could use. Now there were any number of people who would buy and pay well for as much of this French medicine as Uggam could get. It was good for what ailed them, and they didn't know how to get it except through him. But he had no store in which to set up an agency and hence no single place where his customers could go to get what they wanted. If he had, he could sell three or four times as much as he did.

King Solomon was in a position to help him now, same as he had helped King Solomon. He would leave a dozen packages of the medicine—just small envelopes that could all be carried in a coat pocket—with King Solomon every day. Then he could simply send his customers to King Solomon at Tony's store. They'd make some trifling purchase, slip him a certain coupon which Uggam had given them, and King Solomon would wrap the little envelope of medicine with their purchase. Mustn't let Tony catch on, because he might object, and then the whole scheme would go gaflooey. Of course it wouldn't really be hurting Tony any. Wouldn't it increase the number of his customers?

Finally, at the end of each day, Uggam would meet King Solomon some place and give him a quarter for each coupon he held. There'd be at least ten or twelve a day—two and a half or three dollars plumb extra! Eighteen or twenty dollars a week!

"Dog-gone!" breathed Gillis.

"Does Tony ever leave you heer alone?"

"M-hm. Jess started dis mawnin'. Doan nobody much come round 'tween ten an' twelve, so he done took to doin' his buyin' right 'long 'bout dat time. Nobody hyeh but me fo' 'n hour or so."

"Good. I'll try to get my folks to come 'round here mostly while Tony's out, see?"

"I doan miss."

"Sure y' get the idea, now?" Uggam carefully explained it all again. By the time he had finished, King Solomon was wallowing in gratitude.

"Mouse, you sho' is been a friend to me. Why, 'f 't hadn' been fo' you—"

"Bottle it," said Uggam. "I'll be round to your room tonight with enough stuff for to-morrer, see? Be sure 'n be there."

"Won't be nowha' else."

"Ah' remember, this is all jess between you 'n me."

"Nobody else but," vowed King Solomon.

Uggam grinned to himself as he went on his way. "Dumb Oscar! Wonder how much can we make before the cops nab him? French medicine—Hmph!"

V

TONY GABRIELLI, AN OBLATE NEAPOLITAN of enormous equator, wabbled heavily out of his store and settled himself over a soap box.

Usually Tony enjoyed sitting out front thus in the evening, when his helper had gone home and his trade was slackest. He liked to watch the little Gabriellis playing over the sidewalk with the little Levys and Johnsons; the trios and quartettes of brightly dressed, dark-skinned girls merrily out for a stroll; the slovenly gaited, darker men, who eyed them up and down and commented to each other with an unsuppressed "Hot damn!" or "Oh no, now!"

But to-night Tony was troubled. Something was wrong in the store; something was different since the arrival of King Solomon Gillis. The new man had seemed to prove himself honest and trustworthy, it was true. Tony had tested him, as he always tested a new man, by apparently leaving him alone in charge for two or three mornings. As a matter of fact, the new man was never under more vigilant observation than during these two or three mornings. Tony's store was a modification of the front rooms of his flat and was in direct communication with it by way of a glass-windowed door in the rear. Tony always managed to get back into his flat via the side-street entrance and watch the new man through this unobtrusive glass-windowed door. If anything excited his suspicion, like unwarranted interest in the cash register, he walked unexpectedly out of this door to surprise the offender in the act. Thereafter he would have no more such trouble. But he had not succeeded in seeing King Solomon steal even an apple.

What he had observed, however, was that the number of customers that came into the store during the morning's slack hour had pronouncedly increased in the last few days. Before, there had been three or four. Now there were twelve or fifteen. The mysterious thing about it was that their purchases totalled little more than those of the original three or four.

Yesterday and to-day Tony had elected to be in the store at the time when, on the other days, he had been out. But Gillis had not been overcharging or short-changing; for when Tony waited on the customers himself—strange faces all—he found that they bought something like a yeast cake or a five-cent loaf of bread. It was puzzling. Why should strangers leave their own neighborhoods and repeatedly come to him for a yeast cake or a loaf of bread? They were not new neighbors. New neighbors would have bought more variously and extensively and at different times of day. Living near by, they would have come in, the men often in shirtsleeves and slippers, the women in kimonos, with boudoir caps covering their lumpy heads. They would have sent in strange children for things like yeast cakes and loaves of bread. And why did not some of them come in at night when the new helper was off duty?

As for accosting Gillis on suspicion, Tony was too wise for that. Patronage had a queer way of shifting itself in Harlem. You lost your temper and let slip a single "*nègre*." A week later you sold your business.

Spread over his soap box, with his pudgy hands clasped on his preposterous paunch, Tony sat and wondered. Two men came up, conspicuous for no other reason than that they were white. They displayed extreme nervousness, looking about as if afraid of being seen; and when one of them spoke to Tony it was in a husky, toneless, blowing voice, like the sound of a dirty phonograph record.

"Are you Antonio Gabrielli?"

"Yes, sure," Strange behavior for such lusty-looking fellows. He who had spoken unsmilingly winked first one eye then the other, and indicated by a gesture of his head that they should enter the store. His companion looked cautiously up and down the Avenue, while Tony, wondering what ailed them, rolled to his feet and puffingly led the way.

Inside, the spokesman snuffled, gave his shoulders a queer little hunch, and asked, "Can you fix us up, buddy?" The other glanced restlessly about the place as if he were constantly hearing unaccountable noises.

Tony thought he understood clearly now. "Booze, 'ey?" he smiled. "Sorry—I no got."

"Booze? Hell, no!" The voice dwindled to a throaty whisper. "Dope. Coke, milk, dice—anything. Name your price. Got to have it."

"Dope?" Tony was entirely at a loss. "What's a dis, dope?"

"Aw, lay off, brother. We're in on this. Here." He handed Tony a piece of paper. "Froggy gave us a coupon. Come on. You can't go wrong."

"I no got," insisted the perplexed Tony; nor could he be budged on that point.

Quite suddenly the manner of both men changed. "All right," said the first angrily, in a voice as robust as his body. "All right, you're clever, You no got. Well, you will get. You'll get twenty years!"

"Twenty year? Whadda you talk?"

"Wait a minute, Mac," said the second caller. "Maybe the wop's on the level. Look here, Tony, we're officers, see? Policemen." He produced a badge. "A couple of weeks ago a guy was brought in dying for the want of a shot, see? Dope—he needed some dope—like this—in his arm. See? Well, we tried to make him tell us where he'd been getting it, but he was too weak. He croaked next day. Evidently he hadn't had money enough to buy any more.

"Well, this morning a little nigger that goes by the name of Froggy was brought into the precinct pretty well doped up. When he finally came to, he swore he got the stuff here at your store. Of course, we've just been trying to trick you into giving yourself away, but you don't bite. Now what's your game? Know anything about this?"

Tony understood. "I dunno," he said slowly; and then his own problem, whose contemplation his callers had interrupted, occurred to him. "Sure!" he exclaimed. "Wait. Maybeso, I know somet'ing."

"All right. Spill it."

"I got a new man, work-a for me." And he told them what he had noted since King Solomon Gillis came.

"Sounds interesting. Where is this guy?"

"Here in da store—all day."

"Be here to-morrow?"

"Sure. All day."

"All right. We'll drop in to-morrow and give him the eye. Maybe he's our man."

"Sure. Come ten o'clock. I show you," promised Tony.

VI

EVEN THE OLDEST AND RATTIEST cabarets in Harlem have sense of shame enough to hide themselves under the ground—for instance, Edwards's. To get into Edwards's you casually enter a dimly lighted corner saloon, apparently—only apparently—a subdued memory of brighter days. What was once the family entrance is now a side entrance for ladies. Supporting yourself against close walls, you crouchingly descend a narrow, twisted staircase until, with a final turn, you find yourself in a glaring, long, low basement. In a moment your eyes become accustomed to the haze of tobacco smoke. You see men and women seated at wire-legged, white-topped tables, which are covered with half-empty bottles and glasses; you trace the slow-jazz accompaniment you heard as you came down the stairs to a pianist, a cornetist, and a drummer on a little platform at the far end of the room. There is a cleared space from the foot of the stairs, where you are standing, to the platform where this orchestra is mounted, and in it a tall brown girl is swaying from side to side and rhythmically proclaiming that she has the world in a jug and the stopper in her hand. Behind a counter at your left sits a fat, bald, tea-colored Negro, and you wonder if this is Edwards— Edwards, who stands in with the police, with the political bosses, with the importers of wines and worse. A white-vested waiter hustles you to a seat and takes your order. The song's tempo changes to a quicker; the drum and the cornet rip out a fanfare, almost drowning the piano; the girl catches up her dress and begins to dance. . .

Gillis's wondering eyes had been roaming about. They stopped.

"Look, Mouse," he whispered. "Look a-yonder!"

"Look at what?"

"Dog-gone if it ain' de self-same gal!"

"Wha' d'ye mean, self-same girl?"

"Over yonder, wi' de green stockin's. Dass de gal made me knock over dem apples fust day I come to town. 'Member? Been wishin' I could see her ev'y sence."

"What for?" Uggam wondered.

King Solomon grew confidential. "Ain' but two things in dis world, Mouse, I really wants. One is to be a policeman. Been wantin' dat ev'y sence I seen dat cullud traffic-cop dat day. Other is to git myse'f a gal lak dat one over yonder!"

"You'll do it," laughed Uggam, "if you live long enough."

"Who dat wid her?"

"How'n hell do I know?"

"He cullud?"

"Don't look like it. Why? What of it?"

"Hm—nuthin'—"

"How many coupons y' got to-night?"

"Ten." King Solomon handed them over.

"Y'ought to 've slipt 'em to me under the table, but it's all right now, long as we got this table to ourselves. Here's y' medicine for to-morrer."

"Wha'?"

"Reach under the table."

Gillis secured and pocketed the medicine.

"An' here's two-fifty for a good day's work." Uggam passed the money over. Perhaps he grew careless; certainly the passing this time was above the table, in plain sight.

"Thanks, Mouse."

Two white men had been watching Gillis and Uggam from a table near by. In the tumult of merriment that rewarded the entertainer's most recent and daring effort, one of these men, with a word to the other, came over and took the vacant chair beside Gillis.

"Is your name Gillis?"

"'Tain' nuthin' else."

Uggam's eyes narrowed.

The white man showed King Solomon a police officer's badge.

"You're wanted for dope-peddling. Will you come along without trouble?"

"Fo' what?"

"Violation of the narcotic law—dope-selling."

"Who—me?"

"Come on, now, lay off that stuff. I saw what happened just now myself." He addressed Uggam. "Do you know this fellow?"

"Nope. Never saw him before to-night."

"Didn't I just see him sell you something?"

"Guess you did. We happened to be sittin' here at the same table and got to talkin'. After a while I says I can't seem to sleep nights, so he offers me sump'n he says'll make me sleep, all right. I don't know what it is, but he says he uses it himself an' I offers to pay him what it cost him. That's how I come to take it. Guess he's got more in his pocket there now."

The detective reached deftly into the coat pocket of the dumfounded King Solomon and withdrew a packet of envelopes. He tore off a corner of one, emptied a half-dozen tiny white tablets into his palm, and sneered triumphantly. "You'll make a good witness," he told Uggam.

The entertainer was issuing an ultimatum to all sweet mammas who dared to monkey round her loving man. Her audience was absorbed and delighted, with the exception of one couple—the girl with the green stockings and her escort. They sat directly in the line of vision of King Solomon's wide eyes, which, in the calamity that had descended upon him, for the moment saw nothing.

"Are you coming without trouble?"

Mouse Uggam, his friend. Harlem. Land of plenty. City of refuge—city of refuge. If you live long enough—

Consciousness of what was happening between the pair across the room suddenly broke through Gillis's daze like flame through smoke. The man was trying to kiss the girl and she was resisting. Gillis jumped up. The detective, taking the act for an attempt at escape, jumped with him and was quick enough to intercept him. The second officer came at once to his fellow's aid, blowing his whistle several times as he came.

People overturned chairs getting out of the way, but nobody ran for the door. It was an old crowd. A fight was a treat; and the tall Negro could fight.

"Judas Priest!"

"Did you see that?"

"Damn!"

White—both white. Five of Mose Joplin's horses. Poisoning a well. A year's crops. Green stockings—white—white—

"That's the time, papa!"

"Do it, big boy!"

"Good night!"

Uggam watched tensely, with one eye on the door. The second cop had blown for help—

Downing one of the detectives a third time and turning to grapple again with the other, Gillis found himself face to face with a uniformed black policeman.

He stopped as if stunned. For a moment he simply stared. Into his mind swept his own words like a forgotten song, suddenly recalled:

"Cullud policemans!"

The officer stood ready, awaiting his rush.

"Even—got—cullud—policemans—"

Very slowly King Solomon's arms relaxed; very slowly he stood erect; and the grin that came over his features had something exultant about it.

VESTIGES

Harlem Sketches

Rudolph Fisher

I

Shepherd! Lead Us

EZEKIEL TAYLOR, PREACHER OF THE gospel of Jesus Christ, walked slowly along One Hundred and Thirty-third Street, conspicuously alien. He was little and old and bent. A short, bushy white beard framed his shiny black face and his tieless celluloid collar. A long, greasy, green-black Prince Albert, with lapels frayed and buttons worn through to their metal hung loosely from his shoulders. His trousers were big and baggy and limp, yet not enough so to hide the dejected bend of his knees.

A little boy noted the beard and gibed, "Hey, Santa Claus! 'Tain't Chris'mas yet!" And the little boy's playmates chorused, "Haw, haw! Lookit the colored Santa Claus!"

"For of such is the kingdom of heaven," mused Ezekiel Taylor. No. The kingdom of Harlem. Children turned into mockers. Satan in the hearts of infants. Harlem—city of the devil—outpost of hell.

Darkness settled, like the gloom in the old preacher's heart; darkness an hour late, for these sinners even tinkered with God's time, substituting their "daylight-saving." Wicked, yes. But sad too, as though they were desperately warding off the inescapable night of sorrow in which they must suffer for their sins. Harlem. What a field! What numberless souls to save!—These very taunting children who knew not even the simplest of the commandments—

But he was old and alone and defeated. The world had called to his best. It had offered money, and they had gone; first the young men whom he had fathered, whom he had brought up from infancy in his little Southern church; then their wives and children, whom they eventually sent for; and finally their parents, loath to leave their shepherd and their dear, decrepit shacks, but dependent and without choice.

ALAIN LOCKE

"Whyn't y' come to New York?" old Deacon Gassoway had insisted. "Martin and Eli and Jim Lee and his fambly's all up da' now an' doin' fine. We'll all git together an' start a chu'ch of our own, an' you'll still be pastor an' it'll be jes' same as 'twas hyeh." Full of that hope, he had come. But where were they? He had captained his little ship till it sank; he had clung to a splint and been tossed ashore; but the shore was cold, gray, hard and rock-strewn.

He had been in barren places before but God had been there too. Was Harlem then past hope? Was the connection between this place and heaven broken, so that the servant of God went hungry while little children ridiculed? Into his mind, like a reply, crept an old familiar hymn, and he found himself humming it softly:

> *The Lord will provide,*
> *The Lord will provide,*
> *In some way or 'nother,*
> *The Lord will provide.*
> *It may not be in your way,*
> *It may not be in mine,*
> *But yet in His own way*
> *The Lord will provide.*

Then suddenly, astonished, he stopped, listening. He had not been singing alone—a chorus of voices somewhere near had caught up his hymn. Its volume was gradually increasing. He looked about for a church. There was none. He covered his deaf ear so that it might not handicap his good one. The song seemed to issue from one of the private houses a little way down the street.

He approached with eager apprehension and stood wonderingly before a long flight of brownstone steps leading to an open entrance. The high first floor of the house, that to which the steps led, was brightly lighted, and the three front windows had their panes covered with colored tissue-paper designed to resemble church windows. Strongly, cheeringly the song came out to the listener:

> *The Lord will provide,*
> *The Lord will provide,*
> *In some way or 'nother,*
> *The Lord will provide.*

Ezekiel Taylor hesitated an incredulous moment, then smiling, he mounted the steps and went in.

The Reverend Shackleton Ealey had been inspired to preach the gospel by the draft laws of 1917. He remained in the profession not out of gratitude to its having kept him out of war, but because he found it a far less precarious mode of living than that devoted to poker, black-jack and dice. He was stocky and flat-faced and yellow, with many black freckles and the eyes of a dogfish. And he was clever enough not to conceal his origin, but to make capital out of his conversion from gambler to preacher and to confine himself to those less enlightened groups that thoroughly believed in the possibility of so sudden and complete a transformation.

The inflow of rural folk from the South was therefore fortune, and Reverend Shackleton Ealey spent hours in Pennsylvania station greeting newly arrived migrants, urging them to visit his meeting-place and promising them the satisfaction of "that old-time religion." Many had come—and contributed.

This was prayer-meeting night. Reverend Ealey had his seat on a low platform at the distant end of the double room originally designed for a "parlor." From behind a pulpit-stand improvised out of soap-boxes and covered with calico, he counted his congregation and estimated his profit.

A stranger entered uncertainly, looked about a moment, and took a seat near the door. Reverend Shackleton Ealey appraised him: a little bent-over old man with a bushy white beard and a long Prince Albert coat. Perfect type—fertile soil. He must greet this stranger at the close of the meeting and effusively make him welcome.

But Sister Gassoway was already by the stranger's side, shaking his hand vigorously and with unmistakable joy; and during the next hymn she came over to old man Gassoway and whispered in his ear, whereupon he jumped up wide-eyed, looked around, and made broadly smiling toward the newcomer. Others turned to see, and many, on seeing, began to whisper excitedly into their neighbor's ear and turned to see again. The stranger was occasioning altogether too great a stir. Reverend Ealey decided to pray.

His prayer was a masterpiece. It besought of God protection for His people in a strange and wicked land; it called down His damnation upon those dens of iniquity, the dance halls, the theaters, the cabarets; it berated the poker-sharp, the blackjack player, the dice-roller; it denounced the drunkard, the bootlegger, the dope-peddler; and it ended in a sweeping tirade against the wolf-in-sheep's clothing, whatever his motive might be.

Another hymn and the meeting came to a close.

The stranger was surrounded before Reverend Ealey could reach him. When finally he approached the old preacher with extended hand and hollow-hearted smile, old man Gassoway was saying:

"Yas, suh, Rev'n Taylor, dass jes' whut we goin' do. Start makin' 'rangements tomorrer. Martin an' Jim Lee's over to Ebeneezer, but dey doan like it 'tall. Says hit's too hifalutin for 'em, de way dese Harlem cullud folks wushup; Ain't got no Holy Ghos' in 'em, dass whut. Jes' come in an' set down an' git up an' go out. Never moans, never shouts, never even says 'amen.' Most of us is hyeh, an' we gonna git together an' start us a ch'ch of our own, wid you f' pastor, like we said. Yas, suh. Hyeh's Brother Ealey now. Brother Ealey, dis hyeh's our old preacher Rev'n Taylor. We was jes' tellin' him—"

The Reverend Shackleton Ealey had at last a genuine revelation— that the better-yielding half of his flock was on the wing. An old oath of frustration leaped to his lips—"God—"but he managed to bite it in the middle—"bless you, my brother," he growled.

II

Majutah

IT WAS ELEVEN O'CLOCK AT night. Majutah knew that Harry would be waiting on the doorstep downstairs. He knew better than to ring the bell so late—she had warned him. And there was no telephone. Grandmother wouldn't consent to having a telephone in the flat—she thought it would draw lightning. As if every other flat in the house didn't have one, as if lightning would strike all the others and leave theirs unharmed! Grandmother was such a nuisance with her old fogeyisms. If if weren't for her down-home ideas there'd be no trouble getting out now to go to the cabaret with Harry. As it was, Majutah would have to steal down the hall past Grandmother's room in the hope that she would be asleep.

Majutah looked to her attire. The bright red sandals and scarlet stockings, she fancied, made her feet look smaller and her legs bigger. This was desirable, since her black crepe dress, losing in width what style had added to its length, would not permit her to sit comfortably and cross her knees without occasioning ample display of everything below them. Her vanity-case mirror revealed how exactly the long pendant earrings matched her red coral beads and how perfectly becoming the new close bob was, and assured her for the tenth time that Egyptian rouge made her skin look lighter. She was ready.

Into the narrow hallway she tipped, steadying herself against the walls, and slowly approached the outside door at the end. Grandmother's room was the last off the hallway. Majutah reached it, slipped successfully past, and started silently to open the door to freedom.

"Jutie?"

How she hated to be called Jutie! Why couldn't the meddlesome old thing say Madge like everyone else?

"Ma'am?"

"Wha' you goin' dis time o' night?"

"Just downstairs to mail a letter."

"You easin' out mighty quiet, if dat's all you goin' do. Come 'eh. Lemme look at you."

Majutah slipped off her pendants and beads and laid them on the floor. She entered her grandmother's room, standing where the foot of the bed would hide her gay shoes and stockings. Useless precautions. The shrewd old woman inspected her granddaughter a minute in disapproving silence, then asked:

"Well, wha's de letter?"

"HELLO, MADGE," SAID HARRY. "WHAT held you up? You look mad enough to bite bricks."

"I am. Grandmother, of course. She's a pest. Always nosing and meddling. I'm grown, and the money I make supports both of us, and I'm sick of acting like a kid just to please her."

"How'd you manage?"

"I didn't manage. I just gave her a piece of my mind and came on out."

"Mustn't hurt the old lady's feelings. It's just her way of looking out for you."

"I don't need any looking out for—or advice either!"

"Excuse me. Which way—Happy's or Edmonds'?"

"Edmonds'—darn it!"

"Right."

It was two o'clock in the morning. Majutah's grandmother closed her Bible and turned down the oil lamp by which she preferred to read it. For a long time she sat thinking of Jutie—and of Harlem, this city of Satan. It was Harlem that had changed Jutie—this great, noisy, heartless, crowded place where you lived under the same roof with a hundred people you never knew; where night was alive and morning dead. It was Harlem—those brazen women with whom Jutie sewed, who swore and shimmied and laughed at the suggestion of going to church. Jutie wore red stockings. Jutie wore dresses that looked like nightgowns. Jutie painted her face and straightened her hair, instead of leaving it as God intended. Jutie—lied—often.

And while Madge laughed at a wanton song, her grandmother knelt by her bed and through the sinful babel of the airshaft, through her own silent tears, prayed to God in heaven for Jutie's lost soul.

III

Learnin'

"Too much learnin' ain' good f' nobody. When I was her age I couldn't write my own name."

"You can't write much mo' 'n that now. Too much learnin'! Whoever heard o' sich a thing!"

Anna's father, disregarding experience in arguing with his wife, pressed his point. "Sho they's sich a thing as too much learnin'! 'At gal's gittin' so she don't b'lieve nuthin'!"

"Hmph! Didn't she jes' tell me las' night she didn' b'lieve they ever was any Adam an' Eve?"

"Well, I ain' so sho they ever was any myself! An' one thing is certain: If that gal o' mine wants to keep on studyin' an' go up there to that City College an' learn how to teach school an' be somebody, I'll work my fingers to the bone to help her do it! Now!"

"That ain' what I'm talkin' 'bout. You ain' worked no harder 'n I is to help her git this far. Hyeh she is ready to graduate from high school. Think of it—high school! When we come along they didn' even *have* no high schools. Fus' thing y' know she be so far above us we can't reach her with a fence-rail. Then you'll wish you'd a listened to me. What I says is, she done gone far enough."

"Ain' no sich thing as far enough when you wants to go farther. 'Tain' as if it was gonna cost a whole lot. That's the trouble with you cullud

folks now. Git so far an' stop—set down—through—don't want no mo'."
Her disgust was boundless. "Y' got too much cotton field in you, that's
what!"

The father grinned. "They sho' ain' no cotton field in yo' mouth, honey."

"No, they ain't. An' they ain' no need o' all this arguin' either, 'cause
all that gal's got to do is come in hyeh right now an' put her arms 'roun'
y' neck, an' you'd send her to Europe if she wanted to go!"

"Well, all I says is, when dey gits to denyin' de Bible hit's time to
stop 'em."

"Well all *I* says is, if Cousin Sukie an' yo' no 'count brother, Jonathan,
can send their gal all the way from Athens to them Howard's an' pay
car-fare an' boa'd an' ev'ything, we can send our gal—"

She broke off as a door slammed. There was a rush, a delightful
squeal, and both parents were being smothered in a cyclone of embraces
by a wildly jubilant daughter.

"Mummy! Daddy! I won it! I won it!"

"What under the sun—?"

"The scholarship, Mummy! The scholarship!"

"No!"

"Yes, I did! I can go to Columbia! I can go to Teachers College! Isn't
it great?"

Anna's mother turned triumphantly to her husband; but he was
beaming at his daughter.

"You sho' is yo' daddy's chile. Teachers College! Why, that's wha' I
been wantin' you to go all along!"

IV

Revival

RARE SIGHT IN A CLOSE-BUILT, top-heavy city—space. A wide open
lot, extending along One Hundred and Thirty-eighth Street almost
from Lenox to Seventh Avenue; baring the mangy backs of a long
row of One Hundred and Thirty-ninth Street houses; disclosing their
gaping, gasping windows, their shameless strings of half-laundered rags,
which gulp up what little air the windows seek to inhale. Occupying the
Lenox Avenue end of the lot, the so-called Garvey tabernacle, wide,
low, squat, with its stingy little entrance; occupying the other, the
church tent where summer camp meetings are held.

Pete and his buddy, Lucky, left their head-to-head game of coon-can as darkness came on. Time to go out—had to save gas. Pete went to the window and looked down at the tent across the street.

"Looks like the side show of a circus. Ever been in?"

"Not me. I'm a preacher's son—got enough o' that stuff when I was a kid and couldn't protect myself."

"Ought to be a pretty good show when some o' them old-time sisters get happy. Too early for the cabarets; let's go in a while, just for the hell of it."

"You sure are hard up for somethin' to do."

"Aw, come on. Somethin' funny's bound to happen. You might even get religion, you dam' bootlegger."

Lucky grinned. "Might meet some o' my customers, you mean."

Through the thick, musty heat imprisoned by the canvas shelter a man's voice rose, leading a spiritual. Other voices chimed eagerly in, some high, clear, sweet; some low, mellow, full,—all swelling, rounding out the refrain till it filled the place, so that it seemed the flimsy walls and roof must soon be torn from their moorings and swept aloft with the song:

> *Where you running, sinner?*
> *Where you running, I say?*
> *Running from the fire—*
> *You can't cross here!*

The preacher stood waiting for the song to melt away. There was a moment of abysmal silence, into which the thousand blasphemies filtering in from outside dropped unheeded.

The preacher was talking in deep, impressive tones. One old patriarch was already supplementing each statement with a matter-of-fact "amen!" of approval.

The preacher was describing hell. He was enumerating without exception the horrors that befall the damned: maddening thirst for the drunkard; for the gambler, insatiable flame, his own greed devouring his soul. The preacher's voice no longer talked—it sang; mournfully at first, monotonously up and down, up and down—a chant in minor mode; then more intensely, more excitedly; now fairly strident.

The amens of approval were no longer matter-of-fact, perfunctory. They were quick, spontaneous, escaping the lips of their own accord;

they were frequent and loud and began to come from the edges of the assembly instead of just the front rows. The old men cried, "Help him, Lord!" "Preach the word!" "Glory!" taking no apparent heed of the awfulness of the description, and the old women continuously moaned aloud, nodding their bonneted heads, or swaying rhythmically forward and back in their seats.

Suddenly the preacher stopped, leaving the old men and old women still noisy with spiritual momentum. He stood motionless till the last echo of approbation subsided, then repeated the text from which his discourse had taken origin; repeated it in a whisper, lugubrious, hoarse, almost inaudible: "'In—hell—'" paused, then without warning, wildly shrieked, "'In hell—'" stopped—returned to his hoarse whisper—"'he lifted up his eyes. . .'"

"WHAT THE HELL YOU WANT to leave for?" Pete complained when he and Lucky reached the sidewalk. "That old bird would 'a' coughed up his gizzard in two more minutes. What's the idea?"

"Aw hell—I don't know.—You think that stuff's funny. You laugh at it. I don't, that's all." Lucky hesitated. The urge to speak outweighed the fear of being ridiculed. "Dam' 'f I know what it is—maybe because it makes me think of the old folks or somethin'—but—hell—it just sorter—gets me—"

Lucky turned abruptly away and started off. Pete watched him for a moment with a look that should have been astonished, outraged, incredulous—but wasn't. He overtook him, put an arm about his shoulders, and because he had to say something as they walked on, muttered reassuringly:

"Well—if you ain't the damndest fool—"

Fog[1]

John Matheus

The stir of life echoed. On the bridge between Ohio and West Virginia was the rumble of heavy trucks, the purr of high power engines in Cadillacs and Paiges, the rattle of Fords. A string of loaded freight cars pounded along on the C. & P. tracks, making a thunderous, if tedious way to Mingo. A steamboat's hoarse whistle boomed forth between the swish, swish, chug, chug of a mammoth stern paddle wheel with the asthmatic poppings of the pistons. The raucous shouts of smutty speaking street boys, the noises of a steam laundry, the clank and clatter of a pottery, the godless voices of women from Water Street houses of ill fame, all these blended in a sort of modern babel, common to all the towers of destruction erected by modern civilization.

These sounds were stirring when the clock sounded six on top of the Court House, that citadel of Law and Order, with the statue of Justice looming out of an alcove above the imposing stone entrance, blindfolded and in her right hand the scales of Judgment. Even so early in the evening the centers from which issued these inharmonious notes were scarcely visible. This sinister cloak of a late November twilight Ohio Valley fog had stealthily spread from somewhere beneath the somber river bed, down from somewhere in the lowering West Virginia hills. The fog extended its tentacles over city and river, gradually obliterating traces of familiar landscapes. At five-thirty the old Panhandle bridge, supported by massive sandstone pillars, stalwart, as when erected fifty years before to serve a generation now passed behind the portals of life, had become a spectral outline against the sky as the toll keepers of the New bridge looked northward up the Ohio River.

Now at six o'clock the fog no longer distorted; it blotted out, annihilated. One by one the street lights came on, giving an uncertain glare in spots, enabling peeved citizens to tread their way homeward without recognizing their neighbor ten feet ahead, whether he might be Jew or Gentile, Negro or Pole, Slav, Croatian, Italian or one hundred per cent American.

---

1. Awarded first prize *Opportunity* contest, 1925.

An impatient crowd of tired workers peered vainly through the gloom to see if the headlights of the interurban car were visible through the thickening haze. The car was due at Sixth and Market at six-ten and was scheduled to leave at six-fifteen for many little towns on the West Virginia side.

At the same time as these uneasy toilers were waiting, on the opposite side of the river the car had stopped to permit some passengers to descend and disappear in the fog. The motorman, fagged and jaded by the monotony of many stoppings and startings, waited mechanically for the conductor's bell to signal, "Go ahead."

The fog was thicker, more impenetrable. It smothered the headlight. Inside the car in the smoker, that part of the seats nearest the motorman's box, partitioned from the rest, the lights were struggling bravely against a fog of tobacco smoke, almost as opaque as the dull gray blanket of mist outside.

A group of red, rough men, sprawled along the two opposite bench-formed seats, parallel to the sides of the car, were talking to one another in the thin, flat colorless English of their mountain state, embellished with the homely idioms of the coal mine, the oil field, the gas well.

"When does this here meetin' start, Bill?"

"That 'air notice read half after seven."

"What's time now?"

"Damned 'f I know. Hey, Lee, what time's that pocket clock of yourn's got?"

"Two past six."

There was the sound of a match scratching against the sole of a rough shoe.

"Gimme a light, Lafe."

In attempting to reach for the burning match before its flame was extinguished, the man stepped forward and stumbled over a cheap suitcase of imitation leather. A vile-looking stogie fell in the aisle.

"God! Your feet're bigger'n Bills's."

The crowd laughed uproariously. The butt of this joke grinned and showed a set of dirty nicotine-stained teeth. He recovered his balance in time to save the flaring match. He was a tremendous man, slightly stooped, with taffy-colored, straggling hair and little pig eyes.

Between initial puffs he drawled: "Now you're barkin' up the wrong tree. I only wear elevens."

"Git off'n me, Lee Cromarty," growled Bill. "You hadn't ought to be rumlin' of *my* feathers the wrong way—and you a-plannin' to ride the goat."

Lake, a consumptive appearing, undersized, bovine-eyed individual, spat out the remark: "Naow, there! You had better be kereful. Men have been nailed to the cross for less than that."

"Ha! ha!—ho! ho! ho!"

There was a joke to arouse the temper of the crowd.

A baby began to cry lustily in the rear and more commodious end of the car reserved for nonsmokers. His infantine wailing smote in sharp contrast upon the ears of the hilarious joshers, filling the silence that followed the subsidence of the laughter.

"Taci, bimba. Non aver paura!"

Nobody understood the musical words of the patient, Madonna-eyed Italian mother, not even the baby, for it continued its yelling. She opened her gay-colored shirt waist and pressed the child to her bosom. He was quieted.

"She can't speak United States, but I bet her Tony Spaghetti votes the same as you an' me. The young 'un 'll have more to say about the future of these United States than your children an' mine unless we carry forward the work such as we are going to accomplish to-night."

"Yeh, you're damned right," answered the scowling companion of the lynx-eyed citizen in khaki clothes, who had thus commented upon the foreign woman's offspring.

"They breed like cats. They'll outnumber us, unless—"

A smell of garlic stifled his speech. Nich and Mike Axaminter, late for the night shift at the La Belle, bent over the irate American, deluging him with the odor of garlic and voluble, guttural explosions of a Slovak tongue.

"What t' hell! Git them buckets out o' my face, you hunkies, you!"

Confused and apologetic the two men moved forward.

"Isn't this an awful fog, Barney," piped a gay, girlish voice.

"I'll tell the world it is," replied her red-haired companion, flinging a half-smoked cigarette away in the darkness as he assisted the girl to the platform.

They made their way to a vacant seat in the end of the car opposite the smoker, pausing for a moment respectfully to make the sign of the cross before two Sisters of Charity, whose flowing black robes and ebon headdress contrasted strikingly with the pale whiteness of their faces.

The nuns raised their eyes, slightly smiled and continued their orisons on dark decades rosaries with pendent crosses of ivory.

"Let's sit here," whispered the girl. "I don't want to be by those niggers."

In a few seconds they were settled. There were cooings of sweet words, limpid-eyed soul glances. They forgot all others. The car was theirs alone.

"Say, boy, ain't this some fog. Yuh can't see the old berg."

"'Sthat so. I hadn't noticed."

Two Negro youths thus exchanged words. They were well dressed and sporty.

"Well, it don't matter, as long as it don't interfere with the dance."

"I hope Daisy will be there. She's some stunnin' high-brown an' I don't mean maybe."

"O boy!"

Thereupon one began to hum "Daddy, O Daddy" and the other whistled softly the popular air from "Shuffle Along" entitled "Old-Fashioned Love."

"Oi, oi! Ven I say vill dis car shtart. Ve must mek dot train fur Pittsburgh."

"Ach, Ish ka bibble. They can't do a thing without us, Laban."

They settled down in their seats to finish the discussion in Yiddish, emphasizing the conversation with shrugs of the shoulder and throaty interjections.

In a seat apart to themselves, for two seats in front and behind were unoccupied, sat an old Negro man and a Negro woman, evidently his wife. Crowded between them was a girl of fourteen or fifteen.

"This heah is suah cu'us weather," complained the old man.

"We all nevah had no sich fog in Oklahoma."

The girl's hair was bobbed and had been straightened by "Poro" treatment, giving her an Egyptian cast of features.

"Gran'pappy," said the girl, "yo' cain't see ovah yander."

"Ain't it de troot, chile."

"Ne' min', sugah," assured the old woman. "Ah done paid dat 'ployment man an' he sayed yo' bound tuh lak de place. Dis here lady what's hirin' yo' is no po' trash an' she wants a likely gal lak yo' tuh ten' huh baby."

Now these series of conversations did not transpire in chronological order. They were uttered more or less simultaneously during the interval that the little conductor stood on tiptoe in an effort to keep one hand on the signal rope, craning his neck in a vain and dissatisfied endeavor to pierce the miasma of the fog. The motorman chafed in his box, thinking of the drudging lot of the laboring man. He registered discontent.

The garrulous group in the smoker were smoldering cauldrons of discontent. In truth their dissatisfaction ran the gamut of hate. It was stretching out to join hands with an unknown and clandestine host to plot, preserve, defend their dwarfed and twisted ideals.

The two foreign intruders in the smoker squirmed under the merciless, half articulate antipathy. They asked nothing but a job to make some money. In exchange for that magic English word job, they endured the terror that walked by day, the boss. They grinned stupidly at profanity, dirt, disease, disaster. Yet they were helping to make America.

Three groups in the car on this foggy evening were united under the sacred mantle of a common religion. Within its folds they sensed vaguely a something of happiness. The Italian mother radiated the joy of her child. Perhaps in honor of her and in reverence the two nuns with downcast eyes, trying so hard to forget the world, were counting off the rosary of the blessed Virgin—"Ave, Maria," "Hail, Mary, full of grace, the Lord is with thee; blessed art thou among women."

The youth and his girl in their tiny circle of mutual attraction and affection could not as in Edwin Markham's poem widen the circle to include all, or even embrace that small circumscribed area of humanity within the car.

And the Negroes? Surely there was no hate in their minds. The gay youths were rather indifferent. The trio from the South, journeying far for a greater freedom philosophically accepted the inevitable "slings and arrows of outrageous fortune."

The Jews were certainly enveloped in a racial consciousness, unerringly fixed on control and domination of money, America's most potent factor in respectability.

The purplish haze of fog contracted. Its damp presence slipped into the car and every passenger shivered and peered forth to see. Their eyes were as the eyes of the blind!

At last the signal bell rang out staccato. The car suddenly lurched forward, shaking from side to side the passengers in their seats. The wheels scraped and began to turn. Almost at once a more chilling wetness filtered in from the river. In the invisibility of the fog it seemed that one was travelling through space, in an aeroplane perhaps, going nobody knew where.

The murmur of voices buzzed in the smoker, interrupted by the boisterous outbursts of laughter. A red glare tinted the fog for a second and disappeared. La Belle was "shooting" the furnaces. Then a denser darkness and the fog.

The car lurched, scintillating sparks flashed from the trolley wire, a terrific crash—silence. The lights went out. Before anybody could think or scream, there came a falling sensation, such as one experiences when dropped unexpectedly in an elevator or when diving through the scenic railways of the city amusements parks, or more exactly when one has nightmare and dreams of falling, falling, falling.

"The bridge has given way. God! The muddy water! The fog! Darkness. Death."

These thoughts flashed spontaneously in the consciousness of the rough ignorant fellows, choking in the fumes of their strong tobacco, came to the garlic scented "hunkies," to the Italian Madonna, to the Sisters of Charity, to the lover boy and his lover girl, to the Negro youths, to the Jews thinking in Yiddish idioms, to the old Negro man and his wife and the Egyptian-faced girl, with the straightened African hair, even to the bored motorman and the weary conductor.

To drown, to strangle, to suffocate, to die! In the dread silence the words screamed like exploding shells within the beating temples of terror-stricken passengers and crew.

Then protest, wild, mad, tumultuous, frantic protest. Life at bay and bellowing furiously against its ancient arch-enemy and antithesis—Death. An oath, screams—dull, paralyzing, vomit-stirring nausea. Holy, unexpressed intimacies, deeply rooted prejudices were roughly shaken from their smug moorings. The Known to be changed for an Unknown, the ever expected, yet unexpected, Death. No! No! Not that.

Lee Cromarty saw things in that darkness. A plain, one-story frame house, a slattern woman on the porch, an overgrown, large-hipped girl with his face. Then the woman's whining, scolding voice and the girl's bashful confidences. What was dimming that picture? What cataract was blurring his vision? Was it the fog?

To Lafe, leader of the crowd, crouched in his seat, his fingers clawing the air for a grasping place, came a vision of a hill-side grave—his wife's—and he saw again how she looked in her coffin—then the fog.

"I'll not report at the mine," thought Bill. "Wonder what old Bunner will say to that."

The mine foreman's grizzled face dangled for a second before him and was swallowed in the fog.

Hoarse, gasping exhalations. Men, old men, young men, sobbing. "Pietà! Madre mia!—Mercy, Virgin Mary! My child!"

No thoughts of fear or pain on the threshold of death, that shadow from whence all children flow, but all the Mother Love focused to save the child.

"*Memorare*, remember, O most gracious Virgin Mary, that never was it known that any one who fled to thy protection, implored thy help and sought thy intercession was left unaided."

The fingers sped over the beads of the rosary. But looming up, unerasable, shuttled the kaleidoscope of youth, love, betrayal, renunciation, the vows. *Miserere, Jesu!*

> *Life is ever lord of Death*
> *And Love can never lose its own.*

The girl was hysterical, weeping, screaming, laughing. Did the poet dream an idle dream, a false mirage? Death is master. Death is stealing Love away. How could a silly girl believe or know the calm of poesy?

The boy crumbled. His swagger and bravado melted. The passionate call of sex became a blur. He was not himself, yet he was looking at himself, a confusion in space, in night, in Fog. And who was she hanging limp upon his arm?

That dance? The jazz dance? Ah, the dance! The dance of Life was ending. The orchestra was playing a dirge and Death was leading the Grand March. Fog! Impenetrable fog!

All the unheeded, forgotten warnings of ranting preachers, all the prayers of simple black mothers, the Mercy-Seat, the Revival, too late. Terror could give no articulate expression to these muffled feelings. They came to the surface of a blunted consciousness, incoherent.

Was there a God in Israel? Laban remembered Russia and the pogrom. He had looked into the eyes of Fate that day and watched God die with his mother and sisters. Here he was facing Fate again. There was no answer. He was silent.

His companion sputtered, fumed, screeched. He clung to Laban in pieces.

Laban remembered the pogrom. The old Negro couple remembered another horror. They had been through the riots in Tulsa. There they had lost their son and his wife, the Egyptian-faced girl's father and mother. They had heard the whine of bullets, the hiss of flame, the howling of human wolves, killing in the most excruciating manner. The water was silent. The water was merciful.

The old woman began to sing in a high quavering minor key:

Lawdy, won't yo' ketch mah groan,
O Lawdy, Lawdy, won't yo' ketch mah groan.

The old man cried out: "Judgment! Judgment!"

The Egyptian-faced girl wept. She was sore afraid, sore afraid. And the fog was round about them.

Time is a relative term. The philosophers are right for once. What happened inside the heads of these men and women seemed to them to have consumed hours instead of seconds. The conductor mechanically grabbed for the trolley rope, the motorman threw on the brakes.

The reaction came. Fear may become inarticulate and paralyzed. Then again it may become belligerent and self-protective, striking blindly in the maze. Darkness did not destroy completely the sense of direction.

"The door! The exit!"

A mad rush to get out, not to be trapped without a chance, like rats in a trap.

"Out of my way! Damn you—out of my way!"

Somebody yelled: "Sit still!"

Somebody hissed: "Brutes! Beasts!"

Another concussion, accompanied by the grinding of steel. The car stopped, lurched backward, swayed, and again stood still. Excited shouts re-echoed from the ends of the bridge. Automobile horns tooted. An age seemed to pass, but the great splash did not come. There was still time—maybe. The car was emptied.

"Run for the Ohio end!" someone screamed.

The fog shut off every man from his neighbor. The sound of scurrying feet reverberated, of the Italian woman and her baby, of the boy carrying his girl, of the Negro youths, of the old man and his wife, half dragging the Egyptian-faced girl, of the Sisters of Charity, of the miners. Flitting like wraiths in Homer's Hades, seeking life.

In a few minutes all were safe on Ohio soil. The bridge still stood.

A street light gave a ghastly glare through the fog. The whore houses on Water Street brooded evilly in the shadows. Dogs barked, the Egyptian-faced girl had fainted. The old Negro woman panted, "Mah Jesus! Mah Jesus!"

The occupants of the deserted car looked at one another. The icy touch of the Grave began to thaw. There was a generous intermingling. Everybody talked at once, inquiring, congratulating.

"Look after the girl," shouted Lee Cromarty. "Help the old woman, boys."

Bells began to ring. People came running. The ambulance arrived. The colored girl had recovered. Then everybody shouted again. Profane miners, used to catastrophe, were strangely moved. The white boy and girl held hands.

"Sing us a song, old woman," drawled Lafe.

"He's heard mah groan. He done heard it," burst forth the old woman in a song flood of triumph.

Yes, he conquered Death and Hell,
An' He never said a mumblin' word,
Not a word, not a word.

"How you feelin', Mike," said Bill to the garlic eater.

"Me fine. Me fine."

The news of the event spread like wildfire. The street was now crowded. The police arrived. A bridge official appeared, announcing the probable cause of the accident, a slipping of certain supports. The girders fortunately had held. A terrible tragedy had been prevented.

"I'm a wash-foot Baptist an' I don't believe in Popery," said Lake, "but, fellers, let's ask them ladies in them air mournin' robes to say a prayer of thanksgiving for the bunch."

The Sisters of Charity did say a prayer, not an audible petition for the ears of men, but a whispered prayer for the ears of God, the Benediction of Thanksgiving, uttered by the Catholic Church through many years, in many tongues and places.

"De profundis," added the silently moving lips of the white-faced nuns. "Out of the depths have we cried unto Thee, O Lord. And Thou hast heard our cries."

The motorman was no longer dissatisfied. The conductor's strength had been renewed like the eagle's.

"Boys," drawled Lake, "I'll be damned if I'm goin' to that meetin' to-night."

"Nor me," affirmed Lee Cromarty.

"Nor me," repeated all the others.

The fog still crept from under the bed of the river and down from the lowering hills of West Virginia—dense, tenacious, stealthy, chilling, but from about the hearts and minds of some rough, unlettered men another fog had begun to lift.

Carma[1]

Jean Toomer

Wind is in the cane. Come along.
Cane leaves swaying, rusty with talk,
Scratching choruses above the guinea's squawk,
Wind is in the cane. Come along.

C arma, in overalls, and strong as any man, stands behind the old brown mule, driving the wagon home. It bumps, and groans, and shakes as it crosses the railroad track. She, riding it easy. I leave the men around the stove to follow her with my eyes down the red dust road. Nigger woman driving a Georgia chariot down an old dust road. Dixie Pike is what they call it. Maybe she feels my gaze, perhaps she expects it. Anyway, she turns. The sun, which has been slanting over her shoulder, shoots primitive rockets into her mangrove-gloomed, yellow flower face. Hi! Yip! God has left the Moses-people for the nigger. "Gedap." Using reins to slap the mule, she disappears in a cloudy rumble at some indefinite point along the road.

(The sun is hammered to a band of gold. Pine-needles, like mazda, are brilliantly aglow. No rain has come to take the rustle from the falling sweet-gum leaves. Over in the forest, across the swamp, a sawmill blows its closing whistle. Smoke curls up. Marvellous web spun by the spider sawdust pile. Curls up and spreads itself pine-high above the branch, a single silver band along the eastern valley. A black boy. . . you are the most sleepiest man I ever seed, Sleeping Beauty. . . cradled on a gray mule, guided by the hollow sound of cowbells, heads for them through a rusty cotton field. From down the railroad track, the chug-chug of a gas engine announces that the repair gang is coming home. A girl in the yard of a whitewashed shack not much larger than the stack of worn ties piled before it, sings. Her voice is loud. Echoes, like rain, sweep the valley. Dusk takes the polish from the rails. Lights twinkle in scattered houses. From far away, a sad strong song. Pungent and composite, the smell of farmyards is the fragrance of the woman. She does not sing; her body is a song. She is in the forest, dancing. Torches flare. . . juju

---

1. From *Cane*.

men, greegree, witch-doctors. . . torches go out. . . The Dixie Pike has grown from a goat path in Africa.

Night.
Foxie, the bitch, slicks back her ears and barks at the rising moon.)

Wind is in the corn. Come along.
Corn leaves swaying, rusty with talk,
Scratching choruses above the guinea's squawk,
Wind is in the corn. Come along.

Carma's tale is the crudest melodrama. Her husband's in the gang. And it's her fault he got there. Working with a contractor, he was away most of the time. She had others. No one blames her for that. He returned one day and hung around the town where he picked up week-old boasts and rumors. . . Bane accused her. She denied. He couldn't see that she was becoming hysterical. He would have liked to take his fists and beat her. Who was strong as a man. Stronger. Words, like corkscrews, wormed to her strength. It fizzled out. Grabbing a gun, she rushed from the house and plunged across the road into a cane-brake. . . There, in quarter heaven shone the crescent moon. . . Bane was afraid to follow till he heard the gun go off. Then he wasted half an hour gathering the neighbor men. They met in the road where lamp-light showed tracks dissolving in the loose earth about the cane. The search began. Moths flickered the lamps. They put them out. Really, because she still might be live enough to shoot. Time and space have no meaning in a canefield. No more than the interminable stalks. . . Someone stumbled over her. A cry went up. From the road, one would have thought that they were cornering a rabbit or a skunk. . . It is difficult carrying dead weight through cane. They placed her on the sofa. A curious, nosey somebody looked for the wound. This fussing with her clothes aroused her. Her eyes were weak and pitiable for so strong a woman. Slowly, then like a flash, Bane came to know that the shot she fired, with averted head, was aimed to whistle like a dying hornet through the cane. Twice deceived,—and one deception proved the other. His head went off. Slashed one of the men who'd helped, the man who'd stumbled over her. Now he's in the gang. Who was her husband. Should she not take others, this Carma, strong as a man, whose tale as I have told it is the crudest melodrama?

ALAIN LOCKE

Wind is in the cane. Come along.
Cane leaves swaying, rusty with talk,
Scratching choruses above the guinea's squawk,
Wind is in the cane. Come along.

FERN[1]

Jean Toomer

Face flowed into her eyes. Flowed in soft cream foam and plaintive ripples, in such a way that wherever your glance may momentarily have rested, it immediately thereafter wavered in the direction of her eyes. The soft suggestion of down slightly darkened, like the shadow of a bird's wing might, the creamy brown color of her upper lip. Why, after noticing it, you sought her eyes, I cannot tell you. Her nose was aquiline, Semitic. If you have heard a Jewish cantor sing, if he has touched you and made your own sorrow seem trivial when compared with his, you will know my feeling when I follow the curves of her profile, like mobile rivers, to their common delta. They were strange eyes. In this, that they sought nothing—that is, nothing that was obvious and tangible and that one could see, and they gave the impression that nothing was to be denied. When a woman seeks, you will have observed, her eyes deny. Fern's eyes desired nothing that you could give her; there was no reason why they should withhold. Men saw her eyes and fooled themselves. Fern's eyes said to them that she was easy. When she was young, a few men took her, but got no joy from it. And then, once done, they felt bound to her (quite unlike their hit and run with other girls), felt as though it would take them a lifetime to fulfill an obligation which they could find no name for. They became attached to her, and hungered after finding the barest trace of what she might desire. As she grew up, new men who came to town felt as almost everyone did who ever saw her: that they would not be denied. Men were everlastingly bringing her their bodies. Something inside of her got tired of them, I guess, for I am certain that for the life of her she could not tell why or how she began to turn them off. A man in fever is no trifling thing to send away. They began to leave her, baffled and ashamed, yet vowing to themselves that some day they would do some fine thing for her: send her candy every week and not let her know whom it came from, watch out for her wedding-day and give her a magnificent something with no name on it, buy a house and deed it to her, rescue her from some unworthy fellow who had tricked her into marrying him. As you know, men are

---

1. From *Cane*.

apt to idolize or fear that which they cannot understand, especially if it be a woman. She did not deny them, yet the fact was that they were denied. A sort of superstition crept into their consciousness of her being somehow above them. Being above them meant that she was not to be approached by anyone. She became a virgin. Now a virgin in a small southern town is by no means the usual thing, if you will believe me. That the sexes were made to mate is the practice of the South. Particularly, black folks were made to mate. And it is black folks whom I have been talking about thus far. What white men thought of Fern I can arrive at only by analogy. They let her alone.

ANYONE, OF COURSE, COULD SEE her, could see her eyes. If you walked up the Dixie Pike most any time of day, you'd be most like to see her resting listless-like on the railing of her porch, back propped against a post, head tilted a little forward because there was a nail in the porch post just where her head came which for some reason or other she never took the trouble to pull out. Her eyes, if it were sunset, rested idly where the sun, molten and glorious, was pouring down between the fringe of pines. Or maybe they gazed at the gray cabin on the knoll from which an evening folk-song was coming. Perhaps they followed a cow that had been turned loose to roam and feed on cotton-stalks and corn leaves. Like as not they'd settle on some vague spot above the horizon, though hardly a trace of wistfulness would come to them. If it were dusk, then they'd wait for the search-light of the evening train which you could see miles up the track before it flared across the Dixie Pike, close to her home. Wherever they looked, you'd follow them and then waver back. Like her face, the whole countryside seemed to flow into her eyes. Flowed into them with the soft listless cadence of Georgia's South. A young Negro, once, was looking at her, spellbound, from the road. A white man passing in a buggy had to flick him with his whip if he was to get by without running him over. I first saw her on her porch. I was passing with a fellow whose crusty numbness (I was from the North and suspected of being prejudiced and stuck-up) was melting as he found me warm. I asked him who she was. "That's Fern," was all that I could get from him. Some folks already thought that I was given to nosing around; I let it go at that, so far as questions were concerned. But at first sight of her I felt as if I heard a Jewish cantor sing. As if his singing rose above the unheard chorus of a folk-song. And I felt bound to her. I too had my dreams: something I would do for her. I have knocked about from town to town too much not to know the futility of mere change of place. Besides, picture if you can, this cream-colored solitary girl sitting at a tenement window looking down on the indifferent throngs of Harlem. Better that she listen to folk-songs at dusk in Georgia, you would say, and so would I. Or, suppose she came up North and married. Even a doctor or a lawyer, say, one who would be sure to get along—that is, make money. You and I know, who have had experience in such things, that love is not a thing like prejudice which can be bettered by changes of town. Could men in Washington, Chicago, or New York, more than the men of Georgia, bring her something left vacant by the bestowal of their bodies? You and I who know men in these cities will have to say, they could not. See her out and out a prostitute along State Street in Chicago. See her move into a southern town where white men are more aggressive. See her become a white man's concubine. . . Something I must do for her. There was myself. What could I do for her? Talk, of course. Push back the fringe of pines upon new horizons. To what purpose? and what for? Her? Myself? Men in her case seem to lose their selfishness. I lost mine before I touched her. I ask you, friend (it makes no difference if you sit in the Pullman or the Jim Crow as the train crosses her road), what thoughts would come to you—that is, after you'd finished with the thoughts that leap into men's minds at the sight of a pretty woman who will not deny them; what thoughts would come to you, had you seen her in a quick flash, keen and intuitively, as she sat there on her porch when your train thundered by? Would you have got off at the next station and come back for her to take her where? Would you have completely forgotten her as soon as you reached Macon, Atlanta, Augusta, Pasadena, Madison, Chicago, Boston, or New Orleans? Would you tell your wife or sweetheart about a girl you saw? Your thoughts can help me, and I would like to know. Something I would do for her. . .

ONE EVENING I WALKED UP the Pike on purpose, and stopped to say hello. Some of her family were about, but they moved away to make room for me. Damn if I knew how to begin. Would you? Mr. and Miss So-and-So, people, the weather, the crops, the new preacher, the frolic, the church benefit, rabbit and possum hunting, the new soft drink they had at old Pap's store, the schedule of the trains, what kind of town Macon was, Negro's migration north, boll-weevils, syrup, the

ALAIN LOCKE

Bible—to all these things she gave a yassur or nassur, without further comment. I began to wonder if perhaps my own emotional sensibility had played one of its tricks on me. "Let's take a walk," I at last ventured. The suggestion, coming after so long an isolation, was novel enough, I guess, to surprise. But it wasn't that. Something told me that men before me had said just that as a prelude to the offering of their bodies. I tried to tell her with my eyes. I think she understood. The thing from her that made my throat catch, vanished. Its passing left her visible in a way I'd thought, but never seen. We walked down the Pike with people on all the porches gaping at us. "Doesn't it make you mad?" She meant the row of petty gossiping people. She meant the world. Through a canebrake that was ripe for cutting, the branch was reached. Under a sweet-gum tree, and where reddish leaves had dammed the creek a little, we sat down. Dusk, suggesting the almost imperceptible procession of giant trees, settled with a purple haze about the cane. I felt strange, as I always do in Georgia, particularly at dusk. I felt that things unseen to men were tangibly immediate. It would not have surprised me had I had vision. People have them in Georgia more often than you would suppose. A black woman once saw the mother of Christ and drew her in charcoal on the courthouse wall. . . When one is on the soil of one's ancestors, most anything can come to one. . . From force of habit, I suppose, I held Fern in my arms—that is, without at first noticing it. Then my mind came back to her. Her eyes, unusually weird and open, held me. Held God. He flowed in as I've seen the countryside flow in. Seen men. I must have done something—what, I don't know, in the confusion of my emotion. She sprang up. Rushed some distance from me. Fell to her knees, and began swaying, swaying. Her body was tortured with something it could not let out. Like boiling sap it flooded arms and fingers till she shook them as if they burned her. It found her throat, and spattered inarticulately in plaintive, convulsive sounds, mingled with calls to Christ Jesus. And then she sang, brokenly. A Jewish cantor singing with a broken voice. A child's voice, uncertain, or an old man's. Dusk hid her; I could hear only her song. It seemed to me as though she were pounding her head in anguish upon the ground. I rushed to her. She fainted in my arms.

THERE WAS TALK ABOUT HER fainting with me in the cane-field. And I got one or two ugly looks from town men who'd set themselves up to protect her. In fact, there was talk of making me leave town. But they never did. They kept a watch-out for me, though. Shortly after, I came back North. From the train window I saw her as I crossed her road. Saw her on her porch, head tilted a little forward where the nail was, eyes vaguely focused on the sunset. Saw her face flow into them, the countryside and something that I call God, flowing into them. . . Nothing ever really happened. Nothing ever came to Fern, not even I. Something I would do for her. Some fine unnamed thing. . . And, friend, you? She is still living, I have reason to know. Her name, against the chance that you might happen down that way, is Fernie May Rosen.

Spunk[1]

Zora Neale Hurston

I

A GIANT OF A BROWN-SKINNED man sauntered up the one street of the Village and out into the palmetto thickets with a small pretty woman clinging lovingly to his arm.

"Looka theah, folkses!" cried Elijah Mosley, slapping his leg gleefully. "Theah they go, big as life an' brassy as tacks."

All the loungers in the store tried to walk to the door with an air of nonchalance but with small success.

"Now pee-eople!" Walter Thomas gasped. "Will you look at 'em!"

"But that's one thing Ah likes about Spunk Banks—he ain't skeered of nothin' on God's green footstool—*nothin'!* He rides that log down at saw-mill jus' like he struts 'round wid another man's wife—jus' don't give a kitty. When Tes' Miller got cut to giblets on that circle-saw, Spunk steps right up and starts ridin'. The rest of us was skeered to go near it."

A round-shouldered figure in overalls much too large, came nervously in the door and the talking ceased. The men looked at each other and winked.

"Gimme some soda-water. Sass'prilla Ah reckon," the newcomer ordered, and stood far down the counter near the open pickled pig-feet tub to drink it.

Elijah nudged Walter and turned with mock gravity to the newcomer.

"Say, Joe, how's everything up yo' way? How's yo' wife?"

Joe started and all but dropped the bottle he held in his hands. He swallowed several times painfully and his lips trembled.

"Aw 'Lige, you oughtn't to do nothin' like that," Walter grumbled. Elijah ignored him.

"She jus' passed heah a few minutes ago goin' thata way," with a wave of his hand in the direction of the woods.

---

1. Awarded second prize, *Opportunity* contest, 1925.

Now Joe knew his wife had passed that way. He knew that the men lounging in the general store had seen her, moreover, he knew that the men knew *he* knew. He stood there silent for a long moment staring blankly, with his Adam's apple twitching nervously up and down his throat. One could actually *see* the pain he was suffering, his eyes, his face, his hands and even the dejected slump of his shoulders. He set the bottle down upon the counter. He didn't bang it, just eased it out of his hand silently and fiddled with his suspender buckle.

"Well, Ah'm goin' after her to-day. Ah'm goin' an' fetch her back. Spunk's done gone too fur."

He reached deep down into his trouser pocket and drew out a hollow ground razor, large and shiny, and passed his moistened thumb back and forth over the edge.

"Talkin' like a man, Joe. Course that's *yo'* fambly affairs, but Ah like to see grit in anybody."

Joe Kanty laid down a nickel and stumbled out into the street.

Dusk crept in from the woods. Ike Clarke lit the swinging oil lamp that was almost immediately surrounded by candle-flies. The men laughed boisterously behind Joe's back as they watched him shamble woodward.

"You oughtn't to said whut you did to him, Lige—look how it worked him up," Walter chided.

"And Ah hope it did work him up. 'Tain't even decent for a man to take and take like he do."

"Spunk will sho' kill him."

"Aw, Ah doan' know. You never kin tell. He might turn him up an' spank him fur gettin' in the way, but Spunk wouldn't shoot no unarmed man. Dat razor he carried outa heah ain't gonna run Spunk down an' cut him, an' Joe ain't got the nerve to go up to Spunk with it knowing he totes that Army .45. He makes that break outa heah to bluff us. He's gonna hide that razor behind the first likely palmetto root an' sneak back home to bed. Don't tell me nothin' 'bout that rabbit-foot colored man. Didn't he meet Spunk an' Lena face to face one day las' week an' mumble sumthin' to Spunk 'bout lettin' his wife alone?"

"What did Spunk say?" Walter broke in—"Ah like him fine but 'tain't right the way he carries on wid Lena Kanty, jus' cause Joe's timid 'bout fightin'."

"You wrong theah, Walter. 'Tain't cause Joe's timid at all, it's cause Spunk wants Lena. If Joe was a passle of wile cats Spunk would tackle the job just the same. He'd go after *anything* he wanted the same way. As Ah wuz sayin' a minute ago, he tole Joe right to his face that Lena was his. 'Call her,' he says to Joe. 'Call her and see if she'll come. A woman knows her boss an' she answers when he calls.' 'Lena, ain't I yo' husband?' Joe sorter whines out. Lena looked at him real disgusted but she don't answer and she don't move outa her tracks. Then Spunk reaches out an' takes hold of her arm an' says: 'Lena, youse mine. From now on Ah works for you an' fights for you an' Ah never wants you to look to nobody for a crumb of bread, a stitch of close or a shingle to go over yo' head, but *me* long as Ah live. Ah'll git the lumber foh owah house to-morrow. Go home an' git yo' things together!'

"'Thass mah house,' Lena speaks up. 'Papa gimme that.'

"'Well,' says Spunk, 'doan give up whut's yours, but when youse inside don't forgit youse mine, an' let no other man git outa his place wid you!'

"Lena looked up at him with her eyes so full of love that they wuz runnin' over, an' Spunk seen it an' Joe seen it too, and his lip started to tremblin' and his Adam's apple was galloping up and down his neck like a race horse. Ah bet he's wore out half a dozen Adam's apples since Spunk's been on the job with Lena. That's all he'll do. He'll be back heah after while swallowin' an' workin' his lips like he wants to say somethin' an' can't."

"But didn't he do *nothin'* to stop 'em?"

"Nope, not a frazzlin' thing—jus' stood there. Spunk took Lena's arm and walked off jus' like nothin' ain't happened and he stood there gazin' after them till they was outa sight. Now you know a woman don't want no man like that. I'm jus' waitin' to see whut he's goin' to say when he gits back."

II

But Joe Kanty never came back, never. The men in the store heard the sharp report of a pistol somewhere distant in the palmetto thicket and soon Spunk came walking leisurely, with his big black Stetson set at the same rakish angle and Lena clinging to his arm, came walking right into the general store. Lena wept in a frightened manner.

"Well," Spunk announced calmly, "Joe come out there wid a meatax an' made me kill him."

He sent Lena home and led the men back to Joe—Joe crumpled and limp with his right hand still clutching his razor.

"See mah back? Mah does cut clear through. He sneaked up an' tried to kill me from the back, but Ah got him, an' got him good, first shot," Spunk said.

The men glared at Elijah, accusingly.

"Take him up an' plant him in 'Stoney lonesome,'" Spunk said in a careless voice. "Ah didn't wanna shoot him but he made me do it. He's a dirty coward, jumpin' on a man from behind."

Spunk turned on his heel and sauntered away to where he knew his love wept in fear for him and no man stopped him. At the general store later on, they all talked of locking him up until the sheriff should come from Orlando, but no one did anything but talk.

A clear case of self-defense, the trial was a short one, and Spunk walked out of the court house to freedom again. He could work again, ride the dangerous log-carriage that fed the singing, snarling, biting, circle-saw; he could stroll the soft dark lanes with his guitar. He was free to roam the woods again; he was free to return to Lena. He did all of these things.

III

"WHUT YOU RECKON, WALT?" ELIJAH asked one night later. "Spunk's gittin' ready to marry Lena!"

"Naw! Why, Joe ain't had time to git cold yit. Nohow Ah didn't figger Spunk was the marryin' kind."

"Well, he is," rejoined Elijah. "He done moved most of Lena's things—and her along wid 'em—over to the Bradley house. He's buying it. Jus' like Ah told yo' all right in heah the night Joe wuz kilt. Spunk's crazy 'bout Lena. He don't want folks to keep on talkin' 'bout her—thass reason he's rushin' so. Funny thing 'bout that bob-cat, wan't it?"

"What bob-cat, 'Lige? Ah ain't heered 'bout none."

"Ain't cher? Well, night befo' las' was the fust night Spunk an' Lena moved together an' jus' as they was goin' to bed, a big black bob-cat, black all over, you hear me, *black,* walked round and round that house and howled like forty, an' when Spunk got his gun an' went to the winder to shoot it, he says it stood right still an' looked him in the eye, an' howled right at him. The thing got Spunk so nervoused up he couldn't shoot. But Spunk says twan't no bob-cat nohow. He says it was Joe done sneaked back from Hell!"

"Humph!" sniffed Walter, "he oughter be nervous after what he done. Ah reckon Joe come back to dare him to marry Lena, or to come out an' fight. Ah bet he'll be back time and agin, too. Know what Ah think? Joe wuz a braver man than Spunk."

There was a general shout of derision from the group.

"Thass a fact," went on Walter. "Lookit whut he done; took a razor an' went out to fight a man he knowed toted a gun an' wuz a crack shot, too; 'nother thing Joe wuz skeered of Spunk, skeered plumb stiff! But he went jes' the same. It took him a long time to get his nerve up. 'Tain't nothin' for Spunk to fight when he ain't skeered of nothin'. Now, Joe's done come back to have it out wid the man that's got all he ever had. Y'll know Joe ain't never had nothin' nor wanted nothin' besides Lena. It musta been a h'ant cause ain' nobody never seen no black bob-cat."

"'Nother thing," cut in one of the men, "Spunk wuz cussin' a blue streak to-day 'cause he 'lowed dat saw wuz wobblin'—almos' got 'im once. The machinist come, looked it over an' said it wuz alright. Spunk musta been leanin' t'wards it some. Den he claimed somebody pushed 'im but 'twant nobody close to 'im. Ah wuz glad when knockin' off time come. I'm skeered of dat man when he gits hot. He'd beat you full of button holes as quick as he's look atcher."

IV

The men gathered the next evening in a different mood, no laughter. No badinage this time.

"Look, 'Lige, you goin' to set up wid Spunk?"

"Naw, Ah reckon not, Walter. Tell yuh the truth, Ah'm a lil bit skittish. Spunk died too wicket—died cussin' he did. You know he thought he wuz done outa life."

"Good Lawd, who'd he think done it?"

"Joe."

"Joe Kanty? How come?"

"Walter, Ah b'leeve Ah will walk up thata way an' set. Lena would like it Ah reckon."

"But whut did he say, 'Lige?"

Elijah did not answer until they had left the lighted store and were strolling down the dark street.

"Ah wuz loadin' a wagon wid scantlin' right near the saw when Spunk fell on the carriage but 'fore Ah could git to him the saw got him in the body—awful sight. Me an' Skint Miller got him off but it was too late. Anybody could see that. The fust thing he said wuz: 'He pushed me, 'Lige—the dirty hound pushed me in the back!'—He was spittin' blood at ev'ry breath. We laid him on the sawdust pile with his face to the East so's he could die easy. He helt mah han' till the last, Walter, and said: 'It was Joe, 'Lige—the dirty sneak shoved me. . . he didn't dare come to mah face. . . but Ah'll git the son-of-a-wood louse soon's Ah get there an' make hell too hot for him. . . Ah felt him shove me. . . !' Thass how he died."

"If spirits kin fight, there's a powerful tussle goin' on somewhere ovah Jordan 'cause Ah b'leeve Joe's ready for Spunk an' ain't skeered any more—yas, Ah b'leeve Joe pushed 'im mahself."

They had arrived at the house. Lena's lamentations were deep and loud. She had filled the room with magnolia blossoms that gave off a heavy sweet odor. The keepers of the wake tipped about whispering in frightened tones. Everyone in the village was there, even old Jeff Kanty, Joe's father, who a few hours before would have been afraid to come within ten feet of him, stood leering triumphantly down upon the fallen giant as if his fingers had been the teeth of steel that laid him low.

The cooling board consisted of three sixteen-inch boards on saw horses, a dingy sheet was his shroud.

The women ate heartily of the funeral baked meats and wondered who would be Lena's next. The men whispered coarse conjectures between guzzles of whiskey.

ALAIN LOCKE

Sahdji

Bruce Nugent

That one now. . . . that's a sketch of a little African girl. . . delightfully black. . . I made it while I was passing through East Africa. . . her name was Sahdji. . . wife of Konombju. . . chieftain. . . of only a small tribe. . . Warpuri was the area of his sovereign domain. . . but to get back to Sahdji. . . with her beautiful dark body. . . rosy black. . . graceful as the tongues of flame she loved to dance around. . . and pretty. . . small features. . . large liquid eyes. . . over-full sensuous lips. . . she knew how to dance too. . . better than any. . .

Sahdji was proud. . . she was the favorite wife. . . as such she had privileges. . . she did love Konombju. . .

Mrabo. . . son of Konombju, loved Sahdji. . . his father. . . fifty-nine. . . too old for her. . . fifty-nine and eighteen. . . he could wait. . . he loved his father. . . but. . . maybe death. . . his father was getting old. . .

Numbo idolized Mrabo. . . Numbo was a young buck. . . would do anything to make Mrabo happy. . .

one day Sahdji felt restless. . . why. . . it was not unusual for Konombju to lead the hunt. . . even at his age. . . Sahdji jangled her bracelets. . . it was so still and warm. . . she'd wait at the door. . . standing there. . . shifting. . . a blurred silhouette against the brown of the hut. . . she waited. . . waited. . .

maybe. . .

she saw the long steaming stream of natives in the distance. . . she looked for Konombju. . . what was that burden they carried. . . why were they so solemn. . . where was Konombju. . .

the column reached her door. . . placed their burden at her feet. . . Konombju. . . an arrow in his back. . . just accident. . . *Goare go shuioa go elui ruri*—(when men die they depart for ever)—they hadn't seen him fall. . . hunting, one watches the hunt. . . a stray arrow. . . Konombju at her feet. . .

preparations for the funeral feast. . . the seven wives of Konombju went to the new chief's hut. . . Mrabo. . . one. . . two. . . three. . . he counted. . . no Sahdji. . . six. . . seven. . . no Sahdji. . .

the funeral procession filed past the door. . . and Mrabo. . . Mrabo went to. . . the drums beat their boom. . . boom. . . deep pulsing heart-quivering boom. . . and the reeds added their weird dirge. . . the procession moved on. . . on to Konombju's hut. . . boom. . . b-o-o-m. . .

there from the doorway stepped Sahdji. . . painted in the funeral red. . . the flames from the ground are already catching the branches. . . slowly to the funeral drums she swayed. . . danced. . . leading Konombju to his grave. . . her grave. . . their grave. . .

they laid the body in the funeral hut. . . *Goa shoa motho go sale motho*—(when a man dies a man remains)—Sahdji danced slowly. . . sadly. . . looked at Mrabo and smiled. . . slowly triumphantly. . . and to the wails of the wives. . . boom-boom of the drums. . . gave herself again to Konombju. . . the grass-strewn couch of Konombju. . .

Mrabo stood unflinching. . . but Numbo, silly Numbo had made an old. . . old man of Mrabo.

The Palm Porch

Eric Walrond

Nobody had ever heard of Miss Buckner before she swept into The Palm Porch. The Palm Porch was not a cantine; it was a house. Still, one was not sure of that, either; for a house, assuredly, is a place where people live. But Miss Buckner did not only live there: She had cut up the house in small, single rooms, each in separate and distinct entities. Each had its armor of leafy laces, its hangings of mauve and cream-gold; each its loadstones and daggers; its glowing dust and scarlet. Each its wine and music, powders and mirrors.

High against the sky, on slender, ant-proof poles, The Palm Porch looked down upon the squalid cosmos of Colon. Facing north—a broad expanse of red, arid land.

Before the Revolution it was a black, evil forest-swamp. Deer, lions, mongooses and tiger cats went prowling through it. Then the Americans came. . . came with saw and spear, tar and lysol. About to rid it. . . molten city. . . of its cancer, fire swept it up on the bosom of the lagoon. Naked, virgin trees; limbless. Gaunt, hollow stalks. Huge shadows falling. Dredges in the golden mist; dredges on the lagoon. Horny iron pipes spouted over the fetid swamp. Noise; grating noise. Earth stones, up from the bowels of the sea, rattled against the ribs of scaly pipes like popping corn. Crackling corn. Water, red, black, gray, gushed out of big, bursting pipes. For miles people heard its lap-lapping. Dark as the earth, it flung up on its crest stones, pearls, sharks' teeth. . . jewels of the sunken sea. Frogs, vermin, tangled things. . .

It browned into a lake of dazzling corals. Slowly the sun began to sop, harden, dry it up. Upon its surface, buoying it, old tree stumps; guava, pine. On them snipes flew. Wild geese came low, dipping up an earth-burned sprat. Off again. River stakes. Venturing to explore it enterprising kids would slip through. . . plop. . . go down. . . seized by the intense suction. Ugly rescue work.

In time it gave in to the insistence of the sun. White and golden; husks shone upon it. Shells; half-shells. It cut, dazed and dazzled you. Queer things, half-seen, on the dry, salty earth. Ghastly white bones; skulls, ear-rings, bangles. Scrambling. Rows. Sea scum fought and slew each other over them.

As time went on it became a bare, vivid plain. City'd soon spring upon it. Of a Sunday blacks would skip over to the beach to bathe or pick cocoanuts on the banks of the lagoon. On the lagoon. . . a slaughter house and a wireless station. Squeaking down at the flat, low city. Pigs being stuck, the unseeing hoofs of cattle. . . the wireless. . .

tang ta-tang, tang ta-tang

stole out of the meridian dusk.

Upon the lake of sea-earth, dusk swept a mantle of majestic coloring.

East of The Palm Porch, roared the city of Colon. Hudson Alley, "G" Street. . . coolies, natives, Island blacks swarming to the Canal. All about, nothing but tenements. . . city word for cabins. . . low, soggy, toppling.

Near the sky rose the Ant's Nest. Six stories high and it took up half a city block. One rickety staircase. . . in the rear. No two of its rooms connected. Each sheltered a family of eight or nine. A balcony ringed each floor. Rooms. . . each room. . . opened out upon it. Only one person at a time dared walk along any point of it. The cages of voiceless yellow birds adorned each window. Boards were stretched at the bottom of doors to stop kids from wandering out. . . to the piazza below. Flower-pots. . . fern, mint, thyme, parsley, water cress. . . sat on the scum-moist sills of the balconies.

Over the hot, low city the Ant's Nest lorded it. Reared its mouth to the heavens. Sneered truculently at it. Offensive, muggy, habitation made it giddy, bilious. Swarms of black folk populated it. . .

Sorry lot. Tugging at the apron strings of life, scabrous, sore-footed natives, spouting saliva into unisolated cisterns. Naked on the floors Chinese rum shops and chow-stands. Nigger-loving Chinks unmoved and unafraid of the consequences of a breed of untarnished. . . seemingly. . . Asiatics growing up around the breasts of West Indian maidens. Pious English peasant blacks. . . perforating the picture. . . going to church, to lodge meetings, to hear fiery orations.

Ant's Nest. On one hand the Ant's Nest. On the other, the sand-gilt lake. In this fashion it was not an unexpected rarity to find The Palm Porch prospering. Austerely entrenched, the rooms on the ground floor went to a one-eyed *baboo* and a Panama witch doctor. Gates at the top of the stairs kept intruders off. A wolf hound insured the logic of the precaution.

Around the porch Miss Buckner had unsheathed a strip of bright enamel cloth. From a man's waist it rose to the roof. It was beyond reason for anyone to peep up from the piazza and see what was taking place up there. Of course there were iron bars below the white screen, but Miss Buckner had covered these with crates of fern and violets strung along it. In addition, Miss Buckner had not been without an eye to a certain tropical exactness.

About Miss Buckner the idea of surfeit. . . oxen hips, long, pliable hands, roving, sun-staring breasts. . . took on the magic of reality. Upon the yellow stalk of her being there shot up into mist and crystal space a head the shape of a sawed-off cocoanut tree top. Pressed close to its rim were tiny wrinkles. . . circles, circlets, half-circles. . . of black, crisp hair. It was even bobbed. . . an unheard of proceeding among the Victorian maidens of the Indian tropics. Unheard of, indeed.

Further to confound the canaille a heretical part slid down the front of it. Strangely anti-sexual, it helped, too, to create a brightly sodden air about Miss Buckner in the ramified circles in which she set her being.

Urged on by the ruthless, crushing spirit which was firmly and innately a part of her, Miss Buckner, consciously unaware of the capers she was cutting amid the synthetic hordes. . . black, brown, yellow folk. . . had, perhaps, a right to insist on such things as a frizzly head of hair. Perhaps to her it was a trivial item of concern—to her and her only. And, by way of sprucing up lagging ends in her native endowments, items such as wavy, sylvan tresses, or a slim, pretty figure, Miss Buckner had an approach to one. . . life. . . that was simply excruciating. Where, oh! where, folk asked, did she acquire it? London. . . Paris. . . Vienna? No! In reality Miss Buckner, a dame of sixty—it was the first time that she had deserted the isle of her birth in an animated raffle across the sea,—would have fallen ill at the very suggestion of having to go to Europe or anywhere in fact beyond the crimson rim of Jamaica in quest of *manners*. Absurd!

And so, like a bit of tape, this manner to Miss Buckner stuck. Upon women Miss Buckner had meager cause to ply it, for at The Palm Porch precious few women, except, of course, Zuline, her Surinam cook, and, of course, her five daughters, were ever allowed. It was a man's house. When, as a result, Miss Buckner, beneath a brilliant lorgnette, condescended to look at a man, she looked sternly, unsmilingly down at him. When, of a Sabbath, Miss Buckner, hair in oily, overt frills, maidenly in a silken shawl of gold and blue, a dab of carmine on her mouth, decided to go to the *mercado,* followed by the slow, trepid steps of Zuline, to buy *achi* and Lucy-yam and cocoa-milk and red peas, she had half of the city gaping at the very wonder of her. Erratically, entirely in command of herself, Miss Buckner, by a word or gesture. . . quick, stabbing, petulant. . . would outbuy a deftly-enshrined Assyrian candymaker, the most abject West Indian fish dealer or the meekest native vendor of *cebada.* Colorful as a pheasant, she swept on, through the mist of crawling folk, the comely Zuline at her elbow, plying her with queries surely she did not expect her to possess enough virginity to answer. Dumping as she swept along vegetables, meats, spices in the bewildered girl's basket. Her head high above the dusky mob, her voice, at best a thing of angel-colors, uncaught by the shreds of *patois* going by her.

In fact, from Colon to Cocoa Grove, Miss Buckner, by the color-crazed folk who swam head-high in the bowl of luring life stirred by her, was a woman to tip one's hat to—regal rite—a woman of taste, culture, value. Executives at Balboa, pilots on the locks, sun-burned sea folk attested to that. They gloried at the languor of Miss Buckner's salon.

Of course, by words that came flashing like meteors out of Miss Buckner's mouth, one got the impression that Miss Buckner would have liked to be white; but, alas! she was only a mulatto. No one had ever heard of her before she and her innocent darlings moved into The Palm Porch. Of course, it was to be expected, the world being what it is, that there were people who—De la Croix, a San Andres wine merchant, De Pass, a Berbice horse breeder—murmured words of treason: that, out of their roving lives they'd seen her at a certain Bar in Matches Lane stringing out from over a broad, clean counter words of rigid cheer to the colonizing English barque men. . . but such, too, were cast to the dogs to be devoured as expressions of useless and undocumented chatter. Whether the result of a union of white and Negro, French or Spanish, English or Maroon. . . no one knew. And her daughters, sculptural marvels of gold and yellow, were enshrined in a similar mystery. Of their father and their ascension to the luxury of one, the least heard, so far as the buzzing community was concerned, the better. And in the absence of data tongues began to wag. Norwegian bos'en. Jamaica lover. . . Island trumph. Crazy Kingston nights. . . To the charming ladies in question, it was a subject of adoring indifference. Miss Buckner herself, who had a contempt for statistics, was a trifle hazy about the whole thing. . .

ALAIN LOCKE

One of the girls, white as a white woman, eyes blue as a Viking maid's, strangely, at sixteen, had eloped, much to Miss Buckner's disgust, with a shiny-armed black who at one time had been sent to the Island jail for the proletarian crime of prædial larceny. Neighbors swore it was love at first sight. But it irked, piqued Miss Buckner. "It a dam' pity shame," she had cried, between dabs at her already cologne-choked nose, "it a dam' pity shame."

Another girl, the eldest of the lot (Miss Buckner had had seven in all), had oh! ages before given birth to a pretty, gray-eyed baby boy, when she was but seventeen, and, much to Miss Buckner's disgrace, had later taken up with a willing young mulatto, a Christian in the Moravian church, and brutishly undertaken the burdens of concubinage. He was able, honest, industrious and wore shoes, but Miss Buckner nearly went mad—groaned at the pain her wayward daughters were bringing her. "Oh, Gahd," she cried, "Oh, Gahd, dem ah send me to de dawgs. . . dem ah send me to de dawgs!" Clerk in the cold storage; sixty dollars a month. . . wages of an accursed "Silver" employee. Silver is nigger; nigger is silver. Nigger-silver. . . blah! Why, debated Miss Buckner, stockings couldn't be bought with that, much more take care of a woman accustomed to "foxy clothes an' such" and a dazzling baby boy. Silver employee! Why couldn't he be a "Gold" employee. . . and get $125 a month, like "de fella nex' tarrim, he?" He did not get coal and fuel free, besides. He had to dig down and pay extra for them. He was not, alas! white. And that hurt, worried Miss Buckner. Caused her nights of anxious sleeplessness. Wretch! "To tink dat a handsome gal like dat would-ah tek up with a dam' black neygah man like him, he? Now, wa' you tink o' dat? H' answer me, no!" Oh, how her poor little ones were going to the dogs!

And so, to dam the flow of tears, Miss Buckner and the remaining ones of her flamingo-like brood, drew up at The Palm Porch. Sense-picture. All day Miss Buckner's brunettes would be there on the veranda posturing nude, half-nude. Exposed to the subdued warmth, sublimated by the courting of fans and shadow-implements, they'd be there, galore. Gorgeous slippers, wrought by some color-drunk Latin, rested on the tips of toes—toes blushing, hungering to be loved and kissed. Brown and silver ones. Purple and orange-colored kimonos fell away from excitably harmless anatomies. Inexhaustible tresses of night-gloss hair, hair—echoes of Miss Buckner's views on the subject—hair the color of a golden moon, gave shade and sun glows to rose-red arms and bosoms. Vases of roses, flowers. . . scented black and green leaves. . . crowned the night. Earth-sod fragrances; old, prematurely old, and crushed, withered flowers. Stale French perfumes. . . Gems. Gems on the tips and hilts of mediæval daggers. Priceless stones strewn on boudoirs. Hair pins of gold; diamond headed hat pins. Shoe heels ablaze with white, frosty diamonds. . .

Upon the porch sat the cream of Miss Buckner's cultivation. Sprawling, legs. . . soft, round, dimpled. . . on the arms of bamboo chairs. . . smoking. . . drinking. . . expostulating.

On the bare floor, dismal gore-spots on various parts of their crash and crocus bag—eyes watering at them—were men, white men. In the dead of night, chased by the crimson glow of dawn, intense white faces, steaming red in the burning tropics, flew madly, fiercely across the icy-flows of the Zone to the luxurious solitude of The Palm Porch.

To-night, the girls, immune to the vultures of despair, lie, sprawled on bamboo lounges, sat at three-legged tables, eyes sparkling, twittering. . .

O! comin' down with a bunch o' roses
Comin' down
Come down when Ah call ya' . . .

Rustle of silks. European taffeta silk. Wrestling-tight. On an open, buxom body, cherished under the breezes of a virgin civilization, it was a trifle unadoring. It pressed and irked one.

"There now, boys, please be quiet. . . the captain is coming. . ."

Anywhere else she'd have slipt up, but here it rippled like an ocean breeze free of timidity or restraint. In the presence of Islanders it might have resulted otherwise, but to strangers—and it was so easy to fool the whites—the color of one's voice went unobserved.

"Skipper, eh? Who is he? Wha' ta hell tub is 'e on?" Expectorations. Noisy-tongued lime juicers. . .

"Let the bleddy bastard go to. . ."

"Now, Tommy, that isn't nice. . ."

"Hell it ain't! Blarst 'im! Gawd blimmah, I'll blow ta holy car load o' yo' . . ."

Again the swift, swift rustle of silks. Olive one of silk; sweating, arranging, eliminating. . .

"Anesta, dear, take Baldy inside. . ."

"But, mother!"

"Do, darling. . . !"

"No, Gawd blarst yo' . . . lemme go! Lemme go, I say!"

"Be a gentleman, Baldy, and behave!"

"What a hell of a ruction it are, eh?"

"Help me wit' 'im, daughter. . ."

"Do, Anesta, dear. . ."

Yielding ungently, he staggered along on the girl's arm. He stept in the crown of Mr. Thingamerry's hat. A day before he had put on a spotless white suit. Laundered by the Occupation, the starch on the edges of it made it dagger-sharp. Now, it was a sight. Ugly wine stains darkened it. Drink, perspiration, tobacco weed moistened his sprigless shirt front. Awry—his tie, collar, trousers. His reddish brown hair was wet, bushy, ruffled. Grimy curses fell from his red, grime-bound lips. Six months on the Isthmus, its nights and the lure of The Palm Porch had caught him in its enervating grip. It held him tight. Sent from Liverpool to the British Postal Agency at Colon, he had fallen for the languor of the sea coast. . . had been seized by the magic glow of The Palm Porch.

He came down from Heaven to earth
Day by day like us He grew. . ."

La la la, la la la la-ah ah
La la la, la la la la-ah ah ah. . .

"John three, sixteen, and the Lord said there was light. 'And the light shineth in darkness, and the darkness comprehendeth it not.' . . ."

Upon a palpitating bosom, Miss Buckner put a young, eager hand. It was wildly in quest of something. . . anchorage, perhaps.

Viewing it—queer, the disorderly temperature of women—Captain Tintero, a local *vigilante*, shot a red, staring eye at her. . . "Well, my good lady, I see you are nervous as usual. . . Is not that so?"

Flattered by the captain's graciousness, Miss Buckner curtsied. Her eyelids giggled coquettishly. "Oh, my dear captain," she said, "it is so splendid of you to come. I've been thinking of you all day—really. Wasn't I, Anesta, dear? Of course! Anesta, dear? Anesta, where are you, my dear? Where oh where are you?"

"It's good to be this way. God blarst mah, it is. 'And the Lord said unto him, this is my beloved Son in whom I'm well pleased.' . . ."

". . . now laddie boys, don't be naughty. . . be quiet, children. Captain, as I was saying. . . naughty. . . naughty boys. . . Harmless, captain. Harmless, playful things. Anesta, Anestita? Is that the way you. . . persuasive captain!"

Cackling like a hen, pitching men to one side, she swept along. One or two British youths, palsied with liquor, desire, glared at her. . . then, at the olive figure, gold and crimson epaulets, high, regal prancing, at the uncovered, wolf-like fangs of the Captain. . .

"Christ, He was your color. Christ was olive. Jesus Christ was a man of olive. . ."

Grimy Britishers. Loquacious lime-juicers. Wine-crazed, women-crazed. . .

Bringing up the rear, Captain Tintero, at best a dandy of the more democratic salons, grew warm at the grandeur of ennui, the beauty of excess. He, too, alas! was not to be outdone when he had set his heart upon a thing. Beau Brummel of the dusky *policia*, he was vain, handsome, sun-colored. He gloried in a razor slash on his right cheek which he had obtained at a brawl over a German maiden in a District cantine. Livid, the claret about to spring out of it, it did not disfigure him. It lit up the glow women fancied in him. When he laughed it would turn pale, starkly pale; when he was angry it oozed red, blood-red. . .

For a *vigilante* the road to gallantry was clear. Heart of iron, nerves of steel—to be able to club a soused Marine to smithereens. . . possessing these, it was logic to exact tribute from the sulky vermin of the salons. . .

Inflated by such authority, the Captain swore, spat, dug his heels in the faces of the English. . .

Applying a Javanese fan to her furious bosom, Miss Buckner, her taffeta silk kicking up an immense racket, returned to the Captain. A bolden smile covered her frank, open face.

"Now, you impetuous Panamanian!" she warmed, the pearls on the top row of her teeth a-glitter, "you must never be too impatient. The Bible says, 'Him that is exalted. . .' The gods will never be kind to you if you keep on that way. . . No use. . . you won't understand the Bible! Come! . . ."

Gathering up the ruffles of her skirt, she sped along. Into a realm of shadowy mists. Darkness. "Too much liquor," she turned, by way of apology, tapping her black bandeau and indicating the tossing figure of the British Postal Agent. . . "too much liquor. . . don't mind. . . *el es Ingles*. . . postal agental. . . *Ingles*. . ."

"*Necios! Barbaridades!*"

". . . no matter what he says. . ."

"Nigger bastard!"

"Baldy! Why, the very itheah! . . . Go quietly, dear. . ."

"Really, Captain," Miss Buckner waved a jewel-flaming wrist, "it is quite comic. Why, the fellow's actually offensive! And all I can do is keep the dear child out of the wretch's filthy embrace. . . advances!"

It didn't matter very much, after all. And brushing the slip aside, Miss Buckner went on, "But of course," she conceded, "one has to be pleasant to one's guests. O! Captain, in dear old Kingston, none of this sort of thing ever occurred. . . None!—And of course it *constrains me profusely!*—

"Anesta, where are you, my dear?"

Out of the dusk the girl came. Her grace, her beauty, the endless dam of color, of emotion that flooded her face bewitched, unnerved the captain. In an attitude of respectful indecision she paused at the door, one hand at her throat, the other held out to the captain. . .

In one's mouth it savored of butter. Miss Buckner, there at the door, viewing the end of an embarrassing quest, felt happy. The captain, after all, was such a naughty boy!

DOWN ON THE CARPETLESS PORCH, dipt in the brine of shadows, the hoarse, catching voice of an Englishman called. "Anesta, Anesta. . . mulatto girl. . . Gawd blarst the bleddy spiggoty to 'ell! Come to me, Anesta! So 'elp me Gawd if 'e goes artah 'er I'll cut the gizzard out. . . hey. . . where's that bleddy Miss Buckner. . . ?"

Sore, briny silence. "And His word is mine. And the word was God, and all things made by Him, and God. . . No. Gawd damn it, that isn't right. Jesus! . . ."

"And the light shineth in darkness, and the darkness comprehendeth it not. . ." Endless emotion. Swung up upon the shores of a spirit-sea, where the owls and saints and the shiny demons of the hideous morass emerged at the low tide to mate and war and converse on the imperishable odes of time. . . ghastly reality!

SCREAM. . . IT TOUCHED NO ONE. Doing its work at a swift, unerring pace. . . A death-rattle, and the descent of shadows and solitude.

AT NOON THE DAY AFTER the cops came and got the body. Over the blood-black hump a sheet was flung. It ate up the scarlet. Native crowds stuck up their chins at it. . . even the tiny drip-drip on the piazza. From the dark roof hanging over the pavement it came. . .

Way back—to be exact, a week after life moved on The Porch—a new white screen-cloth had been put together and pelted out that way. A slow, rigid procession of them. Now, its edge—that is the novelty of it—taken off, Miss Buckner, firm in the graces of the Captain drunk in Anesta's boudoir, was so busy with sundry affairs she did not have space to devote to the commotion the spectacle had undoubtedly created. To put it briefly, Miss Buckner, while Zuline sewed a button on her suede shoes, was absorbed in the task of deciding whether to have chocolate soufflé or maiden hair custard at lunch that afternoon. . .

POETRY

To a Brown Girl

What if his glance is bold and free,
    His mouth the lash of whips?
So should the eyes of lovers be,
    And so a lover's lips.

What if no puritanic strain
    Confines him to the nice?
He will not pass this way again
    Nor hunger for you twice.

Since in the end consort together
    Magdalen and Mary,
Youth is the time for careless weather;
    Later, lass, be wary.

—Countée Cullen

To a Brown Boy

That brown girl's swagger gives a twitch
    To beauty like a queen;
Lad, never dam your body's itch
    When loveliness is seen.

For there is ample room for bliss
    In pride in clean, brown limbs,
And lips know better how to kiss
    Than how to raise white hymns.

And when your body's death gives birth
    To soil for spring to crown,
Men will not ask if that rare earth
    Was white flesh once, or brown.

—Countée Cullen

Tableau

Locked arm in arm they cross the way,
The black boy and the white,
The golden splendor of the day
The sable pride of night.

From lowered blinds the dark folk stare
And here the fair folk talk,
Indignant that these two should dare
In unison to walk.

Oblivious to look and word
They pass, and see no wonder
That lightning brilliant as a sword
Should blaze the path of thunder.

—Countée Cullen

Harlem Wine

This is not water running here,
These thick rebellious streams
That hurtle flesh and bone past fear
Down alleyways of dreams.

This is a wine that must flow on
Not caring how or where,
So it has ways to flow upon
Where song is in the air.

So it can woo an artful flute
With loose, elastic lips,
Its measurement of joy compute
With blithe, ecstatic hips.

—Countée Cullen

She of the Dancing Feet Sings

And what would I do in heaven, pray,
Me with my dancing feet,
And limbs like apple boughs that sway
When the gusty rain winds beat?

And how would I thrive in a perfect place
Where dancing would be sin,
With not a man to love my face,
Nor an arm to hold me in?

The seraphs and the cherubim
Would be too proud to bend
To sing the faery tunes that brim
My heart from end to end.

The wistful angels down in hell
Will smile to see my face,
And understand, because they fell
From that all-perfect place.

—Countée Cullen

A Brown Girl Dead

With two white roses on her breasts,
White candles at head and feet,
Dark Madonna of the grave she rests;
Lord Death has found her sweet.

Her mother pawned her wedding ring
To lay her out in white;
She'd be so proud she'd dance and sing
To see herself to-night.

—Countée Cullen

Fruit of the Flower

My father is a quiet man
With sober, steady ways;
For simile, a folded fan;
His nights are like his days.

My mother's life is puritan,
No hint of cavalier,
A pool so calm you're sure it can
Have little depth to fear.

And yet my father's eyes can boast
How full his life has been;
There haunts them yet the languid ghost
Of some still sacred sin.

And though my mother chants of God,
And of the mystic river,
I've seen a bit of checkered sod
Set all her flesh aquiver.

Why should he deem it pure mischance
A son of his is fain
To do a naked tribal dance
Each time he hears the rain?

Why should she think it devil's art
That all my songs should be
Of love and lovers, broken heart,
And wild sweet agony?

Who plants a seed begets a bud,
Extract of that same root;
Why marvel at the hectic blood
That flushes this wild fruit?

—*Countée Cullen*

ALAIN LOCKE

In Memory of Colonel Charles Young

Along the shore the tall, thin grass
That fringes that dark river,
While sinuously soft feet pass,
Begins to bleed and quiver.

The great dark voice breaks with a sob
Across the womb of night;
Above your grave the tom-toms throb,
And the hills are weird with light.

The great dark heart is like a well
Drained bitter by the sky,
And all the honeyed lies they tell
Come there to thirst and die.

No lie is strong enough to kill
The roots that work below;
From your rich dust and slaughtered will
A tree with tongues will grow.

—Countée Cullen

Baptism

Into the furnace let me go alone;
Stay you without in terror of the heat.

I will go naked in—for thus 'tis sweet—
Into the weird depths of the hottest zone.
I will not quiver in the frailest bone,
You will not note a flicker of defeat;
My heart shall tremble not its fate to meet,
Nor mouth give utterance to any moan.
The yawning oven spits forth fiery spears;
Red aspish tongues shout wordlessly my name.
Desire destroys, consumes my mortal fears,
Transforming me into a shape of flame.

I will come out, back to your world of tears,
A stronger soul within a finer frame.

—*Claude McKay*

White Houses

Your door is shut against my tightened face,
And I am sharp as steel with discontent;
But I possess the courage and the grace
To bear my anger proudly and unbent.
The pavement slabs burn loose beneath my feet,
A chafing savage, down the decent street,
And passion rends my vitals as I pass,
Where boldly shines your shuttered door of glass.
Oh I must search for wisdom every hour,
Deep in my wrathful bosom sore and raw,
And find in it the superhuman power
To hold me to the letter of your law!
Oh I must keep my heart inviolate
Against the potent poison of your hate.

—*Claude McKay*

Like a Strong Tree

Like a strong tree that in the virgin earth
Sends far its roots through rock and loam and clay,
And proudly thrives in rain or time of dearth,
When the dry waves scare rainy sprites away;
Like a strong tree that reaches down, deep, deep,
For sunken water, fluid underground,
Where the great-ringed unsightly blind worms creep,
And queer things of the nether world abound:

So would I live in rich imperial growth,
Touching the surface and the depth of things,
Instinctively responsive unto both,
Tasting the sweets of being and the stings,

Sensing the subtle spell of changing forms,
Like a strong tree against a thousand storms.

—*Claude McKay*

Russian Cathedral

Bow down my soul in worship very low
And in the holy silences be lost.
Bow down before the marble man of woe,
Bow down before the singing angel host.

What jewelled glory fills my spirit's eye!
What golden grandeur moves the depths of me!
The soaring arches lift me up on high
Taking my breath with their rare symmetry.

Bow down my soul and let the wondrous light
Of Beauty bathe thee from her lofty throne
Bow down before the wonder of man's might.
Bow down in worship, humble and alone;
Bow lowly down before the sacred sight
Of man's divinity alive in stone.

—*Claude McKay*

The Tropics in New York

Bananas ripe and green, and ginger root,
    Cocoa in pods and alligator pears,
And tangerines and mangoes and grape fruit,
    Fit for the highest prize at parish fairs.

Set in the window, bringing memories
    Of fruit-trees laden by low-singing rills,
And dewy dawns, and mystical blue skies
    In benediction over nun-like hills.

My eyes grew dim, and I could no more gaze;
    A wave of longing through my body swept,
And, hungry for the old familiar ways,
    I turned aside and bowed my head and wept.

          —Claude McKay

GEORGIA DUSK

The sky, lazily disdaining to pursue
    The setting sun, too indolent to hold
    A lengthened tournament for flashing gold,
Passively darkens for night's barbecue,

A feast of moon and men and barking hounds,
    An orgy for some genius of the South
    With blood-hot eyes and cane-lipped scented mouth,
Surprised in making folk-songs from soul sounds.

The sawmill blows its whistle, buzz-saws stop,
    And silence breaks the bud of knoll and hill,
    Soft settling pollen where ploughed lands fulfill
Their early promise of a bumper crop.

Smoke from the pyramidal sawdust pile
    Curls up, blue ghosts of trees, tarrying low
    Where only chips and stumps are left to show
The solid proof of former domicile.

Meanwhile, the men, with vestiges of pomp,
    Race memories of king and caravan,
    High-priests, an ostrich, and a juju-man,
Go singing through the footpaths of the swamp.

Their voices rise. . . the pine trees are guitars,
    Strumming, pine-needles fall like sheets of rain. . .
    Their voices rise. . . the chorus of the cane
Is carolling a vesper to the stars.

                                ALAIN LOCKE

O singers, resinous and soft your songs
    Above the sacred whisper of the pines,
    Give virgin lips to cornfield concubines,
Bring dreams of Christ to dusky cane-lipped throngs.

—Jean Toomer

SONG OF THE SON

Pour, O pour that parting soul in song,
O pour it in the saw-dust glow of night,
Into the velvet pine-smoke air to-night,
And let the valley carry it along,
And let the valley carry it along.

O land and soil, red soil and sweet-gum tree,
So scant of grass, so profligate of pines,
Now just before an epoch's sun declines
Thy son, in time, I have returned to thee,
Thy son, I have in time returned to thee.

In time, although the sun is setting on
A song-lit race of slaves, it has not set;
Though late, O soil, it is not too late yet
To catch thy plaintive soul, leaving, soon gone,
Leaving, to catch thy plaintive soul soon gone.

O Negro slaves, dark purple ripened plums,
Squeezed, and bursting in the pine-wood air,
Passing, before they strip the old tree bare
One plum was saved for me, one seed becomes

An everlasting song, a singing tree,
Caroling softly souls of slavery,
What they were, and what they are to me,
Carolling softly souls of slavery.

—Jean Toomer

The Creation

A Negro Sermon

And God stepped out on space,
And He looked around and said,
"I'm lonely
I'll make me a world."

And as far as the eye of God could see
Darkness covered everything,
Blacker than a hundred midnights
Down in a cypress swamp.

Then God smiled,
And the light broke,
And the darkness rolled up on one side,
And the light stood shining on the other,
And God said, *"That's good!"*

Then God reached out and took the light in His hands,
And God rolled the light around in His hands
Until He made the sun;
And He set that sun a-blazing in the heavens.
And the light that was left from making the sun
God gathered it up in a shining ball
And flung it against the darkness,
Spangling the night with the moon and stars.
Then down between
The darkness and the light
He hurled the world;
And God said, *"That's good."*

Then God Himself stepped down—
And the sun was on His right hand
And the moon was on His left;
The stars were clustered about His head,
And the earth was under His feet.
And God walked, and where He trod

ALAIN LOCKE

His footsteps hollowed the valleys out
And bulged the mountains up.

Then He stopped and looked, and saw
That the earth was hot and barren.
So God stepped over to the edge of the world
And He spat out the seven seas;
He batted His eyes, and the lightnings flashed;
He clapped His hands, and the thunders rolled;
And the waters above the earth came down,
The cooling waters came down.

Then the green grass sprouted,
And the little red flowers blossomed,
The pine tree pointed his finger to the sky,
And the oak spread out his arms,
And the lakes cuddled down in the hollows of the ground,
And the rivers ran to the sea;
And God smiled again,
And the rainbow appeared,
And curled itself around His shoulder.

Then God raised His arm and He waved His hand,
Over the sea and over the land,
And He said, *"Bring forth. Bring forth."*
And quicker than God could drop His hand
Fishes and fowls
And beasts and birds
Swam the rivers and the seas,
Roamed the forests and the woods,
And split the air with their wings.
And God said, *"That's good."*

Then God walked around,
And God looked around
On all that He had made.
He looked at His sun,
And He looked at His moon,
And He looked at His little stars;

He looked on His world,
With all its living things,
And God said, *"I'm lonely still."*

Then God sat down
On the side of a hill where He could think;
By a deep, wide river He sat down;
With His head in His hands,
God thought and thought,
Till He thought, *"I'll make me a man."*

Up from the bed of a river
God scooped the clay;
And by the bank of the river
He kneeled Him down;
And there the great God Almighty
Who lit the sun and fixed it in the sky,
Who flung the stars to the most far corner of the night,
Who rounded the earth in the middle of His hand;
This Great God,
Like a mammy bending over her baby,
Kneeled down in the dust
Toiling over a lump of clay
Till He shaped it in His own image;

Then into it He blew the breath of life,
And man became a living soul.
Amen. Amen.

—*James Weldon Johnson*

THE NEGRO SPEAKS OF RIVERS

I've known rivers. . .
I've known rivers ancient as the world and older than the flow of
    human blood in human veins.
My soul has grown deep like the rivers.

ALAIN LOCKE

I bathed in the Euphrates when dawns were young,
I built my hut near the Congo and it lulled me to sleep,
I looked upon the Nile and raised the pyramids above it.

I heard the singing of the Mississippi when
    Abe Lincoln went down to New Orleans,
And I've seen its muddy bosom turn all golden in the sunset.

I've known rivers:
Ancient, dusky rivers,
My soul has grown deep like the rivers.

—Langston Hughes

An Earth Song

It's an earth song,—
And I've been waiting long for an earth song.
It's a spring song,—
And I've been waiting long for a spring song.
    Strong as the shoots of a new plant
    Strong as the bursting of new buds
    Strong as the coming of the first child from its mother's womb.
It's an earth song,
A body-song,
A spring song,
I have been waiting long for this spring song.

—Langston Hughes

Poem

Being walkers with the dawn and morning
Walkers with the sun and morning,
We are not afraid of night,
Nor days of gloom,
Nor darkness,
Being walkers with the sun and morning.

—Langston Hughes

Youth

We have to-morrow
Bright before us
Like a flame

Yesterday, a night-gone thing
A sun-down name

And dawn to-day
Broad arch above the road we came,
We march.

—*Langston Hughes*

Song

Lovely, dark, and lonely one,
Bare your bosom to the sun,
Do not be afraid of light
You who are a child of night.

Open wide your arms to life,
Whirl in the wind of pain and strife,
Face the wall with the dark closed gate,
Beat with bare, brown fists
And wait.

—*Langston Hughes*

Dream Variation

To fling my arms wide
In some place of the sun,
To whirl and to dance
Till the bright day is done.
Then rest at cool evening
Beneath a tall tree
While night comes gently
Dark like me.
That is my dream.

To fling my arms wide
In the face of the sun.
Dance! Whirl! Whirl!
Till the quick day is done.
Rest at pale evening,
A tall, slim tree,
Night coming tenderly
Black like me.

—Langston Hughes

MINSTREL MAN

Because my mouth
Is wide with laughter
And my throat
Is deep with song,
You do not think
I suffer after
I have held my pain
So long.

Because my mouth
Is wide with laughter,
You do not hear
My inner cry,
Because my feet
Are gay with dancing,
You do not know
I die.

—Langston Hughes

OUR LAND

We should have a land of sun,
Of gorgeous sun,
And a land of fragrant water
Where the twilight is a soft bandanna handkerchief
Of rose and gold,

And not this land
Where life is cold.

We should have a land of trees,
Of tall thick trees,
Bowed down with chattering parrots
Brilliant as the day,
And not this land where birds are gray.

Ah, we should have a land of joy,
Of love and joy and wine and song,
And not this land where joy is wrong.

—Langston Hughes

I Too

I, too, sing America.

I am the darker brother.
They send me to eat in the kitchen
When company comes.
But I laugh,
And eat well,
And grow strong.

To-morrow
I'll sit at the table
When company comes
Nobody'll dare
Say to me,
"Eat in the kitchen"
Then.

Besides, they'll see how beautiful I am
And be ashamed,—

I, too, am America.

—Langston Hughes

To Samuel Coleridge Taylor, upon Hearing his

Strange to a sensing motherhood,
Loved as a toy—not understood,
Child of a dusky father, bold;
Frail little captive, exiled, cold.

Oft when the brooding planets sleep,
You through their drowsy empires creep,
Flinging your arms through their empty space,
Seeking the breast of an unknown face.

—Georgia Douglas Johnson

The Ordeal

Ho: my brother,
Pass me not by so scornfully
I'm doing this living of being black,
Perhaps I bear your own life-pack,
And heavy, heavy is the load
That bends my body to the road.

But I have kept a smile for fate,
I neither cry, nor cringe, nor hate,
Intrepidly, I strive to bear
This handicap: The planets wear
The Maker's imprint, and with mine
I swing into their rhythmic line;
I ask—only for destiny,
Mine, not thine.

—Georgia Douglas Johnson

ESCAPE

Shadows, shadows,
Hug me round
So that I shall not be found
By sorrow:
She pursues me
Everywhere,
I can't lose her
Anywhere.

Fold me in your black
Abyss,
She will never look
In this,—
Shadows, shadows,
Hug me round
In your solitude
Profound.

—*Georgia Douglas Johnson*

THE RIDDLE

White men's children spread over the earth—
A rainbow suspending the drawn swords of birth,
Uniting and blending the races in one
The world man—cosmopolite—everyman's son!

He channels the stream of the red blood and blue,
Behold him! A Triton—the peer of the two;
Unriddle this riddle of "outside in"
White men's children in black men's skin.

—*Georgia Douglas Johnson*

LADY, LADY

Lady, Lady, I saw your face,
Dark as night withholding a star. . .
The chisel fell, or it might have been
You had borne so long the yoke of men.

Lady, Lady, I saw your hands,
Twisted, awry, like crumpled roots,
Bleached poor white in a sudsy tub,
Wrinkled and drawn from your rub-a-dub.

Lady, Lady, I saw your heart,
And altared there in its darksome place
Were the tongues of flame the ancients knew,
Where the good God sits to spangle through.

—Anne Spencer

THE BLACK FINGER

I have just seen a most beautiful things
    Slim and still,
  Against a gold, gold sky,
  A straight black cypress,
    Sensitive,
    Exquisite,
    A black finger
    Pointing upwards.
Why, beautiful still finger, are you black?
And why are you pointing upwards?

—Angelina Grimke

ENCHANTMENT

Part I

Night

The moonlight:
Juice flowing from an over-ripe pomegranate
bursting

The cossack-crested palm trees:
motionless

The leopard spotted shade:
inciting fear

silence seeds sown. . .

Part II

Medicine Dance

A body smiling with black beauty
Leaping into the air
Around a grotesque hyena-faced monster:
The Sorcerer—
A black body—dancing with beauty
Clothed in African moonlight,
Smiling more beauty into its body.
The hyena-faced monster yelps!
Echo!
Silence—
The dance
Leaps—
Twirls—
The twirling body comes to a fall
At the feet of the monster.
Yelps—
Wild—

Terror-filled—
Echo—
The hyena-faced monster jumps
starts,
runs,
chases his own yelps back to the wilderness.
The black body clothed in moonlight
Raises up its head,
Holding a face dancing with delight.

Terror reigns like a new crowned king.

—Lewis Alexander

DRAMA

The Drama of Negro Life

Montgomery Gregory

P resident-Emeritus Charles William Eliot of Harvard University recently expressed the inspiring thought that America should not be a "melting-pot" for the diverse races gathered on her soil but that each race should maintain its essential integrity and contribute its own special and peculiar gift to our composite civilization: not a "melting-pot" but a symphony where each instrument contributes its particular quality of music to an ensemble of harmonious sounds. Whatever else the Negro may offer as his part there is already the general recognition that his folk-music, born of the pangs and sorrows of slavery, has made America and the world his eternal debtor. The same racial characteristics that are responsible for this music are destined to express themselves with similar excellence in the kindred art of drama. The recent notable successes of Negro actors and of plays of Negro life on Broadway point to vast potentialities in this field. Eugene O'Neill, who more than any other person has dignified and popularized Negro drama, gives testimony to the possibilities of the future development of Negro drama as follows: "I believe as strongly as you do that the gifts the Negro can—and will—bring to our native drama are invaluable ones. The possibilities are limitless and to a dramatist open up new and intriguing opportunities." Max Reinhardt, the leading continental producer, while on his recent visit to New York commented enthusiastically upon the virgin riches of Negro drama and expressed a wish to utilize elements of it in one of his projected dramas.

Before considering contemporary interest in Negro drama it will be well to discover its historical background. William Shakespeare was the first dramatist to appreciate the "intriguing opportunities" in the life of the darker races and in his master-tragedy *Othello*, he has given us the stellar rôle of the Moor in a study of the effect of jealousy upon a nature of simple and overpowering emotion. So great an embarrassment has this "Black-a-moor" been to the Anglo-Saxon stage that the "supreme tragedy of English drama" has suffered a distinct unpopularity, and its chief interpreters have been compelled to give a bleached and an adulterated presentation of the black commander of the Venetian army. Thus O'Neill had an excellent precedent for his *Emperor Jones*.

The example of Shakespeare was not followed by his immediate successors. In fact, a character of sable hue does not appear in the pages of English literature until a century later when Aphra Behn wrote that sentimental romance, *Oronooko*, portraying the unhappy lot of a noble Negro prince in captivity. This tearful tragedy had numerous imitators in both fiction and drama, an example of the latter being the *Black Doctor*, written by Thomas Archer and published in London in 1847. It was not long after this publication that London and the continent were treated to an extraordinary phenomenon,—the appearance of a Maryland Negro in *Othello* and other Shakespearean rôles in the royal theaters. Ira Aldridge is thus the first Negro to surmount the bars of race prejudice and to receive recognition on the legitimate English-speaking stage.

Up until the Civil War, then, there was but meager interest in the drama of the African or Negro in England, and practically none in the United States. That great sectional conflict aroused a tremendous sentimental interest in the black population of the South and gave us Harriet Beecher Stowe's *Uncle Tom's Cabin*, which also enjoyed a wide popularity as a drama. *The Octoroon*, written on the same pattern, soon followed on the American stage. These works mark the first instance where an attempt is made to present to the American public in a realistic manner the authentic life of the Negro. They accustomed the theater-goer to the appearance of a number of Negro characters (played by blacked-face white actors) on the stage, and this fact was in itself a distinct gain for Negro drama.

Although *Uncle Tom's Cabin* passed into obscurity, "Topsy" survived. She was blissfully ignorant of any ancestors, but she has given us a fearful progeny. With her, popular dramatic interest in the Negro changed from serious moralistic drama to the comic phase. We cannot say that as yet the public taste has generally recovered from this descent from sentimentalism to grotesque comedy, and from that in turn to farce, mimicry and sheer burlesque. The earliest expression of Topsy's baneful influence is to be found in the minstrels made famous by the Callenders, Lew Dockstader, and Primrose and West. These comedians, made up into grotesque caricatures of the Negro race, fixed in the public taste a dramatic stereotype of the race that has been almost fatal to a sincere and authentic Negro drama. The earliest Negro shows were either imitations of these minstrels or slight variations from them. In fact, the average play of Negro life to-day, whether employing white or black actors, reeks with this pernicious influence.

It was not until 1895 that the Negro attempted to break with the minstrel tradition, when John W. Isham formed *The Octoroons*, a musical show. Minor variety and vaudeville efforts followed, but the first all-Negro comedy to receive Broadway notice was Williams and Walker's *In Dahomey*, which played at the Forty-sixth Street Theatre for several weeks. Williams and Walker, Cole and Johnson, S. H. Dudley, and Ernest Hogan now presented a succession of shows in which the Negro still appeared in caricature but which offered some compensation by the introduction of a slight plot and much excellent music and dancing. Such shows as *Abyssinia, Rufus Rastus, Bandana Land*, and *Mr. Lode of Coal*, are still familiar names to the theater-goers between 1900 and 1910. During the latter year "Bert" Williams' inimitable genius was fully recognized, and from then until his death he was an idol of the American public. It may not be amiss to state that it was Williams' ambition to appear in a higher type of drama, and David Belasco states in the introduction to *The Son of Laughter*, a biography of "Bert" Williams by Margaret Rowland, that his death probably prevented him from appearing under his direction as a star. Negro drama will always be indebted to the genius of this great comedian and appreciative of the fact that by breaking into *The Follies* "Bert" Williams unlocked the doors of the American theater to later Negro artists.

The reader will probably be familiar with the extraordinary successes of the latest Negro musical comedies, *Shuffle Along, Runnin' Wild*, and *From Dixie to Broadway*, and with the names of their stars—Sissle and Blake, Miller and Lyles, and Florence Mills. In many respects these shows represent notable advances over the musical shows that preceded them, yet fundamentally they carry-on the old minstrel tradition. Ludwig Lewisohn, the eminent New York critic, thus evaluates their work: "Much of this activity, granting talent and energy, is of slight interest; much of it always strikes me as an actual imitation of the white 'blacked-face' comedian—an imitation from the Negro's point of view of a caricature of himself. All of these things have little or no value as art, as an expression of either the Negro individual or the Negro race." Yet in all justice it should be said that these shows have given a large number of talented Negroes their only opportunity for dramatic expression and have resulted in the development of much stage ability. "Bert" Williams and Florence Mills are examples of dramatic geniuses who have elevated their work in these productions to the highest art. Certainly historically these musical shows are a significant element in the groping of the Negro for dramatic expression, and who knows but that they may be the genesis for an important development of our drama in the future?

Serious Negro drama is a matter of recent growth and still is in its infancy. It is in this field of legitimate drama that the Negro must achieve success if he is to win real recognition in the onward sweep of American drama. The year 1910 may be said to mark the first significant step in this direction, for it witnessed the production with a distinguished cast, including Guy Bates Post and Annie Russell, at the New Theatre in New York City, of Edward Sheldon's *The Nigger* (later called *The Governor*), a somewhat melodramatic treatment of the tragedy of racial admixture in the South. It marks the first sincere attempt to sound the depths of our racial experience for modern drama. A more sympathetic and poetic utilization of this dramatic material appears a few years later in the composition of three one-act plays (*Granny Maumee, The Rider of Dreams,* and *Simon the Cyrenian*), by Ridgely Torrence. Of equal importance was the artistic staging of these plays with a cast of talented Negro actors by Sheldon, Mrs. Norman Hapgood, and others. The venture was a pleasing artistic success, and but for the intervention of the World War might have resulted in the establishment of a permanent Negro Little Theatre in New York City. Not only had the public been impressed with the artistic value of such plays, but it also had been given its first demonstration of the ability of the Negro actor in other than burlesque parts. Opal Cooper especially won the plaudits of the critics, and, like John the Baptist, he proved to be only the forerunner of one who was to touch the peaks of histrionic accomplishment.

Then by a *tour-de-force* of genius—for the histrionic ability of Charles Gilpin has been as effective as the dramatic genius of Eugene O'Neill—the serious play of Negro life broke through to public favor and critical recognition. Overnight this weird psychological study of race experience was hailed as a dramatic masterpiece and an unknown Negro was selected by the Drama League as one of the ten foremost actors on the American stage. In any further development of Negro drama, *The Emperor Jones*, written by O'Neill, interpreted by Gilpin, and produced by the Provincetown Players, will tower as a beacon-light of inspiration. It marks the breakwater plunge of Negro drama into the main stream of American drama.

In 1923 Raymond O'Neill assembled a noteworthy group of Negro actors in Chicago and formed the "Ethiopian Art Theatre." Following successful presentation there he launched his interesting theater on Broadway. Whereas Torrence started out with several original race plays, O'Neill attempted the adaptation of Oscar Wilde's *Salome* and Shakespeare's *Comedy of Errors*. His chief success was the production of *The Chip Woman's Fortune*, a one-act race play by the young Negro dramatist, Willis Richardson. The acting of Evelyn Preer, the Kirkpatricks, Olden and Solomon Bruce was equal to the best traditions of the American theater—but even great acting could not atone for an unwise selection of plays. This untimely collapse of a most promising enterprise should hold a valuable lesson for other promoters of Negro drama.

Since these passing successes of the Negro on the regular stage, there have been several hopeful experiments in the Little Theatre and educational fields, with larger likelihood of permanent results. At Howard University, in Washington, D. C., the writer, with the enthusiastic co-operation of Marie-Moore-Forrest, Cleon Throckmorton, Alain Leroy Locke and the University officials, undertook to establish on an enduring basis the foundations of Negro drama through the institution of a dramatic laboratory where Negro youth might receive sound training in the arts of the theater. The composition of original race plays formed the pivotal element in the project. The Howard Players have given ample evidence of having the same significance for Negro drama that the erstwhile "47 Workshop" at Harvard University and the North Carolina University Players have had for American drama in general. Atlanta University, Hampton Institute, and Tuskegee Institute have been making commendable efforts in the same direction. In Harlem, the Negro quarter of New York City, Anne Wolter has associated with her an excellent corps of dramatic workers in the conduct of "The Ethiopian Art Theatre School."

Finally, mention must be made of two young Negro actors who have been maintaining the same high standard of artistic performance as established by Gilpin. Paul Robeson has succeeded to the rôle of *The Emperor Jones*, and has appeared in the leading part in O'Neill's latest Negro drama, *All God's Chillun Got Wings*. Eugene Corbie has likewise given a creditable performance as the "Witch Doctor" in *Cape Smoke*. Thus a sufficient demonstration has been made that Gilpin's achievement was not merely a comet-flare across the dramatic horizon but a trustworthy sign of the histrionic gift of his race.

The past and present of Negro drama lies revealed before us. It is seen that the popular musical comedies with their unfortunate minstrel inheritance have been responsible for a fateful misrepresentation of Negro life. However, the efforts toward the development of a sincere and artistic drama have not been altogether in vain. O'Neill and Torrence have shown that the ambitious dramatist has a rich and virgin El Dorado in the racial experiences of black folk. As the spirituals have risen from the folk-life of the race, so too will there develop out of the same treasure-trove a worthy contribution to a native American drama. The annual prizes now being offered through the vision of Charles S. Johnson of *The Opportunity* magazine and of W. E. B. DuBois and Jessie Fauset of *The Crisis* magazine for original racial expression in the various literary forms are acting as a splendid stimulus to Negro writers to begin the adequate expression of their race life.

Our ideal is a national Negro Theater where the Negro playwright, musician, actor, dancer, and artist in concert shall fashion a drama that will merit the respect and admiration of America. Such an institution must come from the Negro himself, as he alone can truly express the soul of his people. The race must surrender that childish self-consciousness that refuses to face the facts of its own life in the arts but prefers the blandishments of flatterers, who render all efforts at true artistic expression a laughing-stock by adorning their characters with the gaudy gowns of cheap romance. However disagreeable the fact may be in some quarters, the only avenue of genuine achievement in American drama for the Negro lies in the development of the rich veins of folk-tradition of the past and in the portrayal of the authentic life of the Negro masses of to-day. The older leadership still clings to the false gods of servile reflection of the more or less unfamiliar life of an alien race. The "New Negro," still few in number, places his faith in the potentialities of his own people—he believes that the black man has no reason to be ashamed of himself, but that in the divine plan he too has a worthy and honorable destiny.

The hope of Negro drama is the establishment of numerous small groups of Negro players throughout the country who shall simply and devotedly interpret the life that is familiar to them for the sheer joy of artistic expression.

The Gift of Laughter

Jessie Fauset

The black man bringing gifts, and particularly the gift of laughter, to the American stage is easily the most anomalous, the most inscrutable figure of the century. All about him and within himself stalks the conviction that like the Irish, the Russian and the Magyar he has some peculiar offering which shall contain the very essence of the drama. Yet the medium through which this unique and intensely dramatic gift might be offered has been so befogged and misted by popular preconception that the great gift, though divined, is as yet not clearly seen.

Popular preconception in this instance refers to the pressure of white opinion by which the American Negro is surrounded and by which his true character is almost submerged. For years the Caucasian in America has persisted in dragging to the limelight merely one aspect of Negro characteristics, by which the whole race has been glimpsed, through which it has been judged. The colored man who finally succeeds in impressing any considerable number of whites with the truth that he does not conform to these measurements is regarded as the striking exception proving an unshakable rule. The medium then through which the black actor has been presented to the world has been that of the "funny man" of America. Ever since those far-off times directly after the Civil War when white men and colored men too, blacking their faces, presented the antics of plantation hands under the caption of "Georgia Minstrels" and the like, the edict has gone forth that the black man on the stage must be an end-man.

In passing one pauses to wonder if this picture of the black American as a living comic supplement has not been painted in order to camouflage the real feeling and knowledge of his white compatriot. Certainly the plight of the slaves under even the mildest of masters could never have been one to awaken laughter. And no genuinely thinking person, no really astute observer, looking at the Negro in modern American life, could find his condition even now a first aid to laughter. That condition may be variously deemed hopeless, remarkable, admirable, inspiring, depressing; it can never be dubbed merely amusing.

It was the colored actor who gave the first impetus away from this buffoonery. The task was not an easy one. For years the Negro was no great frequenter of the theater. And no matter how keenly he felt the insincerity in the presentation of his kind, no matter how ridiculous and palpable a caricature such a presentation might be, the Negro auditor with the helplessness of the minority was powerless to demand something better and truer. Artist and audience alike were in the grip of the minstrel formula. It was at this point in the eighteen-nineties that Ernest Hogan, pioneer comedian of the better type, changed the tradition of the merely funny, rather silly "end-man" into a character with a definite plot in a rather loosely constructed but none the less well outlined story. The method was still humorous, but less broadly, less exclusively. A little of the hard luck of the Negro began to creep in. If he was a buffoon, he was a buffoon wearing his rue. A slight, very slight quality of the Harlequin began to attach to him. He was the clown making light of his troubles but he was a wounded, a sore-beset clown.

This figure became the prototype of the plays later presented by those two great characters, Williams and Walker. The ingredients of the comedies in which these two starred usually consisted of one dishonest, overbearing, flashily dressed character (Walker) and one kindly, rather simple, hard-luck personage (Williams). The interest of the piece hinged on the juxtaposition of these two men. Of course these plays, too, were served with a sauce of humor because the public, true to its carefully taught and rigidly held tradition, could not dream of a situation in which colored people were anything but merely funny. But the hardships and woes suffered by Williams, ridiculous as they were, introduced with the element of folk comedy some element of reality.

Side by side with Williams and Walker, who might be called the apostles of the "legitimate" on the stage for Negroes, came the merriment and laughter and high spirits of that incomparable pair, Cole and Johnson. But they were essentially the geniuses of musical comedy. At that time their singers and dancers outsang and outdanced the neophytes of contemporary white musical comedies even as their followers to this day out-sing and outdance in their occasional appearances on Broadway their modern neighbors. Just what might have been the ultimate trend of the ambition of this partnership, the untimely death of Mr. Cole rendered uncertain; but speaking offhand I should say that the relation of their musical comedy idea to the fixed plot and defined dramatic concept of the Williams and Walker plays molded the form of the Negro musical show which still persists and thrives on the contemporary stage. It was they who capitalized the infectious charm of so much rich dark beauty, the verve and abandon of Negro dancers, the glorious fullness of Negro voices. And they produced those effects in the *Red Shawl* in a manner still unexcelled, except in the matter of setting, by any latter-day companies.

But Williams and Walker, no matter how dimly, were seeking a method whereby the colored man might enter the "legitimate." They were to do nothing but pave the way. Even this task was difficult but they performed it well.

THOSE WHO KNEW BERT WILLIAMS say that his earliest leanings were toward the stage; but that he recognized at an equally early age that his color would probably keep him from ever making the "legitimate." Consequently, deliberately, as one who desiring to become a great painter but lacking the means for travel and study might take up commercial art, he turned his attention to minstrelsy. Natively he possessed the art of mimicry; intuitively he realized that his first path to the stage must lie along the old recognized lines of "funny man." He was, as few of us recall, a Jamaican by birth; the ways of the American Negro were utterly alien to him and did not come spontaneously; he set himself therefore to obtaining a knowledge of them. For choice he selected, perhaps by way of contrast, the melancholy out-of-luck Negro, shiftless, doleful, "easy"; the kind that tempts the world to lay its hand none too lightly upon him. The pursuit took him years, but at length he was able to portray for us not only that "typical Negro" which the white world thinks is universal but also the special types of given districts and localities with their own peculiar foibles of walk and speech and jargon. He went to London and studied under Pietro, greatest pantomimist of his day, until finally he, too, became a recognized master in the field of comic art.

But does anyone who realizes that the foibles of the American Negro were painstakingly acquired by this artist, doubt that Williams might just as well have portrayed the Irishman, the Jew, the Englishman abroad, the Scotchman or any other of the vividly etched types which for one reason or another lend themselves so readily to caricature? Can anyone presume to say that a man who travelled *north, east, south* and *west* and even abroad in order to acquire accent and jargon, aspect and characteristic of a people to which he was bound by ties of blood but from whom he was natively separated by training and tradition, would not have been able to portray with equal effectiveness what, for lack of a better term, we must call universal rôles?

There is an unwritten law in America that though white may imitate black, black, even when superlatively capable, must never imitate white. In other words, grease-paint may be used to darken but never to lighten.

Williams' color imposed its limitations upon him even in his chosen field. His expansion was always upward but never outward. He might portray black people along the gamut from roustabout to unctuous bishop. But he must never stray beyond those limits. How keenly he felt this few of us knew until after his death. But it was well known to his intimates and professional associates. W. C. Fields, himself an expert in the art of amusing, called him "the funniest man I ever saw and the saddest man I ever knew."

He was sad with the sadness of hopeless frustration. The gift of laughter in his case had its source in a wounded heart and in bleeding sensibilities.

THAT LAUGHTER FOR WHICH WE are so justly famed has had in late years its over-tones of pain. Now for some time past it has been used by colored men who have gained a precarious footing on the stage to conceal the very real dolor raging in their breasts. To be by force of circumstances the most dramatic figure in a country; to be possessed of the wells of feeling, of the most spontaneous instinct for effective action and to be shunted no less always into the rôle of the ridiculous and funny,—that is enough to create the quality of bitterness for which we are ever so often rebuked. Yet that same laughter influenced by these same untoward obstacles has within the last four years known a deflection into another channel, still productive of mirth, but even more than that of a sort of cosmic gladness, the joy which arises spontaneously in the spectator as a result of the sight of its no less spontaneous bubbling in others. What hurt most in the spectacle of the Bert Williams' funny man and his forerunners was the fact that the laughter which he created must be objective. But the new "funny man" among black comedians is essentially funny himself. He is joy and mischief and rich, homely native humor personified. He radiates good feeling and happiness; it is with him now a state of being purely subjective. The spectator is infected with his high spirits and his excessive good will; a stream of well-being is projected across the footlights into the consciousness of the beholder.

ALAIN LOCKE

This phenomenon has been especially visible in the rendition of the colored musical "shows," *Shuffle Along, Runnin' Wild, Liza*, which livened up Broadway recently for a too brief season. Those of us who were lucky enough to compare with the usual banality of musical comedy, the verve and pep, the liveliness and gayety of those productions will not soon forget them. The medley of shades, the rich colorings, the abundance of fun and spirits on the part of the players all combined to produce an atmosphere which was actually palpable, so full was it of the ecstasy and joy of living. The singing was inimitable; the work of the chorus apparently spontaneous and unstudied. Emotionally they garnished their threadbare plots and comedy tricks with the genius of a new comic art.

The performers in all three of these productions gave out an impression of sheer happiness in living such as I have never before seen on any stage except in a riotous farce which I once saw in Vienna and where the same effect of superabundant vitality was induced. It is this quality of vivid and untheatrical portrayal of sheer emotion which seems likely to be the Negro's chief contribution to the stage. A comedy made up of such ingredients as the music of Sissle and Blake, the quaint, irresistible humor of Miller and Lyles, the quintessence of jazzdom in the Charleston, the superlativeness of Miss Mills' happy abandon could know no equal. It would be the line by which all other comedy would have to be measured. Behind the banalities and clap-trap and crudities of these shows, this supervitality and joyousness glow from time to time in a given step or gesture or in the teasing assurance of such a line as: "If you've never been vamped by a brown-skin, you've never been vamped at all."

And as Carl van Vechten recently in his brilliant article, *Prescription for the Negro Theater*, so pointedly advises and prophesies, once this spirit breaks through the silly "childish adjuncts of the minstrel tradition" and drops the unworthy formula of unoriginal imitation of the stock revues, there will be released on the American stage a spirit of comedy such as has been rarely known.

THE REMARKABLE THING ABOUT THIS gift of ours is that it has its rise, I am convinced, in the very woes which beset us. Just as a person driven by great sorrow may finally go into an orgy of laughter, just so an oppressed and too hard driven people breaks over into compensating laughter and merriment. It is our emotional salvation. There would be no point in mentioning this rather obvious fact were it not that it argues also the possession on our part of a histrionic endowment for the portrayal of tragedy. Not without reason has tradition made comedy and tragedy sisters and twins, the capacity for one argues the capacity for the other. It is not surprising then that the period that sees the Negro actor on the verge of great comedy has seen him breaking through to the portrayal of serious and legitimate drama. No one who has seen Gilpin and Robeson in the portrayal of *The Emperor Jones* and of *All God's Chillun* can fail to realize that tragedy, too, is a vastly fitting rôle for the Negro actor. And so with the culminating of his dramatic genius, the Negro actor must come finally through the very versatility of his art to the universal role and the main tradition of drama, as an artist first and only secondarily as a Negro.

NOR WHEN WITHIN THE NEXT few years, this question comes up,— as I suspect it must come up with increasing insistence, will the more obvious barriers seem as obvious as they now appear. For in this American group of the descendants of Mother Africa, the question of color raises no insuperable barrier, seeing that with chameleon adaptability we are able to offer white colored men and women for *Hamlet, The Doll's House* and the *Second Mrs. Tanqueray;* brown men for *Othello*; yellow girls for *Madam Butterfly*; black men for *The Emperor Jones*. And underneath and permeating all this bewildering array of shades and tints is the unshakable precision of an instinctive and spontaneous emotional art.

All this beyond any doubt will be the reward of the "gift of laughter" which many black actors on the American stage have proffered. Through laughter we have conquered even the lot of the jester and the clown. The parable of the one talent still holds good and because we have used the little which in those early painful days was our only approach we find ourselves slowly but surely moving toward that most glittering of all goals, the freedom of the American stage. I hope that Hogan realizes this and Cole and Walker, too, and that lastly Bert Williams the inimitable, will clap us on with those tragic black-gloved hands of his now that the gift of his laughter is no longer tainted with the salt of chagrin and tears.

Compromise

A Folk Play

By Willis Richardson

Characters

JANE LEE, *a widow*
ALEC, *her son*
ANNIE, *her daughter*
RUTH, *her younger daughter*
BEN CARTER, *a white neighbor*

This room at the home of JANE LEE *and her children in a country district of Maryland has at its center a rectangular table, at the right and left of which are chairs. Left side is an open fireplace, above which stands a chair against the wall and a door leading to the kitchen. At the center of the rear wall stands a bench on which is a water bucket and dipper. At the right of the bench a door leads outside. Right side, a door leads to the stairs, and below this door another chair stands against the wall. At first the room is vacant, but presently* JANE, *a woman of five-and-forty, enters from the kitchen. Taking the bucket, she goes to the outer door and calls her son,* ALEC.

JANE: (*Calling*)
    Alec!
ALEC: Ma'am?
JANE: Come here!
(*Presently* ALEC, *a youth of twenty, appears. He is in his shirt sleeves and is wearing a slouch hat. She hands him the bucket*)
    Get me a bucket o' water.
(*Taking the bucket,* ALEC *goes out to the right and* JANE *comes back to the table. Looking towards the kitchen*)
    Come on, children, Ah ain't got all day to wait.
(*Her two daughters,* ANNIE, *eighteen, and* RUTH, *fourteen, enter from the kitchen. Both are pretty girls but shabbily dressed.* ANNIE *is carrying a small market basket*)
(*Taking money from her pocket and giving it to* ANNIE)

Be sure and don't forget the coffee.

(*Looking closely at* ANNIE)

What's the matter with you, gal? You ain't smiled in the last two days.

ANNIE: Nothin'.

JANE: It must be somethin'. You ain't been actin' like that all the time. It's enough for me and Alec to be goin' around with heavy hearts. You'-all ain't old enough to have no troubles yet.

ANNIE: (*Looking away*)

Ain't nothin' the matter with me.

JANE: All right, go on; and don't forget to hurry back.

(*They go out. She stands in the doorway watching them and shaking her head*)

(*To* ALEC *as he returns with the bucket of water and is on his way to the kitchen with it*)

When you get done cuttin' the wood come in and Ah'll have a good cup o' coffee for you.

ALEC: (*Returning from the kitchen*)

Ah thought you said the coffee was out.

JANE: Ah had enough left for one pot and Annie's gone after more. Boy,—you notice anything strange about Annie lately?

ALEC: Ah notice she's mighty gloomy. Ah seen huh behind the house cryin' yesterday.

JANE: (*Interested*)

You didn't say nothin' about it.

ALEC: She said she just dropped a stick o' wood on huh foot.

JANE: Ah was just tellin' huh a minute ago she was too young to be mopin' around, that she don't know nothin' about trouble yet. It's enough for you an' me to be worryin'.

ALEC: You're right, Ma (*going out*), I ain't done chopping yet.

(*He goes back to the yard.* JANE *stands watching him for a few moments, then goes to the kitchen. The regular fall of* ALEC'S *ax can be heard as he cuts wood outside. Presently* BEN CARTER *enters from the yard. He is a white man between forty-five and fifty, wearing a coat but no necktie in his soft collar*)

CARTER: (*Calling out as he throws his hat on the bench*)

Anybody home!

JANE: (*Appearing at the kitchen door*)

Mornin', Ben Carter.

CARTER: Mornin', Jane. Got any good coffee?

JANE: Ah don't never have no other kind.

CARTER: I know you don't. You make the best coffee in this county.
I 'clare I can't get my wife—

JANE: Sit down and Ah'll get you a cup.

(*He sits at the left of the table and she goes into the kitchen*)

CARTER: I kin smell it all the way in here, Jane.

JANE: (*Appearing with a cup of coffee and placing it on the table before him*)

Ef there's anything men-folks is pertic'ler about, it's coffee.
Jim was moughty pertic'ler about his'n—if he was good for
nuthin'.

CARTER: Now, Jane—lay off Jim. Jim wasn't the wust husban' in these
parts.

JANE: Jim was big and strong enuf—and good natured, 'cept drinkin'—
but Jim was nuthin' up here (*taps her forehead*)

CARTER: Oh, well, Jim's gone now. Ferget it, Jane.

JANE: If he'd had any brains he wouldn't a tuk that hund'ed dollars and
drunk hisself ter death, would he?

CARTER: (*Nervously*)

Ferget it, Jane. You're like my wife, yer mouth spoils yer
cookin'—ef I do say so. Now you got Alec, and he's good an' strong,
and soon he'll—

JANE: (*Interrupting*)

Ben Carter, you sit there an' tell me I got Alec. (*Excitedly*)
What about Jim? What about Joe?

CARTER: Now, Jane—you're such out o' sorts. Don't bring up poor Joe.

JANE: (*Bitterly*)

Yer hund'ed dollars didn't shut me up. Yer com'permised with Jim.

CARTER: (*Getting up*)

Ef you will keep throwin' up that accident, why, I'll gie yer my
house-room. Naggin' won't bring Joe back.

JANE: Ah know it—but if I 'a' killed him, I'd be skeered to call his
name.

CARTER: (*Excitedly*)

Killed him! Don't talk like that, Jane. You talk like I killed that
boy on pu'pose (*shouting*), when you know I didn't.

JANE: Maybe you didn't kill him on purpose, but killin' is killin'; an'
you got off with payin' Jim a hund'ed dollars.

CARTER: (*Bringing his cup down with a bang on the table*)
I done what I thought was fair. If you'-all had 'a' gone to law
maybe you wouldn't 'a' got nothin'.

JANE: Maybe we wouldn't—you bein' white and we bein' black.

CARTER: I didn't mean it like that. You know we've been neighbors for
years and never had no kind o' trouble. I mean if your boy Joe had
'a' been white and you all had 'a' been white—

JANE: If our boy Joe had 'a' been white, we'd 'a' been white anyhow.

CARTER: I know you would, and that's what I'm sayin'. If you'-all had
'a' been white, you couldn't 'a' got nothin' by goin' to law cause it
wasn't nothin' but a accident out and out. When I shot up in that
tree I didn't have no idea Joe was up there.

JANE: You didn't have to shoot.

CARTER: I told you a hundred times, Jane, I done it to scare the boys.
I told 'em to keep out o' my orchard, and when I seen a gang of
'em there, pickin' up apples under that tree, I got my gun and shot
up in the tree to scare 'em. God knows I didn't know nobody was
up there till Joe fell. I didn't know he was up there shakin' apples
down.

JANE: That accident killed a lot o' hope in me. Ma man, Jim, took that
hund'ed dollars and soon drunk hisself to death and that's two o'
ma men-folks gone on account o' you.

CARTER: Nobody felt it more than I did, Jane, unless it was you. And
I hope you ain't harborin' no bad feelin's.

JANE: No, Ah ain't got no bad feelin's for you, Ben Carter. Ah always
found you a pretty good square man, good as the average and
better 'n some Ah know; but you might 'a' done more by us than a
hund'ed dollars. Ah know you could 'a' spared more.

CARTER: I know I could 'a' spared more, but Jim agreed when I said a
hund'ed and I couldn't 'a' paid as much as the boy's life was worth
nohow.

JANE: 'Deed you couldn't.

CARTER: And ain't no man, black or white, goin' to give up more
money than he has to.

JANE: Ah reckon you're right there. All men is pretty near alike when
it comes to payin' out money.

(*She goes to the door and stands with her back to him looking out*)

CARTER: I don't see no use in you bein' so gloomy about a thing that's
done and been done for seven years.

ALAIN LOCKE

JANE: (*Turning to him*)

> You can't expect for me to go around smilin' with the hopes Ah had for that boy. If he had 'a' lived till now he'd 'a' been twenty-five, wouldn't he?

CARTER: Yes.

JANE: He'd 'a' been a man now and able to work and help me educate the younger ones, Alec and Annie and Ruth. That's what Ah wanted most of all—to educate ma children.

CARTER: Ain't none of us can get everything we want.

JANE: But seems like Ah don't get nothin' *Ah* want.

CARTER: You're just feelin' gloomy to-day, that's all. You won't be feelin' like that to-morrow. (*Giving her some change*) Get me another cup o' coffee, won't you?

JANE: (*Taking the cup*)

> You might think Ah'll be feelin' all right to-morrow but Ah don't think so. Ah been feelin' the same way for near seven years.

(*She goes to the kitchen with the cup*)

CARTER: (*Speaking to her from where he sits*)

> If there's anything I kin do, or anything my wife kin do— anything that's reasonable, we'll do it.

JANE: (*Returning with the coffee*)

> No, there ain't nothin' you'-all kin do. Ah ain't got no claim on you now, Ben.

CARTER: I don't want no hard feelin's with none o' my neighbors, white or black.

JANE: Ah told you once Ah didn't have no hard feelin's against you.

CARTER: Maybe you ain't, but your boy, Alec, acts like he is. He never speaks to me on the road, and when he looks at me seems like he hates me.

JANE: You can't expect Alec to go around smilin' at you after what's happened.

CARTER: He might act a little more friendly.

JANE: Maybe he might and maybe he mightn't. There's a lots o' things about us you don't know, Ben Carter, and never dreamed of. Ah'm goin' to tell you one of 'em now.

(*She goes just outside the door which leads to the stairway and brings back a gun*)

> See this gun?

CARTER: Yes.

JANE: This gun's been loaded for seven years, ever since Joe was killed. Alec was fourteen then, and he wanted to go out and shoot you.

CARTER: Shoot me for somethin' I couldn't help?

JANE: He didn't see it the way you see it. He thought you could 'a' helped it.

CARTER: He wasn't a thing but a boy. Why didn't you'-all explain it to him?

JANE: We done the best we could. We persuaded him not to do no shootin' so it didn't take long to wear off his mind, he bein' a kid; but he never liked none o' you'-all after that.

CARTER: Kept hate in his heart for seven years?

JANE: (*Putting the gun in the corner*)
Ah wouldn't call it hate out and out, but you couldn't expect him to love you after you shot his big brother.

CARTER: Can't he see yet that I didn't mean to do it?

JANE: Seems like he can't.

CARTER: I'm glad you kin see I didn't mean it.

JANE: Yes, Ah kin see it, Ben. If Ah couldn't see you didn't mean to do it you'd 'a' been dead years ago.

CARTER: (*Starting*)
Dead!

JANE: Yes.

CARTER: You mean you'd 'a' killed me?

JANE: That's what Ah would. If Ah had 'a' thought you killed ma oldest boy on purpose do you think you could 'a' come in here and drunk ma coffee without me p'izonin' you? Ah'd 'a' put enough p'izon in you to kill ten horses, Ben. You'd 'a' been dead so long your bones would 'a' been dust.

CARTER: Ah never thought it of you, Jane.

JANE: Could you blame me if Ah had 'a' thought you killed Joe on purpose?

CARTER: I can't say I could 'a' blamed you if you had 'a' thought that.

JANE: You just go home and pray and thank your Gawd Ah didn't think that.

CARTER: I'll have to talk to Alec and see if I can't get him to see it like you do.

JANE: Ah wish you could get him to see it that a way.

(RUTH *enters with the basket on her arm*)

JANE: Where's Annie?

RUTH: (*Looking from her mother to* CARTER)

She stopped to talk to Jack Carter.

JANE: She ought to come on home. Take them things in the kitchen.

(RUTH *goes into the kitchen with the basket*)

JANE: Ah don't like too much friendship between Annie and your boy Jack.

CARTER: I can't see no harm in it. They played together when they was kids and growed up together.

JANE: Ah know that, but they ain't kids now. It'll have to stop.

RUTH: (*Who has returned from the kitchen*)

Ma, is anything between Annie and Jack?

JANE: (*Looking at her closely*)

Anything how? Why?

RUTH: Annie was cryin' while she was talkin' to him.

(CARTER *stops the cup on the way to his lips and listens carefully*)

JANE: Cryin'? What's she cryin' for?

RUTH: Ah don't know 'm.

JANE: You go and tell huh to come right home.

(RUTH *goes out*)

JANE: Ah don't like the looks o' things, Ben Carter; Ah don't like it a bit.

CARTER: Don't reckon it's nothin' but a few cross words.

JANE: She wouldn't cry about no cross words—not Annie.

CARTER: What else could it be?

JANE: Ah don't know. Ah hope there ain't nothin' wrong. Ah hope to Gawd it ain't.

CARTER: It can't be nothin' wrong. All them children but Alec's been playin' together like brothers and sisters all their lives.

JANE: (*Who has gone to the door*)

Here she comes now.

(CARTER *drinks the last of his coffee and they wait in silence until* ANNIE *enters.* JANE *has come back to the table and* ANNIE, *although it is summer, closes the door behind her by backing against it*)

What you shuttin' the door for an' it roastin' like this? What you wipin' yo' eyes about? (*ANNIE reopens the door*) Where you been? Ah just sent Ruth after you.

ANNIE: Ah've been to the store.

JANE: (*More impatiently as the argument advances*)

You been pass the store.

ANNIE: (*Sullenly*)

You sent me to the store and that's where Ah've been.

JANE: Ah tell you, you been pass the store! What's that mud doin' on your shoes if you ain't been pass the store? Ain't no mud like that 'tween here and the store!

(ANNIE *is silent*)

What's the matter with you—can't you talk?

ANNIE: Ah walked down the road a little piece with Jack.

JANE: Ah sent you to the store! Ah didn't send you to walk with Jack!

ANNIE: We wanted to talk.

JANE: Talk about what? (ANNIE *is silent*) What you doin' cryin'?

ANNIE: Ah ain't cryin'.

JANE: You *been* cryin'! Can't Ah see where the tears been runnin' down your face?

(ANNIE *looks down*)

Now what you been cryin' about?

(ANNIE *is silent*)

Don't you hear me talkin' to you?

(ANNIE *is still silent. Pause. Almost in tears herself*)

Is there anything between you and Jack Carter?

(ANNIE *bends her head still lower.* JANE *leans closer, trying to look into* ANNIE's *face, and speaks almost pleadingly*)

For mercy's sake, child, tell me if anything's wrong between you and Jack!

(*Unable to keep silent any longer,* ANNIE, *with a quick look at* CARTER, *who has been an attentive listener, hides her face with her arms and runs out towards the stairway.* JANE *turns to* CARTER *and speaks excitedly*)

You see how things is, Ben Carter! You see!

(*She follows* ANNIE *out and* CARTER, *who has half risen from his chair, sits again perplexed. There is a silence until* RUTH's *laughter is heard as she is being chased about the yard by* ALEC. *Presently she runs in and goes towards the stairs with* ALEC *after her. He stops in surprise and starts out when he sees* CARTER, *but* CARTER *rises*)

CARTER: (*As* ALEC *starts out*)

Alec!

(ALEC *stops and looks at him without speaking*)

What you got against me, Alec?

ALEC: Ah ain't got nothin' particular against you.

CARTER: You ain't friendly.

ALEC: Ah ain't got much cause to be friendly.

CARTER: Me and your people here been livin' side by side for years and we always got along all right, but you always seem like you're mad.

ALEC: I cain't help that—that ain't nuthin' ter do with me.

CARTER: Yer mother jus' told me—'twas cause that accident—y' member—that accident 'bout Joe—Well, you know I didn't mean to do it, don't yer?

ALEC: You done it just the same, and you can't expect me to go around laughin' and grinnin' afterwards.

CARTER: You might speak to a person on the road.

ALEC: If ma old man had 'a' shot your boy, Jack, down out a tree like you done Joe, would you be so friendly? Would you be laughin' and grinnin' at us on the road?

CARTER: Ain't no use o' bringin' up nothin' like that.

ALEC: Ah know it ain't. The shoe always fits awkward on the other foot. If he had 'a' done that to your boy, Jack, he'd 'a' been lucky to get off with a hund'ed years in the pen.

CARTER: After what happened I done all I could.

ALEC: You compromised with that fool daddy o' mine for a hund'ed dollars to drink hisself to death with, and that's two counts against you.

(*He goes quickly back to the yard without awaiting* CARTER'S *reply.* CARTER *is still standing by the table when* JANE *comes downstairs*)

JANE: (*Controlling herself with an effort*)
    It's true, Ben Carter, just like Ah was scared it was.

CARTER: What's true?

JANE: Annie's in trouble, and it's Jack.

CARTER: How do you know it's Jack?

JANE: (*Looking straight at him*)
    She just told me!

CARTER: That ain't no proof.

JANE: (*Advancing to him and shaking her finger in his face*)
    Wait a minute, Ben Carter! Wait right there! Ah ain't goin' to have you throwin' out no slurs about ma child! She says it's Jack, and Jack it is! This is the third thing that's happened to us on account o' you and your'n! And this time you're goin' to pay! If you compermise this time you're goin' to compermise for somethin'!

CARTER: I'm a fair man, Jane Lee; you know that. And if Jack's in fault I'll do all I kin do, but I won't be bullied. I've got to know he's in fault.

JANE: Jack is in fault!

CARTER: Your gal must be in fault, too.

JANE: Ah ain't denyin' that!

CARTER: She must 'a' liked him a little or it wouldn't 'a' happened.

JANE: And he must 'a' liked huh a little, too!

CARTER: Why should I have to pay, then, if she's as much to blame as he is?

JANE: You kin stand there and talk like that if you want to, but if Ah'd say let's punish 'em both and make 'em get married you'd set up a big howl!

CARTER: Wouldn't I have a right to?

JANE: Ah don't know that you would! She's as good as he is, and it wouldn't be the first time that ever happened in these parts!

CARTER: But it ain't goin' to happen this time.

JANE: Ah know it ain't, and that ain't what Ah'm after. Ah don't believe in no forced marriages.

CARTER: What is you after?

JANE: Ah want you to do somethin' for ma children to make up for the harm that's come to us by you and yours.

CARTER: I'll do what's reasonable, but it's got to be fair. I ain't for makin' enemies.

JANE: Then, educate ma children.

CARTER: What you mean?

JANE: Ah mean pay for Alec and Ruth to go to school. That's been ma plan all the time but you spoiled it when you shot Joe.

CARTER: Ain't you askin' a whole lot, Jane?

JANE: Askin' a whole lot! You think you kin pay for Joe's life with a little money? You think you kin pay for Annie bein' ruined with a little money?

CARTER: I ain't tryin' to pay for neither one. I just want to be fair.

JANE: Three of us is done for on account o' you all, but Ah won't count that no good husband o' mine. Just count the two children, Joe and Annie. Now—don't you think you ought to do somethin' for us?

CARTER: That's what I'm willin' to do.

JANE: Look at me and look at yourself. Ah'm a lone woman and poor with three children; you're one o' the richest men in the county, if not the richest, with a wife and one child. Does that seem fair to you, Ben Carter; when Ah'm just as honest as you and just as good a Christian?

CARTER: Ain't nobody denyin' about you bein' honest, and ain't nobody denyin' about you bein' a good Christian.

JANE: Where's ma reward for bein' honest and bein' good?

CARTER: I reckon you'll get your reward in heaven.

JANE: Ah know that well enough; but Ah want ma children to have somethin' in this worl'.

CARTER: I can't blame you much for that. I'll talk to my wife and Jack, and I reckon we kin come to terms.

(*He starts out*)

JANE: Wait a minute.

(*She brings out the gun again*)

Ah believe you mean to be fair, and Ah want to show you that Ah mean to be fair. This old gun's loaded, and when Alec finds out what's happened Ah can't tell what he might do. The Lawd hisself moughtn't be able to hold him back this time—so Ah'll unload it.

(*She unloads the gun and puts the cartridges in her bosom*)

CARTER: All right, Jane, I see you mean well and I'll do what I kin for you. 'Deed I will, Jane.

(*He goes out. She puts the gun back and returns to the table where she sits weakly, and, losing control of herself, breaks into a flood of tears. Presently* ALEC *enters from the yard, bringing an armful of wood*)

ALEC: What's the good o' lettin' Ben Carter come in here and drink our coffee up every day or so? He don't give you nothin' for it, does he, or nothin' much, I'll bet—

(*She looks up and he notices her tears*)

What you doin'—cryin'?

JANE: Nothin'. Ah ain't feelin' good.

ALEC: (*Putting the wood on the bench*)

What's the matter?

JANE: Don't ask a lot o' questions, now. Ah ain't feelin' good.

(*With this she goes through the door which leads to the stairs.* RUTH *passes her in the doorway and stops to look around at her*)

ALEC: (*Calling* RUTH *in subdued tones*)

Come here.

RUTH: (*Going to him*)

What you want?

ALEC: What's the matter with Ma?

RUTH: Ah don't know. Why?

ALEC: Ah found huh in here cryin'.

RUTH: Ah don't know what's the matter 'less she's cryin' about Annie.

ALEC: (*Going closer and speaking more earnestly*)
    What's the matter with Annie?

RUTH: Seems like somethin's between huh and Jack Carter.

ALEC: Somethin' what?

RUTH: Ah don't know what. She was standin' down the road cryin'
    while she was talkin' to him.

(ALEC *goes out towards the stairway and* RUTH *goes to the door and stands looking out. Presently* ALEC *returns. He has heard the bad news and his face is set. He looks first towards the place where the gun is, then towards* RUTH)

ALEC: (*In a husky voice*)
    Ma wants you to bring huh a dipper o' water up there.

(RUTH *goes out through the kitchen and* ALEC *quickly gets the gun and goes outside. Presently* JANE *comes from towards the stairway and, not seeing anyone, goes to the door and looks out.* RUTH *returns from the kitchen with a dipper of water*)

RUTH: Here's the water.

JANE: (*Looking at her puzzled*)
    What water?

RUTH: Alec said you wanted a dipper o' water.

JANE: Alec! Where's Alec?

RUTH: He was in here a minute ago.

JANE: Where's he now?

RUTH: Ah don't know 'm.

(JANE *looks quickly in the place and finds that the gun is no longer there*)

JANE: He's got the gun, but, thank Gawd, he can't do no harm. It ain't
    loaded.

RUTH: What's he got the gun for?

JANE: He's got his temper up. You know how Alec is when he gets his
    temper up.

RUTH: Ah believe he fooled me out o' here so he could get out with
    the gun.

JANE: He'll be back in a minute.

RUTH: What's he got his temper up about? Is it about Annie?

JANE: Yes.

RUTH: When Ah asked you a while ago you said there wasn't nothin' between Annie and Jack.

JANE: (*Moving to the door to get away from* RUTH's *questions*)
Ah didn't know it then.

(*There is a pause and* JANE *changes the subject*)
How'd you like to go away to school?

RUTH: Ah'd sure be glad to.

JANE: Ah'm goin' to see if Ah can't send you away.

RUTH: How you goin' to send me away, poor as we is.

JANE: That's all right, Ah'm goin' to find a way. Ah'm goin' to find a way for you and Alec both to go.

RUTH: How about Annie?

JANE: (*With a catch in her voice*)
Ah reckon Annie'll stay home with me.

(ALEC *backs into the doorway with the gun in his hand. He is holding it by the barrel as one would hold a club. Still looking outside he has not seen those in the room*)

JANE: Where you been with that gun?

ALEC: (*Turning quickly*)
Ah went out fer Jack Carter, an' Ben Carter, too. Who's been foolin' with this gun?

JANE: What you want to shoot him for? Ain't Ah already compermised?

ALEC: (*Very angrily*)
Compermised! What good will it do to compermise? You compermised about Joe and didn't get nothin' out o' that, did yuh?

JANE: Your fool daddy done that! Ah'll get somethin' out o' this!

ALEC: What you think you goin' to get?

JANE: Ah made Ben Carter give his word to educate you and Ruth, and Ben Carter always keeps his word.

ALEC: You won't edjercate me with any o' his money! Ah won't have it!

JANE: Why won't you?

ALEC: Ah just won't, that's all!

JANE: Ah'll see that you will! Ah know Ah ain't wasted all ma breath on Ben Carter for nothin'!

ALEC: He ain't goin' to give you nothin', nohow. Not after what Ah done to Jack!

JANE: (*Going to him and catching him by the arm*)
Done to Jack! What did you do to Jack?

ALEC: Ah fixed him even if the gun wasn't loaded.

JANE: Fixed him, how?

ALEC: (*Showng her*)

Ah made a swipe at his head with this gun and he th'owed his arm er he'd 'a' got it proper, but Ah bet Ah broke sumpin'.

JANE: Beat Jack up after Ah compermised with his daddy?

ALEC: Ah'd 'a' broke his head if he hadn't 'a' been down. Ah didn't hit him but one lick; but it was a good 'un.

JANE: Now you are in a mess, Alec Lee. Ben Carter'll put the sheriff on you sure! Get out o' here and go to Aunt Dinah's and hide!

ALEC: (*Slowly putting the gun away*)

Hide for what! He didn't hide after he shot Joe, did he?

JANE: That's diff'ent! Can't you see that's diff'ent! He ain't goin' to let you beat Jack up and get away with it! Get out o' here and hide till this thing blows over!

(ALEC *starts outside*)

JANE: (*Catching him by the arm*)

Not that 'a way!

(*Pointing to the door which leads to the stairway*)

Go th'u' there and jump out o' the back window so nobody won't see you!

(ALEC *goes through the door which leads to the stairs*)

(*Fondling* RUTH)

You'll get educated just the same, Ruth; see if you don't. Ben Carter'll keep his word!

RUTH: Ah don't know what he'll do after what Alec's done.

JANE: Yes, he will. He ain't never broke his word.

(CARTER, *hatless and coatless, rushes in angrily*)

CARTER: What kind o' business is this, Jane Lee?

JANE: What?

CARTER: That boy o' yours broke Jack's arm! I'm goin' to put the sheriff on him sure as a gun's iron!

JANE: Put the sheriff on him what for? You know Alec's hotheaded!

CARTER: Hot-headed or not hot-headed! He'll go up for it if he's caught! And that bargain I made with you about sendin' 'em to school is all off! It don't go! Wasn't nothin' in it about breakin' ma boy's arm! I'm done with you! I'm done with you all—'ceptin' Alec—Yer hear me.

(*He hurries out*)

JANE: (*Running to the door and calling him*)

      Ben Carter! Ben Carter!

(*As he does not answer, she slowly returns to* RUTH, *then takes the cartridges out of her bosom, where she has tucked them. She looks for the gun—picks it up—sits down at centre table—starts to reload it—fumbles the cartridges—and then suddenly as she says "Oh Lawd," puts them in her bosom again*)

      I oughtn't 'a' compermised. I oughtn't 'a' compermised.

(*Suddenly*)

      Ruth, come here.

      Ruth, yer must help mammy get Alec's things tergether,—
quick, yer hear. We must get Alec out o' here. Ben Carter shan't
get Alec. I'll face him myself, an' I don't mean no foolin' this time.

(*As she begins to stuff* ALEC's *clothes into a valise*)

CURTAIN

MUSIC

THE NEGRO SPIRITUALS

Alain Locke

The Spirituals are really the most characteristic product of the race genius as yet in America. But the very elements which make them uniquely expressive of the Negro make them at the same time deeply representative of the soil that produced them. Thus, as unique spiritual products of American life, they become nationally as well as racially characteristic. It may not be readily conceded now that the song of the Negro is America's folk-song; but if the Spirituals are what we think them to be, a classic folk expression, then this is their ultimate destiny. Already they give evidence of this classic quality. Through their immediate and compelling universality of appeal, through their untarnishable beauty, they seem assured of the immortality of those great folk expressions that survive not so much through being typical of a group or representative of a period as by virtue of being fundamentally and everlastingly human. This universality of the Spirituals looms more and more as they stand the test of time. They have outlived the particular generation and the peculiar conditions which produced them; they have survived in turn the contempt of the slave owners, the conventionalizations of formal religion, the repressions of Puritanism, the corruptions of sentimental balladry, and the neglect and disdain of second-generation respectability. They have escaped the lapsing conditions and the fragile vehicle of folk art, and come firmly into the context of formal music. Only classics survive such things.

In its disingenuous simplicity, folk art is always despised and rejected at first; but generations after, it flowers again and transcends the level of its origin. The slave songs are no exception; only recently have they come to be recognized as artistically precious things. It still requires vision and courage to proclaim their ultimate value and possibilities. But while the first stage of artistic development is yet uncompleted, it appears that behind the deceptive simplicity of Negro song lie the richest undeveloped musical resources anywhere available. Thematically rich, in idiom of rhythm and harmony richer still, in potentialities of new musical forms and new technical traditions so deep as to be accessible only to genius, they have the respect of the connoisseur even while still under the sentimental and condescending patronage of the amateur. Proper understanding and full appreciation of the Spirituals, in spite of their present vogue, is still rare. And the Negro himself has shared many of the common and widespread limitations of view with regard to them. The emotional intuition which has made him cling to this folk music has lacked for the most part that convinced enlightenment that eventually will treasure the Spirituals for their true musical and technical values. And although popular opinion and the general conception have changed very materially, a true estimate of this body of music cannot be reached until many prevailing preconceptions are completely abandoned. For what general opinion regards as simple and transparent about them is in technical ways, though instinctive, very intricate and complex, and what is taken as whimsical and child-like is in truth, though naïve, very profound.

It was the great service of Dr. Du Bois in his unforgettable chapter on the Sorrow Songs in *The Souls of the Black Folk* to give them a serious and proper social interpretation, just as later Mr. Krehbiel in his *Afro-American Folk Songs* gave them their most serious and adequate musical analysis and interpretation. The humble origin of these sorrow songs is too indelibly stamped upon them to be ignored or overlooked. But underneath broken words, childish imagery, peasant simplicity, lies, as Dr. Du Bois pointed out, an epic intensity and a tragic profundity of emotional experience, for which the only historical analogy is the spiritual experience of the Jews and the only analogue, the Psalms. Indeed they transcend emotionally even the very experience of sorrow out of which they were born; their mood is that of religious exaltation, a degree of ecstasy indeed that makes them in spite of the crude vehicle a classic expression of the religious emotion. They lack the grand style, but never the sublime effect. Their words are colloquial, but their mood is epic. They are primitive, but their emotional artistry is perfect. Indeed, spiritually evaluated, they are among the most genuine and outstanding expressions of Christian mood and feeling, fit musically and emotionally, if not verbally, of standing with the few Latin hymns, the handful of Gregorian tunes, and the rarest of German chorals as a not negligible element in the modicum of strictly religious music that the Christian centuries have produced.

Perhaps there is no such thing as intrinsically religious music; certainly the traceable interplay of the secular and the religious in music would scarcely warrant an arbitrary opinion in the matter. And just as certainly as secular elements can be found in all religious music are there discoverable sensuous and almost pagan elements blended into the Spirituals. But something so intensely religious and so essentially Christian dominates the blend that they are indelibly and notably of this quality. The Spirituals are spiritual. Conscious artistry and popular conception alike should never rob them of this heritage, it is untrue to their tradition and to the folk genius to give them another tone. That they are susceptible of both crude and refined secularization is no excuse. Even though their own makers worked them up from the "shout" and the rhythmic elements of the sensuous dance, in their finished form and basic emotional effect all of these elements were completely sublimated in the sincere intensities of religious seriousness. To call them Spirituals and treat them otherwise is a travesty.

It was the Negro himself who first took them out of their original religious setting, but he only anticipated the inevitable by a generation— for the folk religion that produced them is rapidly vanishing. Noble as the purpose of this transplanting was, damage was done to the tradition. But we should not be ungrateful, for surely it was by this that they were saved to posterity at all. Nevertheless it was to an alien atmosphere that the missionary campaigning of the Negro schools and colleges took these songs. And the concert stage has but taken them an inevitable step further from their original setting. We should always remember that they are essentially congregational, not theatrical, just as they are essentially a choral not a solo form. In time, however, on another level, they will get back to this tradition,—for their next development will undoubtedly be, like that of the modern Russian folk music, their use in the larger choral forms of the symphonic choir, through which they will reachieve their folk atmosphere and epic spirituality.

It is a romantic story told in the *Story of the Jubilee Singers*, and retold in Professor Work's *Folk Song of the American Negro*; the tale of that group of singers who started out from Fisk University in 1871, under the resolute leadership of George L. White, to make this music the appeal of the struggling college for philanthropic support. With all the cash in the Fisk treasury, except a dollar held back by Principal Adam K. Spence, the troupe set out to Oberlin, where, after an unsuccessful concert of current music, they instantly made an impression by a program of Negro Spirituals. Henry Ward Beecher's invitation to Brooklyn led to fame for the singers, fortune for the college, but more important than these things, recognition for the Spirituals. Other schools, Hampton, Atlanta, Calhoun, Tuskegee joined the movement, and spread the knowledge of these songs far and wide in their concert campaigns. Later they recorded and published important collections of them. They thus were saved over that critical period of disfavor in which any folk product is likely to be snuffed out by the false pride of the second generation. Professor Work rightly estimates it as a service worth more racially and nationally than the considerable sums of money brought to these struggling schools. Indeed, as he says, it saved a folk art and preserved as no other medium could the folk temperament, and by maintaining them introduced the Negro to himself. Still the predominant values of this period in estimating the Spirituals were the sentimental, degenerating often into patronizing curiosity on the one side, and hectic exhibitionism on the other. Both races condescended to meet the mind of the Negro slave, and even while his moods were taking their hearts by storm, discounted the artistry of genius therein.

It was only as the musical appreciation of the Spirituals grew that this interest changed and deepened. Musically I think the Spirituals are as far in advance of their moods as their moods are in advance of their language. It is as poetry that they are least effective. Even as folk poetry, they cannot be highly rated. But they do have their quaint symbolisms, and flashes, sometimes sustained passages of fine imagery, as in the much quoted

> *I know moonlight, I know starlight*
> *I lay dis body down*
> *I walk in de graveyard, I walk troo de graveyard*
> *To lay dis body down.*
>
> *I lay in de grave an' stretch out my arms,*
> *I lay dis body down.*
> *I go to de judgment in de evenin' of de day*
> *When I lay dis body down,*
> *An' my soul an' yo' soul will meet de day*
> *I lay dis body down.*

or

> *Bright sparkles in de churchyard*
> *Give light unto de tomb;*
> *Bright summer, spring's over—*

> *Sweet flowers in their bloom.*

> *My mother once, my mother twice, my mother,*
> *she'll rejoice,*
> *In the Heaven once, in the Heaven twice,*
> *she'll rejoice.*
> *May the Lord, He will be glad of me*
> *In the Heaven, He'll rejoice.*

or again

> *My Lord is so high, you can't get over Him,*
> *My Lord is so low, you can't get under Him,*
> *You must come in and through de Lamb.*

In the latter passages, there is a naïveté, and also a faith and fervor, that are mediæval. Indeed one has to go to the Middle Ages to find anything quite like this combination of childlike simplicity of thought with strangely consummate artistry of mood. A quaintly literal, lisping, fervent Christianity, we feel it to be the evangelical and Protestant counterpart of the naïve Catholicism of the tenth to the thirteenth centuries. And just as there we had quaint versions of Bernard of Clairvaux and Saint Francis in the Virgin songs and Saints Legends, so here we have Bunyan and John Wesley percolated through a peasant mind and imagination, and concentrated into something intellectually less, but emotionally more vital and satisfying. If the analogy seems forced, remember that we see the homely colloquialism of the one through the glamorous distance of romance, and of the other, through the disillusioning nearness of social stigma and disdain. How regrettable though, that the very qualities that add charm to the one should arouse mirthful ridicule for the other.

Over-keen sensitiveness to this reaction, which will completely pass within a half generation or so, has unfortunately caused many singers and musicians to blur the dialect and pungent colloquialisms of the Spirituals so as not to impede with irrelevant reactions their proper artistic and emotional effect. Some have gone so far as to advocate the abandonment of the dialect versions to insure their dignity and reverence. But for all their inadequacies, the words are the vital clues to the moods of these songs. If anything is to be changed, it should be the popular attitude. One thing further may be said, without verging upon apologetics, about their verbal form. In this broken dialect and grammar there is almost invariably an unerring sense of euphony. Mr. Work goes so far as to suggest—rightly, I think—that in many instances the dropped, elided, and added syllables, especially the latter, are a matter of instinctive euphonic sense following the requirements of the musical rhythm, as, for example, "The Blood came a twinklin' down" from "The Crucifixion" or "Lying there fo' to be heal" from "Blind Man at the Pool." Mr. Work calls attention to the extra beat syllable, as in "De trumpet soun's it in-a' my soul," which is obviously a singing device, a subtle phrase-molding element from a musical point of view, even if on verbal surface value, it suggests illiteracy.

Emotionally, these folks songs are far from simple. They are not only spread over the whole gamut of human moods, with the traditional religious overtone adroitly insinuated in each instance, but there is further a sudden change of mood in the single song, baffling to formal classification. Interesting and intriguing as was Dr. Du Bois's analysis of their emotional themes, modern interpretation must break with that mode of analysis, and relate these songs to the folk activities that they motivated, classifying them by their respective song-types. From this point of view we have essentially four classes, the almost ritualistic prayer songs or pure Spirituals, the freer and more unrestrained evangelical "shouts" or camp-meeting songs, the folk ballads so overlaid with the tradition of the Spirituals proper that their distinctive type quality has almost been unnoticed until lately, and the work and labor songs of strictly secular character. In choral and musical idiom closely related, these song types are gradually coming to be regarded as more and more separate, with the term Spiritual reserved almost exclusively for the songs of intensest religious significance and function. Indeed, in the pure Spirituals one can trace the broken fragments of an evangelical folk liturgy, with confession, exhortation, "mourning," conversion and "love-feast" rejoicing as the general stages of a Protestant folk-mass. The instinctive feeling for these differences is almost wholly lost, and it will require the most careful study of the communal life as it still lingers in isolated spots to set the groupings even approximately straight. Perhaps after all the final appeal will have to be made to the sensitive race interpreter, but at present many a half secularized ballad is mistaken for a "spiritual," and many a camp-meeting shout for a folk hymn. It is not a question of religious content or allusion,—for the great majority of the Negro songs have this—but a more delicate question of caliber of feeling and type of folk use. From this important point of view, Negro folk song has yet to be studied.

The distinctiveness of the Spirituals after all, and their finest meaning resides in their musical elements. It is pathetic to notice how late scientific recording has come to the task of preserving this unique folk art. Of course the earlier four-part hymn harmony versions were travesties of the real folk renditions. All competent students agree in the utter distinctiveness of the melodic, harmonic and rhythmic elements in this music. However, there is a regrettable tendency, though a very natural one in view of an inevitable bias of technical interest, to over-stress as basically characteristic one or other of these elements in their notation and analysis. Weldon Johnson thinks the characteristic beauty of the folk song is harmonic, in distinction to the more purely rhythmic stress in the secular music of the Negro, which is the basis of "ragtime" and "jazz"; while Krehbiel, more academically balances these elements, regarding the one as the African component in them, and the other as the modifying influence of the religious hymn. "In the United States," he says, "the rhythmic element, though still dominant, has yielded measurably to the melodic, the dance having given way to religious worship, sensual bodily movement to emotional utterance." But as a matter of fact, if we separate or even over-stress either element in the Spirituals, the distinctive and finer effects are lost. Strain out and emphasize the melodic element *a la* Foster, and you get only the sentimental ballad; emphasize the harmonic idiom; and you get a cloying sentimental glee; over-emphasize the rhythmic idiom and instantly you secularize the product into syncopated dance elements. It is the fusion, and that only, that is finely characteristic; and so far as possible, both in musical settings and in the singing of the Negro Spirituals, this subtle balance of musical elements should be sought after and maintained. The actual mechanics of the native singing, with its syllabic quavers, the off-tones and tone glides, the improvised interpolations and, above all, the subtle rhythmic phrase balance, has much to do with the preservation of the vital qualities of these songs.

Let us take an example. There is no more careful and appreciative student of the Spirituals than David Guion; as far as is possible from a technical and outside approach, he has bent his skill to catch the idiom of these songs. But contrast his version of "God's Goin' to Set Dis Worl' on Fire" with that of Roland Hayes. The subtler rhythmic pattern, the closer phrase linkage, the dramatic recitative movement, and the rhapsodic voice glides and quavers of the great Negro tenor's version are instantly apparent. It is more than a question of musicianship, it is a question of feeling instinctively qualities put there by instinct. In the process of the art development of this material the Negro musician has not only a peculiar advantage but a particular function and duty. Maintaining spiritual kinship with the best traditions of this great folk art, he must make himself the recognized vehicle of both its transmission and its further development.

At present the Spirituals are at a very difficult point in their musical career; for the moment they are caught in the transitional stage between a folk-form and an art-form. Their increasing concert use and popularity, as Carl van Vechten has clearly pointed out in a recent article, has brought about a dangerous tendency toward sophisticated over-elaboration. At the same time that he calls attention to the yeoman service of Mr. Henry T. Burleigh in the introduction of the Spirituals to the attention and acceptance of the concert stage, Mr. Van Vechten thinks many of his settings tincture the folk spirit with added concert furbelows and alien florid adornments. This is true. Even Negro composers have been perhaps too much influenced by formal European idioms and mannerisms in setting these songs. But in calling for the folk atmosphere, and insisting upon the folk quality, we must be careful not to confine this wonderfully potential music to the narrow confines of "simple versions" and musically primitive molds. While it is proper to set up as a standard the purity of the tradition and the maintenance of idiom, it is not proper to insist upon an arbitrary style or form. When for similar reasons, Mr. van Vechten insists in the name of the folk spirit upon his preference for the "evangelical renderings" of Paul Robeson's robust and dramatic style as over against the subdued, ecstatic and spiritually refined versions of Roland Hayes, he overlooks the fact that the folk itself has these same two styles of singing, and in most cases discriminates according to the mood, occasion and song type, between them. So long as the peculiar quality of Negro song is maintained, and the musical idiom kept unadulterated, there is and can be no set limitation. Negro folk song is not midway its artistic career as yet, and while the preservation of the original folk forms is for the moment the most pressing necessity, an inevitable art development awaits them, as in the past it has awaited all other great folk music.

The complaint to be made is not against the art development of the Spirituals, but against the somewhat hybrid treatment characteristic of the older school of musicians. One of the worst features of this period has been the predominance of solo treatment and the loss of the vital sustained background of accompanying voices. In spite of the effectiveness of the solo versions, especially when competently sung by Negro singers, it must be realized more and more that the proper idiom of Negro folk song calls for choral treatment. The young Negro musicians, Nathaniel Dett, Carl Diton, Ballanta Taylor, Edward Boatner, Hall Johnson, Lawrence Brown and others, while they are doing effective solo settings, are turning back gradually to the choral form. Musically speaking, only the superficial resources in this direction have been touched as yet; just as soon as the traditional conventions of four-part harmony and the oratorio style and form are broken through, we may expect a choral development of Negro folk song that may equal or even outstrip the phenomenal choral music of Russia. With its harmonic versatility and interchangeable voice parts, Negro music is only conventionally in the four-part style, and with its skipped measures and interpolations it is at the very least potentially polyphonic. It can therefore undergo without breaking its own boundaries, intricate and original development in directions already the line of advance in modernistic music.

Indeed one wonders why something vitally new has not already been contributed by Negro folk song to modern choral and orchestral musical development. And if it be objected that it is too far a cry from the simple folk spiritual to the larger forms and idioms of modern music, let us recall the folk song origins of the very tradition which is now classic in European music. Up to the present, the resources of Negro music have been tentatively exploited in only one direction at a time,—melodically here, rhythmically there, harmonically in a third direction. A genius that would organize its distinctive elements in a formal way would be the musical giant of his age. Such a development has been hampered by a threefold tradition, each aspect of which stands in the way of the original use of the best in the Negro material. The dominance of the melodic tradition has played havoc with its more original harmonic features, and the oratorio tradition has falsely stereotyped and overlaid its more orchestral choral style, with its intricate threading in and out of the voices. Just as definitely in another direction has the traditional choiring of the orchestra stood against the opening up and development of the Negro and the African idioms in the orchestral forms. Gradually these barriers are being broken through. Edgar Varese's *Integrales*, a "study for percussion instruments," presented last season by the International Composers' Guild, suggests a new orchestral technique patterned after the characteristic idiom of the African "drum orchestra." The modernistic, *From the Land of Dreams*, by Grant Still, a young Negro composer who is his student and protégé, and Louis Grünberg's setting for baritone and chamber orchestra of Weldon Johnson's *The Creation: a Negro Sermon*, are experimental tappings in still other directions into the rich veins of this new musical ore. In a recent article (*The Living Age*, October, 1924), Darius Milhaud sums up these characteristic traits as "the possibilities of a thoroughgoing novelty of instrumental technique." Thus Negro music very probably has a great contribution yet to make to the substance and style of contemporary music, both choral and instrumental. If so, its thematic and melodic contributions from Dvorák to Goldmark's recent *Negro Rhapsody* and the borrowings of rhythmical suggestions by Milhaud and Stravinsky are only preluding experiments that have proclaimed the value of the Negro musical idioms, but have not fully developed them. When a body of folk music is really taken up into musical tradition, it is apt to do more than contribute a few new themes. For when the rhythmic and harmonic basis of music is affected, it is more than a question of superstructure, the very foundations of the art are in process of being influenced.

In view of this very imminent possibility, it is in the interest of musical development itself that we insist upon a broader conception and a more serious appreciation of Negro folk song, and of the Spiritual which is the very kernel of this distinctive folk art. We cannot accept the attitude that would merely preserve this music, but must cultivate that which would also develop it. Equally with treasuring and appreciating it as music of the past, we must nurture and welcome its contribution to the music of to-morrow. Mr. Work has aptly put it in saying: "While it is now assured that we shall always preserve these songs in their original forms, they can never be the last word in the development of our music. . . They are the starting point, not our goal; the source, not the issue, of our musical tradition."

NEGRO DANCERS

Claude McKay

I

Lit with cheap colored lights a basement den,
　　With rows of chairs and tables on each side,
And, all about, young, dark-skinned women and men
　　Drinking and smoking, merry, vacant-eyed.
A Negro band, that scarcely seems awake,
　　Drone out half-heartedly a lazy tune,
While quick and willing boys their orders take
　　And hurry to and from the near saloon.
Then suddenly a happy, lilting note
　　Is struck, the walk and hop and trot begin,
Under the smoke upon foul air afloat;
　　Around the room the laughing puppets spin
　　　　To sound of fiddle, drum and clarinet,
　　　　Dancing, their world of shadows to forget.

II

'Tis best to sit and gaze; my heart then dances
　　To the lithe bodies gliding slowly by,
The amorous and inimitable glances
　　That subtly pass from roguish eye to eye,
The laughter gay like sounding silver ringing,
　　That fills the whole wide room from floor to ceiling,—
A rush of rapture to my tried soul bringing—
　　The deathless spirit of a race revealing.
Not one false step, no note that rings not true!
　　Unconscious even of the higher worth
Of their great art, they serpent-wise glide through
　　The syncopated waltz. Dead to the earth
　　　　And her unkindly ways of toil and strife,
　　　　For them the dance is the true joy of life.

III

And yet they are the outcasts of the earth,
 A race oppressed and scorned by ruling man;
How can they thus consent to joy and mirth
 Who live beneath a world-eternal ban?
No faith is theirs, no shining ray of hope,
 Except the martyr's faith, the hope that death
Some day will free them from their narrow scope
 And once more merge them with the infinite breath.
But, oh! they dance with poetry in their eyes
 Whose dreamy loveliness no sorrow dims,
And parted lips and eager, gleeful cries,
 And perfect rhythm in their nimble limbs.
  The gifts divine are theirs, music and laughter;
  All other things, however great, come after.

ALAIN LOCKE

JAZZ AT HOME

J. A. Rogers

Jazz is a marvel of paradox: too fundamentally human, at least as modern humanity goes, to be typically racial, too international to be characteristically national, too much abroad in the world to have a special home. And yet jazz in spite of it all is one part American and three parts American Negro, and was originally the nobody's child of the levee and the city slum. Transplanted exotic—a rather hardy one, we admit—of the mundane world capitals, sport of the sophisticated, it is really at home in its humble native soil wherever the modern unsophisticated Negro feels happy and sings and dances to his mood. It follows that jazz is more at home in Harlem than in Paris, though from the look and sound of certain quarters of Paris one would hardly think so. It is just the epidemic contagiousness of jazz that makes it, like the measles, sweep the block. But somebody had to have it first: that was the Negro.

What after all is this taking new thing, that, condemned in certain quarters, enthusiastically welcomed in others, has nonchalantly gone on until it ranks with the movie and the dollar as a foremost exponent of modern Americanism? Jazz isn't music merely, it is a spirit that can express itself in almost anything. The true spirit of jazz is a joyous revolt from convention, custom, authority, boredom, even sorrow—from everything that would confine the soul of man and hinder its riding free on the air. The Negroes who invented it called their songs the "Blues," and they weren't capable of satire or deception. Jazz was their explosive attempt to cast off the blues and be happy, carefree happy, even in the midst of sordidness and sorrow. And that is why it has been such a balm for modern ennui, and has become a safety valve for modern machine-ridden and convention-bound society. It is the revolt of the emotions against repression.

The story is told of the clever group of "Jazz-specialists" who, originating dear knows in what scattered places, had found themselves and the frills of the art in New York and had been drawn to the gay Bohemias of Paris. In a little cabaret of Montmartre they had just "entertained" into the wee small hours fascinated society and royalty; and, of course, had been paid royally for it. Then, the entertainment over and the guests away, the "entertainers" entertained themselves with their very best, which is always impromptu, for the sheer joy of it. That is jazz.

In its elementals, jazz has always existed. It is in the Indian war-dance, the Highland fling, the Irish jig, the Cossack dance, the Spanish fandango, the Brazilian *maxixe*, the dance of the whirling dervish, the hula hula of the South Seas, the *danse du vêntre* of the Orient, the *carmagnole* of the French Revolution, the strains of Gypsy music, and the ragtime of the Negro. Jazz proper, however, is something more than all these. It is a release of all the suppressed emotions at once, a blowing off of the lid, as it were. It is hilarity expressing itself through pandemonium; musical fireworks.

The direct predecessor of jazz is ragtime. That both are atavistically African there is little doubt, but to what extent it is difficult to determine. In its barbaric rhythm and exuberance there is something of the bamboula, a wild, abandoned dance of the West African and the Haytian Negro, so stirringly described by the anonymous author of *Untrodden Fields of Anthropology*, or of the *ganza* ceremony so brilliantly depicted in Maran's *Batouala*. But jazz time is faster and more complex than African music. With its cowbells, auto horns, calliopes, rattles, dinner gongs, kitchen utensils, cymbals, screams, crashes, clankings and monotonous rhythm it bears all the marks of a nerve-strung, strident, mechanized civilization. It is a thing of the jungles—modern man-made jungles.

The earliest jazz-makers were the itinerant piano players who would wander up and down the Mississippi from saloon to saloon, from dive to dive. Seated at the piano with a carefree air that a king might envy, their box-back coats flowing over the stool, their Stetsons pulled well over their eyes, and cigars at an angle of forty-five degrees, they would "whip the ivories" to marvellous chords and hidden racy, joyous meanings, evoking the intense delight of their hearers who would smother them at the close with huzzas and whiskey. Often wholly illiterate, these humble troubadours knowing nothing of written music or composition, but with minds like cameras, would listen to the rude improvisations of the dock laborers and the railroad gangs and reproduce them, reflecting perfectly the sentiments and the longings of these humble folk. The improvised bands at Negro dances in the South, or the little boys with their harmonicas and jews'-harps, each one putting his own individuality into the air, played also no inconsiderable part in its evolution. "Poverty," says J. A. Jackson of the *Billboard*, "compelled improvised instruments.

Bones, tambourines, make-shift string instruments, tin can and hollow wood effects, all now utilized as musical novelties, were among early Negroes the product of necessity. When these were not available 'patting juba' prevailed. Present-day 'Charleston' is but a variation of this. Its early expression was the 'patting' for the buck dance."

The origin of the present jazz craze is interesting. More cities claim its birthplace than claimed Homer dead. New Orleans, San Francisco, Memphis, Chicago, all assert the honor is theirs. Jazz, as it is to-day, seems to have come into being this way, however: W. C. Handy, a Negro, having digested the airs of the itinerant musicians referred to, evolved the first classic, *Memphis Blues*. Then came Jasbo Brown, a reckless musician of a Negro cabaret in Chicago, who played this and other blues, blowing his own extravagant moods and risqué interpretations into them, while hilarious with gin. To give further meanings to his veiled allusions he would make the trombone "talk" by putting a derby hat and later a tin can at its mouth. The delighted patrons would shout, "More, Jasbo. More, Jas, more." And so the name originated.

As to the jazz dance itself: at this time Shelton Brooks, a Negro comedian, invented a new "strut," called "Walkin' the Dog." Jasbo's anarchic airs found in this strut a soul mate. Then as a result of their union came "The Texas Tommy," the highest point of brilliant, acrobatic execution and nifty footwork so far evolved in jazz dancing. The latest of these dances is the "Charleston," which has brought something really new to the dance step. The "Charleston" calls for activity of the whole body. One characteristic is a fantastic fling of the legs from the hip downwards. The dance ends in what is known as the "camel-walk"—in reality a gorilla-like shamble—and finishes with a peculiar hop like that of the Indian war dance. Imagine one suffering from a fit of rhythmic ague and you have the effect precisely.

The cleverest "Charleston" dancers perhaps are urchins of five and six who may be seen any time on the streets of Harlem, keeping time with their hands, and surrounded by admiring crowds. But put it on a well-set stage, danced by a bobbed-hair chorus, and you have an effect that reminds you of the abandon of the Furies. And so Broadway studies Harlem. Not all of the visitors of the twenty or more well-attended cabarets of Harlem are idle pleasure seekers or underworld devotees. Many are serious artists, actors and producers seeking something new, some suggestion to be taken, too often in pallid imitation, to Broadway's lights and stars.

This makes it difficult to say whether jazz is more characteristic of the Negro or of contemporary America. As was shown, it is of Negro origin plus the influence of the American environment. It is Negro-American. Jazz proper, however, is in idiom—rhythmic, musical and pantomimic—thoroughly American Negro; it is his spiritual picture on that lighter comedy side, just as the spirituals are the picture on the tragedy side. The two are poles apart, but the former is by no means to be despised and it is just as characteristically the product of the peculiar and unique experience of the Negro in this country. The African Negro hasn't it, and the Caucasian never could have invented it. Once achieved, it is common property, and jazz has absorbed the national spirit, that tremendous spirit of go, the nervousness, lack of conventionality and boisterous good-nature characteristic of the American, white or black, as compared with the more rigid formal natures of the Englishman or German.

But there still remains something elusive about jazz that few, if any of the white artists, have been able to capture. The Negro is admittedly its best expositor. That elusive something, for lack of a better name, I'll call Negro rhythm. The average Negro, particularly of the lower classes, puts rhythm into whatever he does, whether it be shining shoes or carrying a basket on the head to market as the Jamaican women do. Some years ago while wandering in Cincinnati I happened upon a Negro revival meeting at its height. The majority present were women, a goodly few of whom were white. Under the influence of the "spirit" the sisters would come forward and strut—much of jazz enters where it would be least expected. The Negro women had the perfect jazz abandon, while the white ones moved lamely and woodenly. This same lack of spontaneity is evident to a degree in the cultivated and inhibited Negro.

In its playing technique, jazz is similarly original and spontaneous. The performance of the Negro musicians is much imitated, but seldom equalled. Lieutenant Europe, leader of the famous band of the "Fifteenth New York Regiment," said that the bandmaster of the Garde Republicaine, amazed at his jazz effects, could not believe without demonstration that his band had not used special instruments. Jazz has a virtuoso technique all its own: its best performers, singers and players, lift it far above the level of mere "trick" or mechanical effects. Abbie Mitchell, Ethel Waters, and Florence Mills; the Blues singers, Clara, Mamie, and Bessie Smith; Eubie Blake, the pianist; "Buddy" Gilmore, the drummer, and "Bill" Robinson, the pantomimic dancer—to mention merely an illustrative few—are inimitable artists, with an inventive, improvising skill that defies imitation. And those who know their work most intimately trace its uniqueness without exception to the folk-roots of their artistry.

Musically jazz has a great future. It is rapidly being sublimated. In the more famous jazz orchestras like those of Will Marion Cook, Paul Whiteman, Sissle and Blake, Sam Stewart, Fletcher Henderson, Vincent Lopez and the Clef Club units, there are none of the vulgarities and crudities of the lowly origin or the only too prevalent cheap imitations. The pioneer work in the artistic development of jazz was done by Negro artists; it was the lead of the so-called "syncopated orchestras" of Tyers and Will Marion Cook, the former playing for the Castles of dancing fame, and the latter touring as a concertizing orchestra in the great American centers and abroad. Because of the difficulties of financial backing, these expert combinations have had to yield ground to white orchestras of the type of the Paul Whiteman and Vincent Lopez, organizations that are now demonstrating the finer possibilities of jazz music. "Jazz," says Serge Koussevitzy, the new conductor of the Boston Symphony, "is an important contribution to modern musical literature. It has an epochal significance—it is not superficial, it is fundamental. Jazz comes from the soil, where all music has its beginning." And Leopold Stokowski says more extendedly of it:

"Jazz has come to stay because it is an expression of the times, of the breathless, energetic, superactive times in which we are living, it is useless to fight against it. Already its new vigor, its new vitality is beginning to manifest itself. . . America's contribution to the music of the past will have the same revivifying effect as the injection of new, and in the larger sense, vulgar blood into dying aristocracy. Music will then be vulgarized in the best sense of the word, and enter more and more into the daily lives of people. . . The Negro musicians of America are playing a great part in this change. They have an open mind, and unbiassed outlook. They are not hampered by conventions or traditions, and with their new ideas, their constant experiment, they are causing new blood to flow in the veins of music. The jazz players make their instruments do entirely new things, things finished musicians are taught to avoid. They are pathfinders into new realms."

And thus it has come about that serious modernistic music and musicians, most notably and avowedly in the work of the French modernists Auric, Satie and Darius Milhaud, have become the confessed debtors of American Negro jazz. With the same nonchalance and impudence with which it left the levee and the dive to stride like an upstart conqueror, almost overnight, into the grand salon, jazz now begins its conquest of musical Parnassus.

Whatever the ultimate result of the attempt to raise jazz from the mob-level upon which it originated, its true home is still its original cradle, the none too respectable cabaret. And here we have the seamy side to the story. Here we have some of the charm of Bohemia, but much more of the demoralization of vice. Its rash spirit is in Grey's popular song, *Runnin' Wild:*

> *Runnin' wild; lost control*
> *Runnin' wild; mighty bold,*
> *Feelin' gay and reckless too*
> *Carefree all the time; never blue*
> *Always goin' I don't know where*
> *Always showin' that I don't care*
> *Don' love nobody, it ain't worth while*
> *All alone; runnin' wild.*

Jazz reached the height of its vogue at a time when minds were reacting from the horrors and strain of war. Humanity welcomed it because in its fresh joyousness men found a temporary forgetfulness, infinitely less harmful than drugs or alcohol. It is partly for some such reasons that it dominates the amusement life of America to-day. No one can sensibly condone its excesses or minimize its social danger if uncontrolled; all culture is built upon inhibitions and control. But it is doubtful whether the "jazz-hounds" of high and low estate would use their time to better advantage. In all probability their tastes would find some equally morbid, mischievous vent. Jazz, it is needless to say, will remain a recreation for the industrious and a dissipater of energy for the frivolous, a tonic for the strong and a poison for the weak.

For the Negro himself, jazz is both more and less dangerous than for the white—less in that, he is nervously more in tune with it; more, in that at his average level of economic development his amusement life is more open to the forces of social vice. The cabaret of better type provides a certain Bohemianism for the Negro intellectual, the artist and the well-to-do. But the average thing is too much the substitute for the saloon and the wayside inn. The tired longshoreman, the porter, the housemaid and the poor elevator boy in search of recreation, seeking in jazz the tonic for weary nerves and muscles, are only too apt to find the bootlegger, the gambler and the demi-monde who have come there for victims and to escape the eyes of the police.

Yet in spite of its present vices and vulgarizations, its sex informalities, its morally anarchic spirit, jazz has a popular mission to perform. Joy, after all, has a physical basis. Those who laugh and dance and sing are better off even in their vices than those who do not. Moreover, jazz with its mocking disregard for formality is a leveller and makes for democracy. The jazz spirit, being primitive, demands more frankness and sincerity. Just as it already has done in art and music, so eventually in human relations and social manners, it will no doubt have the effect of putting more reality in life by taking some of the needless artificiality out. . . Naturalness finds the artificial in conduct ridiculous. "Cervantes smiled Spain's chivalry away," said Byron. And so this new spirit of joy and spontaneity may itself play the rôle of reformer. Where at present it vulgarizes, with more wholesome growth in the future, it may on the contrary truly democratize. At all events, jazz is rejuvenation, a recharging of the batteries of civilization with primitive new vigor. It has come to stay, and they are wise, who instead of protesting against it, try to lift and divert it into nobler channels.

Jazzonia

Langston Hughes

Oh, silver tree!
Oh, shining rivers of the soul!

In a Harlem cabaret
Six long-headed jazzers play.
A dancing girl whose eyes are bold
Lifts high a dress of silken gold.

Oh, singing tree!
Oh, shining rivers of the soul!

Were Eve's eyes
In the first garden
Just a bit too bold?
Was Cleopatra gorgeous
Is a gown of gold?

Oh, shining tree!
Oh, silver rivers of the soul!

In a whirling cabaret
Six long-headed jazzers play.

Nude Young Dancer

What jungle tree have you slept under,
    Midnight dancer of the jazzy hour?
What great forest has hung its perfume
    Like a sweet veil about your bower?

What jungle tree have you slept under,
    Dark brown girl of the swaying hips?
What star-white moon has been your lover?
    To what mad faun have you offered your lips?

The Negro Digs up his Past

Arthur A. Schomburg

The American Negro must remake his past in order to make his future. Though it is orthodox to think of America as the one country where it is unnecessary to have a past, what is a luxury for the nation as a whole becomes a prime social necessity for the Negro. For him, a group tradition must supply compensation for persecution, and pride of race the antidote for prejudice. History must restore what slavery took away, for it is the social damage of slavery that the present generations must repair and offset. So among the rising democratic millions we find the Negro thinking more collectively, more retrospectively than the rest, and apt out of the very pressure of the present to become the most enthusiastic antiquarian of them all.

Vindicating evidences of individual achievement have as a matter of fact been gathered and treasured for over a century: Abbé Gregoire's liberal-minded book on Negro notables in 1808 was the pioneer effort; it has been followed at intervals by less known and often less discriminating compendiums of exceptional men and women of African stock. But this sort of thing was on the whole pathetically over-corrective, ridiculously over-laudatory; it was apologetics turned into biography. A true historical sense develops slowly and with difficulty under such circumstances. But to-day, even if for the ultimate purpose of group justification, history has become less a matter of argument and more a matter of record. There is the definite desire and determination to have a history, well documented, widely known at least within race circles, and administered as a stimulating and inspiring tradition for the coming generations.

Gradually as the study of the Negro's past has come out of the vagaries of rhetoric and propaganda and become systematic and scientific, three outstanding conclusions have been established:

First, that the Negro has been throughout the centuries of controversy an active collaborator, and often a pioneer, in the struggle for his own freedom and advancement. This is true to a degree which makes it the more surprising that it has not been recognized earlier.

Second, that by virtue of their being regarded as something "exceptional," even by friends and well-wishers, Negroes of attainment and genius have been unfairly disassociated from the group, and group credit lost accordingly.

Third, that the remote racial origins of the Negro, far from being what the race and the world have been given to understand, offer a record of credible group achievement when scientifically viewed, and more important still, that they are of vital general interest because of their bearing upon the beginnings and early development of culture.

With such crucial truths to document and establish, an ounce of fact is worth a pound of controversy. So the Negro historian to-day digs under the spot where his predecessor stood and argued. Not long ago, the Public Library of Harlem housed a special exhibition of books, pamphlets, prints and old engravings, that simply said, to skeptic and believer alike, to scholar and school-child, to proud black and astonished white, "Here is the evidence." Assembled from the rapidly growing collections of the leading Negro book-collectors and research societies, there were in these cases, materials not only for the first true writing of Negro history, but for the rewriting of many important paragraphs of our common American history. Slow though it be, historical truth is no exception to the proverb.

Here among the rarities of early Negro Americana was Jupiter Hammon's Address to the Negroes of the State of New York, edition of 1787, with the first American Negro poet's famous "If we should ever get to Heaven, we shall find nobody to reproach us for being black, or for being slaves." Here was Phyllis Wheatley's Mss. poem of 1767 addressed to the students of Harvard, her spirited encomiums upon George Washington and the Revolutionary Cause, and John Marrant's St. John's Day eulogy to the "Brothers of African Lodge No. 459" delivered at Boston in 1784. Here too were Lemuel Haynes' Vermont commentaries on the American Revolution and his learned sermons to his white congregation in Rutland, Vermont, and the sermons of the year 1808 by the Rev. Absalom Jones of St. Thomas Church, Philadelphia, and Peter Williams of St. Philip's, New York, pioneer Episcopal rectors who spoke out in daring and influential ways on the Abolition of the Slave Trade. Such things and many others are more than mere items of curiosity: they educate any receptive mind.

Reinforcing these were still rarer items of Africana and foreign Negro interest, the volumes of Juan Latino, the best Latinist of Spain in the reign of Philip V, incumbent of the chair of Poetry at the University of Granada, and author of Poems printed Granatae 1573 and a book on the Escurial published 1576; the Latin and Dutch treatises of Jacobus Eliza Capitein, a native of West Coast Africa and graduate of the University of Leyden, Gustavus Vassa's celebrated autobiography that supplied so much of the evidence in 1796 for Granville Sharpe's attack on slavery in the British colonies, Julien Raymond's Paris exposé of the disabilities of the free people of color in the then (1791) French colony of Hayti, and Baron de Vastey's *Cry of the Fatherland*, the famous polemic by the secretary of Christophe that precipitated the Haytian struggle for independence. The cumulative effect of such evidences of scholarship and moral prowess is too weighty to be dismissed as exceptional.

But weightier surely than any evidence of individual talent and scholarship could ever be, is the evidence of important collaboration and significant pioneer initiative in social service and reform, in the efforts toward race emancipation, colonization and race betterment. From neglected and rust-spotted pages comes testimony to the black men and women who stood shoulder to shoulder in courage and zeal, and often on a parity of intelligence and talent, with their notable white benefactors. There was the already cited work of Vassa that aided so materially the efforts of Granville Sharpe, the record of Paul Cuffee, the Negro colonization pioneer, associated so importantly with the establishment of Sierra Leone as a British colony for the occupancy of free people of color in West Africa; the dramatic and history-making exposé of John Baptist Phillips, African graduate of Edinburgh, who compelled through Lord Bathhurst in 1824 the enforcement of the articles of capitulation guaranteeing freedom to the blacks of Trinidad. There is the record of the pioneer colonization project of Rev. Daniel Coker in conducting a voyage of ninety expatriates to West Africa in 1820, of the missionary efforts of Samuel Crowther in Sierra Leone, first Anglican bishop of his diocese, and that of the work of John Russwurm, a leader in the work and foundation of the American Colonization Society.

When we consider the facts, certain chapters of American history will have to be reopened. Just as black men were influential factors in the campaign against the slave trade, so they were among the earliest instigators of the abolition movement. Indeed there was a dangerous calm between the agitation for the suppression of the slave trade and the beginning of the campaign for emancipation. During that interval colored men were very influential in arousing the attention of public

ALAIN LOCKE

men who in turn aroused the conscience of the country. Continuously between 1808 and 1845, men like Prince Saunders, Peter Williams, Absalom Jones, Nathaniel Paul, and Bishops Varick and Richard Allen, the founders of the two wings of African Methodism, spoke out with force and initiative, and men like Denmark Vesey (1822), David Walker (1828) and Nat Turner (1831) advocated and organized schemes for direct action. This culminated in the generally ignored but important conventions of Free People of Color in New York, Philadelphia and other centers, whose platforms and efforts are to the Negro of as great significance as the nationally cherished memories of Faneuil and Independence Halls. Then with Abolition comes the better documented and more recognized collaboration of Samuel R. Ward, William Wells Brown, Henry Highland Garnett, Martin Delaney, Harriet Tubman, Sojourner Truth, and Frederick Douglass with their great colleagues, Tappan, Phillips, Sumner, Mott, Stowe and Garrison.

But even this latter group who came within the limelight of national and international notice, and thus into open comparison with the best minds of their generation, the public too often regards as a group of inspired illiterates, eloquent echoes of their Abolitionist sponsors. For a true estimate of their ability and scholarship, however, one must go with the antiquarian to the files of the *Anglo-African Magazine*, where page by page comparisons may be made. Their writings show Douglass, McCune Smith, Wells Brown, Delaney, Wilmot Blyden and Alexander Crummell to have been as scholarly and versatile as any of the noted publicists with whom they were associated. All of them labored internationally in the cause of their fellows; to Scotland, England, France, Germany and Africa, they carried their brilliant offensive of debate and propaganda, and with this came instance upon instance of signal foreign recognition, from academic, scientific, public and official sources. Delaney's *Principia of Ethnology* won public reception from learned societies, Penington's discourses an honorary doctorate from Heidelberg, Wells Brown's three year mission the entrée of the salons of London and Paris, and Douglass' tours receptions second only to Henry Ward Beecher's.

After this great era of public interest and discussion, it was Alexander Crummell, who, with the reaction already setting in, first organized Negro brains defensively through the founding of the American Negro Academy in 1874 at Washington. A New York boy whose zeal for education had suffered a rude shock when refused admission to the

Episcopal Seminary by Bishop Onderdonk, he had been befriended by John Jay and sent to Cambridge University, England, for his education and ordination. On his return, he was beset with the idea of promoting race scholarship, and the Academy was the final result. It has continued ever since to be one of the bulwarks of our intellectual life, though unfortunately its members have had to spend too much of their energy and effort answering detractors and disproving popular fallacies. Only gradually have the men of this group been able to work toward pure scholarship. Taking a slightly different start, The Negro Society for Historical Research was later organized in New York, and has succeeded in stimulating the collection from all parts of the world of books and documents dealing with the Negro. It has also brought together for the first time co-operatively in a single society African, West Indian and Afro-American scholars. Direct offshoots of this same effort are the extensive private collections of Henry P. Slaughter of Washington, the Rev. Charles D. Martin of Harlem, of Arthur Schomburg of Brooklyn, and of the late John E. Bruce, who was the enthusiastic and far-seeing pioneer of this movement. Finally and more recently, the Association for the Study of Negro Life and History has extended these efforts into a scientific research project of great achievement and promise. Under the direction of Dr. Carter G. Woodson, it has continuously maintained for nine years the publication of the learned quarterly, *The Journal of Negro History*, and with the assistance and recognition of two large educational foundations has maintained research and published valuable monographs in Negro history. Almost keeping pace with the work of scholarship has been the effort to popularize the results, and to place before Negro youth in the schools the true story of race vicissitude, struggle and accomplishment. So that quite largely now the ambition of Negro youth can be nourished on its own milk.

Such work is a far cry from the puerile controversy and petty braggadocio with which the effort for race history first started. But a general as well as a racial lesson has been learned. We seem lately to have come at last to realize what the truly scientific attitude requires, and to see that the race issue has been a plague on both our historical houses, and that history cannot be properly written with either bias or counterbias. The blatant Caucasian racialist with his theories and assumptions of race superiority and dominance has in turn bred his Ethiopian counterpart—the rash and rabid amateur who has glibly tried to prove half of the world's geniuses to have been Negroes and to trace the pedigree of nineteenth century Americans from the Queen of Sheba. But fortunately to-day there is on both sides of a really common cause less of the sand of controversy and more of the dust of digging.

Of course, a racial motive remains—legitimately compatible with scientific method and aim. The work our race students now regard as important, they undertake very naturally to overcome in part certain handicaps of disparagement and omission too well-known to particularize. But they do so not merely that we may not wrongfully be deprived of the spiritual nourishment of our cultural past, but also that the full story of human collaboration and interdependence may be told and realized. Especially is this likely to be the effect of the latest and most fascinating of all of the attempts to open up the closed Negro past, namely the important study of African cultural origins and sources. The bigotry of civilization which is the taproot of intellectual prejudice begins far back and must be corrected at its source. Fundamentally it has come about from that depreciation of Africa which has sprung up from ignorance of her true rôle and position in human history and the early development of culture. The Negro has been a man without a history because he has been considered a man without a worthy culture. But a new notion of the cultural attainment and potentialities of the African stocks has recently come about, partly through the corrective influence of the more scientific study of African institutions and early cultural history, partly through growing appreciation of the skill and beauty and in many cases the historical priority of the African native crafts, and finally through the signal recognition which first in France and Germany, but now very generally, the astonishing art of the African sculptures has received. Into these fascinating new vistas, with limited horizons lifting in all directions, the mind of the Negro has leapt forward faster than the slow clearings of scholarship will yet safely permit. But there is no doubt that here is a field full of the most intriguing and inspiring possibilities. Already the Negro sees himself against a reclaimed background, in a perspective that will give pride and self-respect ample scope, and make history yield for him the same values that the treasured past of any people affords.

American Negro Folk Literature

Arthur Huff Fauset

Most people are acquainted with Negro Folk Literature even if they do not recognize it as such. There are few children who have not read the Uncle Remus stories of Joel Chandler Harris, which were based upon the original folk tales of the African slaves. But the great storehouse from which they were gleaned, that treasury of folk lore which the American Negro inherited from his African forefathers, is little known. It rivals in amount as well as in quality that of any people on the face of the globe, and is not confined to stories of the Uncle Remus type, but includes a rich variety of story forms, legends, saga cycles, songs, proverbs and phantastic, almost mythical, material.

It simply happens that the one type of Negro story has struck the popular fancy, and becoming better known, blurred out the remaining types. For this result, we are indebted to Joel Chandler Harris, who saw the popular possibilities of the "B'rer Rabbit" tales, and with his own flair for literature, adapted them with such remarkable skill and individuality that to-day they rank with the best known and most highly appreciated works of American literature.

Familiar as he was with his material, and with an instinct for its value—even in his day these tales were fast disappearing among "modern" colored folk—his approach was nevertheless that of the journalist and literary man rather than the folk-lorist. "Written," as has been said, "with no thought of the ethnological bearing which critics were so quick to discern in them, they established themselves at a bound as among the most winsome of folk tales." There is some possibility of their having passed out unnoticed and thus being lost to posterity if he had not done the work which drew attention to them. Yet in spite of the happy providence that produced a Harris, and although his intentions were of the best, we are forced to recognize the harm as well as the good that these stories have done. This query may come as a shock to some, but on further analysis we shall see there is reason for wondering.

In the first place, the Uncle Remus Stories, as the Harris tales have become known, are not folk tales, but adaptations. This fact alone is enough to warrant some hesitancy about placing them in the category of folk lore. To be sure, folk lore was their background, but this can be said of many literary works (Dracula, for example) which we would not think of classifying with folk literature.

The misrepresentation goes further than simply the name, however. The very dialect of the Uncle Remus Stories is questionable, statements to the contrary notwithstanding. Scholars have tried to show that Harris very faithfully recorded the dialect of his time, in its truly intimate expressions, mannerisms and colloquialisms, but it is doubtful whether Negroes generally ever used the language employed in the works of Joel Chandler Harris. Rather, in these works we observe the consciously devised, artistically wrought, patiently carved out expressions of a story writer who knew his art and employed it well. They have too much the flavor of the popular trend of contemporary writing of the Thomas Nelson Page tradition, and though they endeavored to give a faithful portrait of the Negro and did so more successfully than any other of these Southern writers, it cannot be denied that such portraits as they gave were highly romanticized, and gave an interpretation of the Negro seen neither objectively nor realistically.

These stories of Chandler Harris made and still make their most powerful impression and appeal through the character of Uncle Remus himself. But it is in just this projection into the picture of this amiable and winsome ante-bellum personality that contorts the Negro folk tale from its true plane. The American Negro folk tale, borrowed as it most certainly was from Africa, is an animal cycle, recounting the exploits of various members of the animal world of which "B'rer Rabbit" was arch-villain or hero, as you please. As in the case of all true folk tales, the story teller himself was inconsequential; he did not figure at all—a talking machine might serve the purpose just as well. As a result the stories take on an impersonal character, more or less lacking in artistic embellishments. The Uncle Remus stories break this tradition, however; instead the story teller plays an important, a too important, role. By that very fact, this type of story ceases to be a folk tale; and becomes in reality a product of the imagination of the author. Of course there is such a thing as an intermediate type; there is a place for Hans Andersen, and Brothers Grimm. But Harris, familiar with his material and genuinely loving it, could not be spiritually saturated with it under the circumstances. And this was more a matter of class than race; for human kinships are spiritual after all, but these stories cannot present Negro folk life and feeling seen and felt on its own level. Enough has been said, perhaps, to show, without in any way detracting from the true service and real charm of the Harris stories, that there are enough incongruous elements insinuated into the situation to make it impossible to accept them as a final rendering of American Negro folk lore.

We would not be so much concerned about a "distinction without a difference" if there were actually no difference. Unfortunately the treatment of these stories by Harris resulted in certain developments which are too noteworthy to pass by. The most striking consequence of the fact that Uncle Remus is written all over and interwoven into the stories which bear his name, is that the Harris variety of the Negro folk tale assumes to interpret Negro character instead of simply telling his stories. The result is a composite picture of the ante-bellum Negro that fits exactly into the conception of the type of Negro which so many white people would like to think once existed, or even now exists; whereas in the material in question there is reflected a quite different folk temperament—apart from the question of what is or what isn't *the* Negro temperament. When we find one critic naïvely suggesting that Uncle Remus "makes clear to every thoughtful reader that the system of slavery pernicious as it may appear to us now, took the dusky savage from his haunts in the African jungle and made of him a Christian and a gentleman," we can clearly see that any writing that can be taken as an *apologia* for a social system, or the idealization of the plantation régime, cannot be taken unsuspiciously as the chronicle of a primitive folk lore.

Nevertheless, Harris wrought well from the standpoint of art, and by so doing let the world know that Negroes possessed a rich folk lore. The unquestionable result of this was a keener interest in the Negro and his lore. Just the same, the intrusion of a dominant note of humor, not by any means as general in the material as one would suppose, fell in line with an arbitrary and unfortunately general procedure of regarding anything which bore the Negro trademark as inherently comic and only worth being laughed at. It is not necessary to draw upon sentiment in order to realize the masterful quality of some of the Negro tales: it is simply necessary to read them. Moralism, sober and almost grim, irony, shrewd and frequently subtle, are their fundamental tone and mood—as in the case of their African originals—and the quaint and sentimental humor so popularly prized is oftener than not an overtone merely. But the unfortunate thing about American thought is the habit of classifying first and investigating after. As a result this misrepresentation of the temper and spirit of Negro folk lore has become traditional, and for all we know, permanent.

There is strong need of a scientific collecting of Negro folk lore before the original sources of this material altogether lapse. Sentimental admiration and amateurish praise can never adequately preserve or interpret this precious material. It is precious in two respects— not only for its intrinsic, but for its comparative value. Some of the precious secrets of folk history are in danger of fading out in its gradual disappearance. American folk-lorists are now recognizing this, and systematic scientific investigation has begun under the influence and auspices of the Society for American Folk Lore and such competent ethnologists as Franz Boas, Elsie Clews Parsons, and others.

Simply because we are considering Negro folk lore, we do not say that it is superior to other folk material, nor even that it is as great as any other folk literature; but we do insist that all folk material, in order to be appraised justly, must be read and considered in the light of those values which go to make up great folk literature. Briefly stated, these values are:

1. Lack of the self-conscious element found in ordinary literature.
2. Nearness to nature.
3. Universal appeal.

Search the body of Negro folk literature and you will find these characteristics dominant. As one writer has well expressed it: "All nature is alive, anthropomorphized as it were, replete with intelligences; the whispering, tinkling, hissing, booming, muttering, zooming around him are full of mysterious hints and suggestions." Out of this primitive intimacy of the mind with nature come those naïve personifications of the rabbits, foxes and wolves, terrapins and turtles, buzzards and eagles which make the animal lore of the world. Many tales ascribed to lands far away find parallels in Negro stories bearing indubitable traces of African origin; opening out into the great question of common or separate origin. Fundamentally, as Lang points out, they prove the common ancestry of man, both with regard to his mental and cultural inheritance. Whichever way the question is solved, the physical contacts of common origins or the psychological similarities of common capacity and endowment, it is essentially the same fundamental point in the end—human kinship and universality. Yet there is much that is distinctively African in animal lore, and of a quality not usually conceded. The African proverb, in its terseness and pith, the shrewd moralisms of the fables, the peculiar whimsicality and turn to the imagination in many of the tales, are notably outstanding. Clive Bell to the contrary, it is by their intelligence, their profound and abstract underlying conceptions, that they possess a peculiar touch and originality that is distinctively African. Æsop, it is claimed was African, but any folk-lorist knows that the African folk fable of indigenous growth outmasters Æsop over and over. Africa in a sense is the home of the fable; the African tales are its classics.

It is interesting, in this connection, to consider the case of the rabbit, which figures so largely in Negro Folk Lore. It was the belief of Harris, and still is the belief of many, that the Negro chose the weak rabbit and glorified him in his stories because this animal was a prototype of himself during slavery times; according to this theory, the stronger, more rapacious animals such as wolves, foxes, etc., represented the white masters. But this cannot be so, for as Ambrose E. Gonzales aptly points out in his volume entitled, *Æsop Along the Black Border,* these stories, or their types at least, came with the Negro from Africa where they had existed for centuries. In the African tales, the hare is the notable figure. Surely, then, the rabbit is none other than the African hare. As a matter of fact, the "B'rer Rabbit" character simply confirms the opinion that Negro Folk Lore is a genuine part of world folk literature, for we find the hare one of the animals most frequently encountered in folk lore the world over. In Scottish and Irish Tales he is associated with witches. In the ancient Druidical mysteries the hare was employed in auguries to indicate the outcome of war. Chinese and East Indian stories feature the hare and he is common even in the tales of the American Indian. The Easter "bunny" shows the hare cropping up in a Teutonic atmosphere. So that when all these instances are added to the African and American Negro we may be reasonably safe in assuming that "B'rer Rabbit" comes into American lore from the level of true primitive folk material.

The antiquity and authentic folk lore ancestry of the Negro tale make it the proper subject for the scientific folk-lorist rather than the literary amateur. It is the ethnologist, the philologist and the student of primitive psychology that are most needed for its present investigation. Of course no one will deny or begrudge the delightful literary by-products of this material. Negro writers themselves will shortly, no doubt, be developing them as arduously as Chandler Harris, and we hope as successfully, or even more so. But a literary treatment based on a scientific recording will have much fresh material to its hand, and cannot transgress so far from the true ways of the folk spirit and the true lines of our folk art.

T'appin[1] (Terrapin)

Told by Cugo Lewis, Plateau, Alabama. Brought to America
from West Coast Africa, 1859.

It was famine time an' T'appin had six chillun. Eagle hide behin' cloud
an' he went crossed de ocean an' go gittin' de palm oil; got de seed to
feed his chillun wid it. T'appin see it, say "hol' on, it har' time. Where
you git all dat to feed your t'ree chillun? I got six chillun, can't you show
me wha' you git all dat food?" Eagle say, "No, I had to fly 'cross de ocean
to git dat." T'appin say, "Well, gimme some o' you wings an' I'll go wid
you." Eagle say, "A' right. When shall we go?" T'appin say, "'Morrow
morning' by de firs' cock crow." So 'morrow came but T'appin didn' wait
till mornin'. T'ree 'clock in de mornin' T'appin come in fron' Eagle's
house say, "Cuckoo—cuckoo—coo." Eagle say, "Oh, you go home. Lay
down. 'Tain't day yit." But he kep' on, "Cuckoo, cuckoo, coo," an' bless de
Lor' Eagle got out, say, "Wha' you do now?" T'appin say, "You put t'ree
wings on this side an' t'ree on udda side." Eagle pull out six feathers an'
put t'ree on one side an' t'ree on de udda. Say, "Fly, le's see." So T'appin
commence to fly. One o' de wings fall out. But T'appin said, "Da's all
right, I got de udda wings. Le's go." So dey flew an' flew; but when dey
got over de ocean all de eagle wings fell out. T'appin about to fall in de
water. Eagle went out an' ketch him. Put him under his wings. T'appin
say, "I don' like dis." Eagle say, "Why so?" T'appin say, "Gee it stink
here." Eagle let him drop in ocean. So he went down, down, down to de
underworl'. De king o' de underworl' meet him. He say, "Why you come
here? Wha' you doin' here?" T'appin say, "King, we in te'bul condition
on de earth. We can't git nothin' to eat. I got six chillun an' I can't git
nothin' to eat for dem. Eagle he on'y got t'ree an' he go 'cross de ocean an'
git all de food he need. Please gimme sumpin' so I kin feed my chillun."
King say, "A' right, a' right, so he go an' give T'appin a dipper. He say
to T'appin, "Take dis dipper. When you want food for your chillun say:

Bakon coleh
Bakon cawbey
Bakon cawhubo lebe lebe.

---

1. "T'appin" and "Brer Buzzard" were collected by Mr. Fauset in the South, August, 1925.

ALAIN LOCKE

So T'appin carry it home an' go to de chillun. He say to dem, "Come here." When dey all come he say:

> Bakon coleh
> Bakon cawbey
> Bakon cawhubo lebe lebe.

Gravy, meat, biscuit, ever'ting in de dipper. Chillun got plenty now. So one time he say to de chillun, "Come here. Dis will make my fortune. I'll sell dis to de King." So he showed de dipper to de King. He say:

> Bakon coleh
> Bakon cawbey
> Bakon cawhubo lebe lebe.

Dey got somet'ing. He feed ev'ryone. So de King went off, he call ev'ryboda. Pretty soon ev'ryboda eatin'. So dey ate an' ate, ev'ryt'ing, meats, fruits, and all like dat. So he took his dipper an' went back home. He say, "Come, chillun." He try to feed his chillun; nothin' came. (You got a pencil dere, ain't you?) When it's out it's out. So T'appin say, "Aw right, I'm going back to de King an' git him to fixa dis up." So he went down to de underworl' an' say to de King, "King, wha' de matter? I can't feeda my chillun no mora." So de King say to him, "You take dis cow hide an' when you want somepin' you say:

> Sheet n oun
> n-jacko
> nou o quaako.

So T'appin went off an' he came to cross roads. Den he said de magic:

> Sheet n oun
> n-jacko
> nou o quaako.

De cowhide commence to beat um. It beat, beat. Cowhide said, "Drop, drop." So T'appin drop an' de cowhide stop beatin'. So he went home. He called his chillun in. He gim um de cowhide an' tell dem what to say, den he went out. De chillun say:

Sheet n oun
n-jacko
nou o quaako.

De cowhide beat de chillun. It say, "Drop, drop." Two chillun dead an' de others sick. So T'appin say, "I will go to de King." He calls de King, he call all de people. All de people came. So before he have de cowhide beat, he has a mortar made an' gets in dere an' gets all covered up. Den de King say:

Sheet n oun
n-jacko
nou o quaako.

So de cowhide beat, beat. It beat everyboda, beat de King too. Dat cowhide beat, beat, beat right t'roo de mortar wha' was T'appin an' beat marks on his back, an' da's why you never fin' T'appin in a clean place, on'y under leaves or a log.

B'rer Rabbit Fools Buzzard

Once upon a time B'rer Rabbit an' B'rer Buzzard. Buzzard say gonna shut up Rabbit five days until he starve to death. So he put him in a hole an' cover him up. Every day he come to him an' sing:

> *Diddledum-diddledum-day-day*
> *Young man, I'm here.*

B'rer Rabbit he sing it after him. Did that five days. Every day Rabbit gittin' lower an' lower. B'rer Buzzard come 'round an' sing louder an' louder:

> *Diddledum-diddledum-day-day*
> *Young man, I'm here.*

De las' day Buzzard sing louder still; but B'rer Rabbit he very faint. He kin jes' barely say:

> *Didd—le—dum—didd—le—dum*
> *d—a—a——d—a—a*

So Buzzard decide it is time to take Rabbit home to his little ones. As he was carryin' Rabbit to his little ones he said:

> *Diddledum-diddledum-day-day*
> *Young man, here he.*

All come 'round de table. Dey meant to eat him. Had knives an' everything, an' were jes' gonna cut him up when de father said:

> *Diddledum-diddledum-day-day*
> *Young man, let's eat.*

But jes' den ol' B'rer Rabbit jumped up from de table an' said:

Diddledum-diddledum-day-day
Young man, I'm gone.

Stepped on a pin
Hit bent
That's the way he went.

HERITAGE

Countee Cullen

What is Africa to me:
Copper sun, a scarlet sea,
Jungle star and jungle track,
Strong bronzed men and regal black
Women from whose loins I sprang
When the birds of Eden sang?
One three centuries removed
From the scenes his fathers loved
Spicy grove and banyan tree,
What is Africa to me?

Africa? A book one thumbs
Listlessly, till slumber comes.
Unremembered are her bats
Circling through the night, her cats
Crouching in the river reeds
Stalking gentle flesh that feeds
By the river brink; no more
Does the bugle-throated roar
Cry that monarch claws have leapt
From the scabbards where they slept.
Silver snakes that once a year
Doff the lovely coats you wear
Seek no covert in your fear
Lest a mortal eye should see:
What's your nakedness to me?

All day long and all night through
One thing only I must do
Quench my pride and cool my blood,
Lest I perish in their flood,
Lest a hidden ember set
Timber that I thought was wet
Burning like the dryest flax,

Melting like the merest wax,
Lest the grave restore its dead.
Stubborn heart and rebel head.
Have you not yet realized
You and I are civilized?

So I lie and all day long
Want no sound except the song
Sung by wild barbaric birds
Goading massive jungle herds,
Juggernauts of flesh that pass
Trampling tall defiant grass
Where young forest lovers lie
Plighting troth beneath the sky.

So I lie, who always hear
Though I cram against my ear
Both my thumbs, and keep them there,
Great drums beating through the air.
So I lie, whose fount of pride,
Dear distress, and joy allied,
Is my somber flesh and skin
With the dark blood dammed within.
Thus I lie, and find no peace
Night or day, no slight release
From the unremittent beat
Made by cruel padded feet,
Walking through my body's street.
Up and down they go, and back
Treading out a jungle track.
So I lie, who never quite
Safely sleep from rain at night
While its primal measures drip
Through my body, crying, "Strip!
Doff this new exuberance,
Come and dance the Lover's Dance."
In an old remembered way
Rain works on me night and day.

Though three centuries removed
From the scenes my fathers loved.

My conversion came high-priced.
I belong to Jesus Christ,
Preacher of humility:
Heathen gods are naught to me—
Quaint, outlandish heathen gods
Black men fashion out of rods,
Clay and brittle bits of stone,
In a likeness like their own.

"Father, Son and Holy Ghost"
Do I make an idle boast,
Jesus of the twice turned cheek,
Lamb of God, although I speak
With my mouth thus, in my heart
Do I not play a double part?
Ever at thy glowing altar
Must my heart grow sick and falter
Wishing He I served were black.
Thinking then it would not lack
Precedent of pain to guide it
Let who would or might deride it;
Surely then this flesh would know
Yours had borne a kindred woe.
Lord, I fashion dark gods, too,
Daring even to give to You
Dark, despairing features where
Crowned with dark rebellious hair,
Patience wavers just so much as
Mortal grief compels, while touches
Faint and slow, of anger, rise
To smitten cheek and weary eyes.

Lord, forgive me if my need
Sometimes shapes a human creed.

THE LEGACY OF THE ANCESTRAL ARTS

Alain Locke

Music and poetry, and to an extent the dance, have been the predominant arts of the American Negro. This is an emphasis quite different from that of the African cultures, where the plastic and craft arts predominate; Africa being one of the great fountain sources of the arts of decoration and design. Except then in his remarkable carry-over of the rhythmic gift, there is little evidence of any direct connection of the American Negro with his ancestral arts. But even with the rude transplanting of slavery, that uprooted the technical elements of his former culture, the American Negro brought over as an emotional inheritance a deep-seated æsthetic endowment. And with a versatility of a very high order, this offshoot of the African spirit blended itself in with entirely different culture elements and blossomed in strange new forms.

There was in this more than a change of art-forms and an exchange of cultural patterns; there was a curious reversal of emotional temper and attitude. The characteristic African art expressions are rigid, controlled, disciplined, abstract, heavily conventionalized; those of the Aframerican,—free, exuberant, emotional, sentimental and human. Only by the misinterpretation of the African spirit, can one claim any emotional kinship between them—for the spirit of African expression, by and large, is disciplined, sophisticated, laconic and fatalistic. The emotional temper of the American Negro is exactly opposite. What we have thought primitive in the American Negro—his naïveté, his sentimentalism, his exuberance and his improvizing spontaneity are then neither characteristically African nor to be explained as an ancestral heritage. They are the result of his peculiar experience in America and the emotional up-heaval of its trials and ordeals. True, these are now very characteristic traits, and they have their artistic, and perhaps even their moral compensations; but they represent essentially the working of environmental forces rather than the outcropping of a race psychology; they are really the acquired and not the original artistic temperament.

A further proof of this is the fact that the American Negro, even when he confronts the various forms of African art expression with a sense of its ethnic claims upon him, meets them in as alienated and misunderstanding an attitude as the average European Westerner. Christianity and all the other European conventions operate to make this inevitable. So there would be little hope of an influence of African art upon the western African descendants if there were not at present a growing influence of African art upon European art in general. But led by these tendencies, there is the possibility that the sensitive artistic mind of the American Negro, stimulated by a cultural pride and interest, will receive from African art a profound and galvanizing influence. The legacy is there at least, with prospects of a rich yield. In the first place, there is in the mere knowledge of the skill and unique mastery of the arts of the ancestors the valuable and stimulating realization that the Negro is not a cultural foundling without his own inheritance. Our timid and apologetic imitativeness and overburdening sense of cultural indebtedness have, let us hope, their natural end in such knowledge and realization.

Then possibly from a closer knowledge and proper appreciation of the African arts must come increased effort to develop our artistic talents in the discontinued and lagging channels of sculpture, painting and the decorative arts. If the forefathers could so adroitly master these mediums, why not we? And there may also come to some creative minds among us, hints of a new technique to be taken as the basis of a characteristic expression in the plastic and pictorial arts; incentives to new artistic idioms as well as to a renewed mastery of these older arts. African sculpture has been for contemporary European painting and sculpture just such a mine of fresh *motifs*, just such a lesson in simplicity and originality of expression, and surely, once known and appreciated, this art can scarcely have less influence upon the blood descendants, bound to it by a sense of direct cultural kinship, than upon those who inherit by tradition only, and through the channels of an exotic curiosity and interest.

But what the Negro artist of to-day has most to gain from the arts of the forefathers is perhaps not cultural inspiration or technical innovations, but the lesson of a classic background, the lesson of discipline, of style, of technical control pushed to the limits of technical mastery. A more highly stylized art does not exist than the African. If after absorbing the new content of American life and experience, and after assimilating new patterns of art, the original artistic endowment can be sufficiently augmented to express itself with equal power in more complex patterns and substance, then the Negro may well become what some have predicted, the artist of American life.

As it is, African art has influenced modern art most considerably. It has been the most influential exotic art of our era, Chinese and Japanese art not excepted. The African art object, a half generation ago the most neglected of ethnological curios, is now universally recognized as a "notable instance of plastic representation," a genuine work of art, masterful over its material in a powerful simplicity of conception, design and effect. This artistic discovery of African art came at a time when there was a marked decadence and sterility in certain forms of European plastic art expression, due to generations of the inbreeding of style and idiom. Out of the exhaustion of imitating Greek classicism and the desperate exploitation in graphic art of all the technical possibilities of color by the Impressionists and Post Impressionists, the problem of form and decorative design became emphasized in one of those reactions which in art occur so repeatedly. And suddenly with this new problem and interest, the African representation of form, previously regarded as ridiculously crude and inadequate, appeared cunningly sophisticated and masterful. Once the strong stylistic conventions that had stood between it and a true æsthetic appreciation were thus broken through, Negro art instantly came into marked recognition. Roger Fry in an essay on Negro Sculpture has the following to say: "I have to admit that some of these things are great sculpture—greater, I think, than anything we produced in the Middle Ages. Certainly they have the special qualities of sculpture in a higher degree. They have indeed complete plastic freedom, that is to say, these African artists really can see form in three dimensions. Now this is rare in sculpture. . . So—far from the clinging to two dimensions, as we tend to do, the African artist actually underlines, as it were, the three-dimensionalness of his forms. It is in some such way that he manages to give to his forms their disconcerting vitality, the suggestion that they make of being not mere echoes of actual figures, but of possessing an inner life of their own. . . Besides the logical comprehension of plastic from which the Negro shows he has also an exquisite taste in the handling of his material." The most authoritative contemporary Continental criticism quite thoroughly agrees with this verdict and estimate.

Indeed there are many attested influences of African art in French and German modernist art. They are to be found in work of Matisse,

Picasso, Derain, Modigliani and Utrillo among the French painters, upon Max Pechstein, Elaine Stern, Franz Marc and others of the German Expressionists, and upon Modigliani, Archipenko, Epstein, Lipschitz, Lembruch, and Zadkine and Faggi among sculptors. In Paris, centering around Paul Guillaume, one of its pioneer exponents, there has grown up an art coterie profoundly influenced by an æsthetic developed largely from the idioms of African art. And what has been true of the African sculptures has been in a lesser degree true of the influence of other African art forms—decorative design, musical rhythms, dance forms, verbal imagery and symbolism. Attracted by the appeal of African plastic art to the study of other modes of African expression, poets like Guillaume Appolinaire and Blaisé Cendrars have attempted artistic re-expression of African idioms in poetic symbols and verse forms. So that what is a recognized school of modern French poetry professes the inspiration of African sources,—Appolinaire, Reverdy, Salmon, Fargue and others. The bible of this coterie has been Cendrars' *Anthologie Nègre,* now in its sixth edition.

The starting point of an æsthetic interest in African musical idiom seems to have been H. A. Junod's work,—*Les Chants et les Contes des Barongas* (1897). From the double source of African folk song and the study of American Negro musical rhythms, many of the leading French modernists have derived inspiration. Berard, Satie, Poulenc, Auric, and even Honneger, are all in diverse ways and degrees affected, but the most explicit influence has been upon the work of Darius Milhaud, who is an avowed propagandist of the possibilities of Negro musical idiom. The importance of these absorptions of African and Negro material by all of the major forms of contemporary art, some of them independently of any transfer that might be dismissed as a mere contagion of fad or vogue, is striking, and ought to be considered as a quite unanimous verdict of the modern creative mind upon the values, actual and potential, of this yet unexhausted reservoir of art material.

There is a vital connection between this new artistic respect for African idiom and the natural ambition of Negro artists for a racial idiom in their art expression. To a certain extent contemporary art has pronounced in advance upon this objective of the younger Negro artists, musicians and writers. Only the most reactionary conventions of art, then, stand between the Negro artist and the frank experimental development of these fresh idioms. This movement would, we think, be well under way in more avenues of advance at present but for the timid conventionalism which racial disparagement has forced upon the Negro mind in America. Let us take as a comparative instance, the painting of the Negro subject and notice the retarding effect of social prejudice. The Negro is a far more familiar figure in American life than in European, but American art, barring caricature and *genre*, reflects him scarcely at all. An occasional type sketch of Henri, or local color sketch of Winslow Homer represents all of a generation of painters. Whereas in Europe, with the Negro subject rarely accessible, we have as far back as the French romanticists a strong interest in the theme, an interest that in contemporary French, Belgian, German and even English painting has brought forth work of singular novelty and beauty. This work is almost all above the plane of *genre*, and in many cases represents sustained and lifelong study of the painting of the particularly difficult values of the Negro subject. To mention but a few, there is the work of Julius Hüther, Max Slevogt, Max Pechstein, Elaine Stern, yon Reuckterschell among German painters; of Dinet, Lucie Cousturier, Bonnard, Georges Rouault, among the French; Klees van Dongen, the Dutch painter; most notably among the Belgians, Auguste Mambour; and among English painters, Neville Lewis, F. C. Gadell, John A. Wells, and Frank Potter. All these artists have looked upon the African scene and the African countenance, and discovered there a beauty that calls for a distinctive idiom both of color and modelling. The Negro physiognomy must be freshly and objectively conceived on its own patterns if it is ever to be seriously and importantly interpreted. Art must discover and reveal the beauty which prejudice and caricature have overlaid. And all vital art discovers beauty and opens our eyes to that which previously we could not see. While American art, including the work of our own Negro artists, has produced nothing above the level of the *genre* study or more penetrating than a Nordicized transcription, European art has gone on experimenting until the technique of the Negro subject has reached the dignity and skill of virtuoso treatment and a distinctive style. No great art will impose alien canons upon its subject matter. The work of Mambour especially suggests this forceful new stylization; he has brought to the Negro subject a modeling of masses that is truly sculptural and particularly suited to the broad massive features and subtle value shadings of the Negro countenance. After seeing his masterful handling of mass and light and shade in bold solid planes, one has quite the conviction that mere line and contour treatment can never be the classical technique for the portrayal of Negro types.

The work of these European artists should even now be the inspiration and guide-posts of a younger school of American Negro artists. They have too long been the victims of the academy tradition and shared the conventional blindness of the Caucasian eye with respect to the racial material at their immediate disposal. Thus there have been notably successful Negro artists, but no development of a school of Negro art. Our Negro American painter of outstanding success is Henry O. Tanner. His career is a case in point. Though a professed painter of types, he has devoted his art talent mainly to the portrayal of Jewish Biblical types and subjects, and has never maturely touched the portrayal of the Negro subject. Warrantable enough—for to the individual talent in art one must never dictate—who can be certain what field the next Negro artist of note will choose to command, or whether he will not be a landscapist or a master of still life or of purely decorative painting? But from the point of view of our artistic talent in bulk—it is a different matter. We ought and must have a school of Negro art, a local and a racially representative tradition. And that we have not, explains why the generation of Negro artists succeeding Mr. Tanner had only the inspiration of his great success to fire their ambitions, but not the guidance of a distinctive tradition to focus and direct their talents. Consequently they fumbled and fell short of his international stride and reach. The work of Henri Scott, Edwin A. Harleson, Laura Wheeler, in painting, and of Meta Warrick Fuller and May Howard Jackson in sculpture, competent as it has been, has nevertheless felt this handicap and has wavered between abstract expression which was imitative and not highly original, and racial expression which was only experimental. Lacking group leadership and concentration, they were wandering amateurs in the very field that might have given them concerted mastery.

A younger group of Negro artists is beginning to move in the direction of a racial school of art. The strengthened tendency toward representative group expression is shared even by the later work of the artists previously mentioned, as in Meta Warrick Fuller's "Ethiopia Awakening," to mention an outstanding example. But the work of young artists like Archibald Motley, Otto Farrill, Cecil Gaylord, John Urquhart, Samuel Blount, and especially that of Charles Keene and Aaron Douglas shows the promising beginning of an art movement instead of just the cropping out of isolated talent. The work of Winold Reiss, fellow-countryman of Slevogt and von Reuckterschell, which has supplied the main illustrative material for this volume has been deliberately conceived and executed as a path-breaking guide and encouragement to this new foray of the younger Negro artists. In idiom, technical treatment and objective social angle, it is a bold iconoclastic break with the current traditions that have grown up about the Negro subject in American art. It is not meant to dictate a style to the young Negro artist, but to point the lesson that contemporary European art has already learned—that any vital artistic expression of the Negro theme and subject in art must break through the stereotypes to a new style, a distinctive fresh technique, and some sort of characteristic idiom.

While we are speaking of the resources of racial art, it is well to take into account that the richest vein of it is not that of portraitistic idiom after all, but its almost limitless wealth of decorative and purely symbolic material. It is for the development of this latter aspect of a racial art that the study and example of African art material is so important. The African spirit, as we said at the outset, is at its best in abstract decorative forms. Design, and to a lesser degree, color, are its original *fortes*. It is this aspect of the folk tradition, this slumbering gift of the folk temperament that most needs reachievement and re-expression. And if African art is capable of producing the ferment in modern art that it has, surely this is not too much to expect of its influence upon the culturally awakened Negro artist of the present generation. So that if even the present vogue of African art should pass, and the bronzes of Benin and the fine sculptures of Gabon and Baoulé, and the superb designs of the Bushongo should again become mere items of exotic curiosity, for the Negro artist they ought still to have the import and influence of classics in whatever art expression is consciously and representatively racial.

ALAIN LOCKE

PART II
THE NEW NEGRO IN A NEW WORLD

The Negro Pioneers

Paul U. Kellogg

In *Vandemark's Folly* and other of his novels, Herbert Quick interpreted the settlement of the Mississippi basin. He gave us its valor and epic qualities. But in that series of remarkable biographical sketches which were cut short by his death, he lamented the cultural wastage of American pioneering. He laid a wreath on the unknown graves of the artists, poets, singers, the talented of youth, who were submerged in the westward trek of peoples on the new continent as, in the course of two hundred and fifty years, they hewed their way through the forests and at last came out on the open prairie. In the northward movement of the Negroes in the last ten years, we have another folk migration which in human significance can be compared only with this pushing back of the Western frontier in the first half of the last century or with the waves of immigration which have swept in from overseas in the last half. Indeed, though numerically far smaller than either of these, this folk movement is unique. For this time we have a people singing as they come—breaking through to cultural expression and economic freedom together.

In our generation the children and grandchildren of the settlers of the Middle West have uprooted themselves as their sires did, but to-day their faces are turned cityward. In this new urban shift, the Negro is sharing, but so swiftly and with such a peculiar quickening as he pours for the first time into this new terrain of American economic and community life, that for him it is more than a migration, it is a rebirth. The full significance of this belated sharing in the American tradition of pioneering by black folk from the South should not escape us; nor the rare fortune that they bring with them cultural talents long buried and only half revealed in the cotton lands from which they come.

In a way, two great modes of impulse have been at work in the settlement of the United States, other than the material one of bettering one's lot.

In no small part, ours has been the history of the under-dog—of common people rising against kings and overlords, of Pilgrims and Puritans and Catholics working loose from religious intolerance, of rebels seeking a new freedom, of adventures breaking away from the fixity of things. This tradition we share with England and Western Europe; the impulse became a dominant force in New England and was at flood throughout the tidewater colonies when in the Revolution they threw off the Georges. We may trace its re-emergence in a new form even in the part which the South took in the Civil War. This may be put in terms of its idealists, as resistance to imposed authority by men who sought the governance of their own lives, however much they might deny it to their slaves.

We have another tradition—or, at least, another mode of the same impulse. Not alone rebellion against what has been, but opportunity for what may be, shaped its course. Set off by three thousand miles of sea, settled on a continent which had been kept in reserve ten thousand years, the spirit of our people has been molded by the frontiers we cleared. It drew and grew from the open spaces, from wildernesses giving way to settlements, from the building processes of countryside and commonwealth and nation. Its like is not known in the older countries of the world, still in the process of shaking loose from old tyrannies. We may abuse this heritage, but it is ours, a broader and more dynamic, more creative conception of liberty. Spiritually we are rebels. But we are also pioneers.

The Civil War may be interpreted in its final outcome, as the clash between these two great streams of impulse in American life and the triumph of this newer native embodiment of the thing that has stirred and molded the American soul.

For, while the record of Western settlement in our dealings with the Indians is a chapter not without black pages which may be compared with our slave trade, nonetheless it was the free play of free men on free land that built up the Middle West; and it was the rapidly mounting weight of men and means of that hinterland, flung into the conflict by common faith in an order which meant opportunity for all, which tipped the scales as between North and South, preserved the Union and freed the slaves. Lincoln was its man; not its leader, merely, but framed of the bone and marrow of its plain people; his spirit, the embodiment of frontiersmen and settlers.

And what has this to do with the northward migration of the Negro— or its counterpart, his partnership in agricultural reconstruction in the South? It has more to do than that children and grandchildren of the emancipated slaves enter the gates of the cities with the children and grandchildren of the old frontier. Or even that in this new generation they are fellow adventurers as never before in the inveterate quest of our people for new horizons—on the land and in industry. These things are in themselves of tremendous import. But my point is, that in the pioneering of this new epoch, they are getting into stride with that of the old. By way of the typical American experience, they became for the first time a part of its living tradition.

The great folkway which is America need no longer be a thing abstract, apart from them. The Negro boy, who with his satchel steps off the train in Pittsburgh or Chicago, Detroit or New York, to make his way in what Robert Woods called the city wilderness, may draw at the same springs of inspiration as the boy next him from Wisconsin or Kansas, or that other who, still westward bent, throws in his lot in the valley of some irrigation project in the mountain states. The same can be said of the Corn Club boys and girls of Georgia or South Carolina, who are building up farm homes with new tools and husbandry in regions which have been held in the mesh of a worn out economy. The Hampton and Tuskegee graduates, the farm demonstrators and co-operators who break that mesh, its tough warp of the one crop and its binding woof of the credit system, and help weave in its stead the texture of a new and more self-reliant rural life, are settlers in a very real sense. And so are the men and women who, in a great city district like Harlem, against the pressure of overcrowding and high rents, against the drag of black exploiters and white, and the hazards of sickness and precariousness of livelihood, odds which all of us face in our great city machines, and which bear down with redoubled force upon youth and childhood—these men and these women, who strand by strand fashion the fabric of the good life in a city neighborhood, are of the breed of the old pioneers. They are builders.

Do not mistake me, the land they come to is not all milk and honey. Nor was the way of the frontiersman, or the frontier woman, or the frontier child. Nor were these all cast in heroic or congenial, or even tolerable, molds. But the new order in the Southern countryside, the new order in the Northern city, offers an economic foothold, as did the old clearing. It calls on the spirit of team play, as did the old settlement with its road building and its barn raisings. There is a smack of opportunity and freedom in the air. The very process as bound up in those changes in individual fortune, is instinct with that group consciousness of common adventure, is fresh with the tang of growth and expansion, which the wagon trains carried with them to the West, and which became the theme of our pioneering.

The vocational schools for Negroes in the South have encouraged, among other things, the vigorous spirit of individual initiative which we like to associate with American character. The recoil among Negroes against political suppression and terrorism which has animated much of their leadership of protest in the last thirty years has been kin to our old rebel tradition. But here in this new pioneering, we have the nascent beginnings of that other great mode of social impulse. And we catch its gleam in a newer, more positive and creative leadership of self-expression.

Those of us who trace our blazed ways to the Atlantic Seaboard, to Pilgrim Rock or James River blockhouse or Dutch trading post, can perhaps not realize what it means to a people to have their vista of the past shut in by whitewashed wall, mud chimney and whipping ring of a slave street. No wonder in his new racial consciousness, the Negro digs up his past and searches out in Africa the genesis of a proud tradition. My thought is that the new opportunities he is broaching in American life and labor throw open another vista of the past, one of the New World, to which he is not alien. This background may not be his to-day, I grant; but by some compensating law of relativity, it will come to meet him as he presses forward.

Seldom in the history of the world have a people moved North. Our history is of Westward expansion. So coursed the great racial waves that swept into Europe from the East. We have had the experiment of peoples moving Southward—Northmen and Frank and the rest, flowering out in a new and milder climate. Here we are witnessing a reversal of that process. What its outcome will be cannot be forecast. But it is something which, points of compass aside, is kin to the whole trend of American experience. It is search for the new and democratic chance. It is pioneering.

It is, also, an adventure in self-expression—not alone in political and economic terms, but in things of the word and spirit. We have witnessed in the United States the duress in which various immigrant groups have been held until their cause was taken up by rare people, as Jane Addams and Jacob Riis, endowed not alone with understanding, but with the art of interpretation. The Negro has had no language barrier; but he has been hemmed in by barbed wire entanglements of prejudice and fixed conceptions. He is learning ways of his own to surmount them. He employs winged gifts that shoot across them. He brings song, music, dance, poetry, story-telling; rhythms and color and drama, ardent feeling and fleet thought. Not alone is his a Northward migration within the confines of America, challenging new communities with his presence. Not alone is it a shift from soil to city. Not alone a breaking-away from the old inhibitions of a fixed and often adverse social environment. He is readdressing himself to America on a cultural plane; and in arenas where the old inhibitions do not hold. A verse that pierces the heart meets no race barriers. A song that lifts the spirit with its lilt wings free in the democracy of art.

It would be difficult to overestimate the significance of the Negro's employment of these cultural gifts. A new generation of both races respond to them. They afford white America a new approach to what we have overlong dourly called the Race Problem. They make for swifter understanding than a multitude of heavy treatises. I speak from experience with our special number of the *Survey Graphic* (Harlem: Mecca of the New Negro: March, 1925) which Dr. Locke edited and which was the forerunner of this book. Harlem presents to the eye the look of any tenement and apartment district of New York so far as its physical make-up is concerned. Occasionally some writer dipped beneath the surface: Negro authors and periodicals had borne witness to it; yet so far as the newspapers were concerned, it had not registered, except as an area of real estate speculation and clashes, and the police news and racial friction of a city quarter. Kipling gave us the High Road to India in Kim. Sinclair Lewis set down America in Main Street. But that contrast is not the whole story of East and West; here was something as alluring as it was portentous happening in our midst; but unobserved and swathed in the commonplace. How to unfold it? Our number was cut from city cloth, it brought out the seams of social problems which underlie it, but also, and in all its sheen, the cultural pattern that gave it texture. It proved a magic carpet which swung the reader not across the minarets and bazaars of some ancient Arabia, but the wells and shrines of a people's renaissance. The pageant of it swept past in pastel and story, poem and epic prose, and the response was instant. In this volume, what was then done fragmentarily is now done in a way which will endure.

For the Negro to thus make himself, and his, articulate to those about him will count for much; but it is the lesser good of two. He is finding himself anew in his own eyes. His self-expression is giving body to his special racial genius; he gains a new sense of its integrity and distinction. I recall a discussion at the Harlem Forum of the work of Winold Reiss which enriches this volume. There were Negroes who protested against his series of racial types; they clung to the prevailing ideals of beauty and these heads were not beautiful to them. As others were quick to point out, from the picture books they were brought up on as children to the newspaper supplements that reached their homes the Sunday before, they had been encompassed by Nordic conventions. Their imagery had been so long thwarted and warped that they could not grasp the rare service rendered by this Bavarian artist, who came with fresh eyes, who is the first in America to break with sentimentality and caricature and delineate racial types with fidelity, and who is encouraging a group of young Negroes to follow through to mastery the path he has broken.

Mr. Reiss's pastels were shown that month in the Harlem Public Library, and at the instigation of Mrs. McDougall, hundreds of Negro school children passed before them. There they saw plain people depicted, such as they knew on the street, and, also, poets, philosophers, teachers and leaders, who are the spearheads of a racial revival; forerunners, whose work might be passed on to them, men and women treated with a dignity and beauty and potency altogether new. Images they could carry with them through their lives. Their pioneers!

But, though this latest experience of the American Negro is properly a promisefully racial revival, more fundamentally even it is an induction into the heritage of the national tradition, a baptism of the American spirit that slavery cheated him out of, a maturing experience that Reconstruction delayed. Now that materially and spiritually the Negro pioneers, and by his own initiative, shares the common experience of all the others of America's composite stock, his venturing Americanism stakes indisputable claims in the benefits and resources of our democracy.

THE NEW FRONTAGE ON AMERICAN LIFE

Charles S. Johnson

I

THE CITIES OF THE NORTH, stern, impersonal and enchanting, needed men of the brawny muscles, which Europe, suddenly flaming with war, had ceased to supply, when the black hordes came on from the South like a silent, encroaching shadow. Five hundred thousand there were in the first three-year period. These had yielded with an almost uncanny unanimity of triumphant approval to this urge to migration, closing in first upon the little towns of the South, then upon the cities near the towns, and, with an unfailing consistency, sooner or later, they boarded a *Special* bound North, to close in upon these cities which lured them, with an ultimate appeal, to their gay lights and high wages, unoppressive anonymity, crowds, excitement, and feverish struggle for life.

There was Chicago in the West, known far and wide for its colossal abattoirs, whose placarded warehouses, set close by the railroad, dotted every sizable town of the South, calling for men; Chicago, remembered for the fairyland wonders of the World's Fair; home of the fearless, taunting "race paper," and above all things, of mills clamoring for men.

And there was Pittsburgh, gloomy, cheerless—bereft of the Poles and Lithuanians, Croatians and Austrians, who had trucked and smelted its steel. And along with Pittsburgh, the brilliant satellite towns of Bethlehem and Duquesne and Homestead. The solid but alert Europeans in 1916 had deserted the lower bases of industry and gone after munitions money, or home to fight. Creeping out, they left a void, which, to fill, tempted industry to desperate measures. One railroad line brought in 12,000 of these new laborers graciously and gratuitously. The road-beds and immense construction projects of the State were in straits and the great mills wanted men.

And there was New York City with its polite personal service and its Harlem—the Mecca of the Negroes the country over. Delightful Harlem of the effete East! Old families, brownstone mansions, a step from worshipful Broadway, the end of the rainbow for early relatives drifting from home into the exciting world; the factories and the docks, the stupendous clothing industries, and buildings to be "superintended," a land of opportunity for musicians, actors and those who wanted to be, the national headquarters of everything but the government.

And there was Cleveland with a faint Southern exposé but with iron mills; and St. Louis, one of the first cities of the North, a city of mixed traditions but with great foundries, brick and terra-cotta works; Detroit, the automobile center, with its sophistication of skill and fancy wages reflecting the daring economic policies of Henry Ford; Hartford, Connecticut, where, indeed, the first experiment with southern labor, was tried on the tobacco plantations skirting the city; Akron and its rubber; Philadelphia, with its comfortable old traditions; and the innumerable little industrial towns where fabulous wages were paid.

White and black these cities lured, but the blacks they lured with a demoniac appeal.

II

MIGRATIONS, THINKS PROFESSOR CARR-SAUNDERS—AND HE is confirmed by history—are nearly always due to the influence of an idea. Population crowding, and economic debasement, are, by their nature, more or less constant. In the case of the Negroes, it was not exclusively an idea, but an idea brought within the pale of possibility. By tradition and probably by temperament the Negro is a rural type. His metier is agriculture. To this economy his mental and social habits have been adjusted. In exact contrast to him is the Jew, who by every aptitude and economic attachment is a city dweller, and in whom modern students of racial behavior are discovering a neurotic constitution traceable to the emotional strain of peculiar racial status and to the terrific pressure of city life.

South, there are few cities. The life of the section is not manufacture but the soil—and more than anything else, the fluffy white bolls of cotton. There is Mississippi where 56 per cent of the population are Negroes and 88 per cent of the Negroes are farmers. Cotton is King. When it lives and grows and escapes the destroying weevil and the droughts and the floods, there is comfort for the owners. When it fails, as is most often, want stalks, and a hobbed heel twists on the neck of the black tenant. The iniquitous credit system breeding dishonesty and holding the Negroes perpetually in debt and virtually enslaved; the fierce hatred of poor whites in frightened and desperate competition; cruelty of the masters who reverently thanked God for the inferior blacks who could labor happily in the sun, with all the unfeeling complaisance of oxen; the barrenness and monotony of rural life; the dawn of hope for something better; distant flashes of a new country, beckoning—these were the soil in which the idea took root—and flowered. There was no slow, deliberate sifting of plans, or measurement of conduct, or inspired leadership, or forces dark and mysterious. To each in his setting came an impulse and an opportunity.

There was Jeremiah Taylor, of Bobo, Mississippi, long since at the age of discretion, gnarled and resigned to his farm, one of whose sons came down one day from the "yellow dog road" with the report that folks were leaving "like Judgment day"; that he had seen a labor man who promised a free ticket to a railroad camp up North. Jeremiah went to town, half doubting and came back aflush and decided. His son left, he followed and in four months his wife and two daughters bundled their possessions, sold their chickens and joined them.

Into George Horton's barber shop in Hattiesburg, Mississippi, came a white man of the North. Said he: "The colored folks are obligated to the North because it freed them. The North is obligated to the colored folks because after freeing them it separated them from their livelihood. Now, this living is offered with interest and a new birth of liberty. Will the colored man live up to his side of the bargain?" The clinching argument was free transportation. George Horton's grievance was in politics. He already earned a comfortable living and could decline the free ride as a needless charity. But his place contributed forty men. The next year the Hattiesburg settlement in Chicago brought up their pastor.

And there was Joshua Ward, who had prayed for these times and now saw God cursing the land and stirring up his people. He would invoke his wrath no longer.

Rosena Shephard's neighbor's daughter, with a savoury record at home, went away. Silence, for the space of six weeks. Then she wrote that she was earning $2 a day packing sausages. "If that lazy, good-for-nothing gal kin make $2 a day, I kin make four," and Mrs. Shephard left.

Clem Woods could not tolerate any fellow's getting ahead of him. He did not want to leave his job and couldn't explain why he wanted to go North and his boss *proved* to him that his chances were better at home. But every departure added to his restlessness. One night a train passed through with two coaches of men from New Orleans. Said one of them: "Good-by, bo, I'm bound for the promised land," and Clem got aboard.

Jefferson Clemons in De Ridder, Louisiana, was one of "1,800 of the colored race" who paid $2 to a "white gentleman" to get to Chicago on the 15th of March. By July he had saved enough to pay his fare and left "bee cars," as he confided, "he was tired of bein' dog and beast."

Mrs. Selina Lennox was slow to do anything, but she was by nature a social creature. The desolation of her street wore upon her. No more screaming, darting children, no more bustle of men going to work or coming home. The familiar shuffle and loud greetings of shopping matrons, the scent of boiled food—all these were gone. Mobile Street, the noisy, was clothed in an ominous quiet, as if some disaster impended. Now and then the Italian storekeeper, bewildered and forlorn, would walk to the middle of the street and look first up and then down and walk back into his store again. Mrs. Lennox left.

George Scott wanted more "free liberty" and accepted a proffered railroad ticket from a stranger who always talked in whispers and seemed to have plenty of money.

Dr. Alexander H. Booth's practice declined, but some of his departed patients, long in his debt paid up with an infuriating air of superiority, adding in their letters such taunts as "home ain't nothing like this" or "nobody what has any grit in his craw would stay," and the Doctor left.

John Felts of Macon was making $1.25 when flour went up to $12 a barrel and the New York *Age* was advertising cheap jobs at $2.50 a day. He had a wife and six children.

Jim Casson in Grabor, Louisiana, had paid his poll taxes, his state and parish taxes and yet children could not get a school.

Miss Jamesie Towns taught fifty children four months for the colored tenants, out near Fort Valley, Georgia. Her salary was reduced from $16.80 to $14.40 a month.

Enoch Scott was living in Hollywood, Mississippi, when the white physician and one of the Negro leaders disputed a small account. The Negro was shot three times in the back and his head battered—all this in front of the high sheriff's office. Enoch says he left because the doctor might sometime take a dislike to him.

When cotton was selling for forty cents a point, Joshua Johnson was offered twenty and was dared to try to sell it anywhere else. Said Joshua: "Next year, I won't have no such trouble," and he didn't.

Chicago's Negro population had dragged along by decades until the upheaval, when suddenly it leaped from 44,000 to 109,000. In a slice of the city between nineteen blocks, 92,000 of them crowded: on the east the waters of Lake Michigan; on the west the great nauseous stretch of the stockyards and the reeking little unpainted dwellings of foreigners; on the north the business district, and on the south the scowling and self-conscious remnant of the whites left behind in the rush of fashion to the North Shore.

Fifteen years ago over 60 per cent of all these working Negroes were engaged in domestic and personal service. There was nothing else to do. Then the fashion had changed in servants as Irish and Swedish and German tides came on. An unfortunate experience with the unions lost for Negroes the best positions in their traditional strongholds as waiters and poisoned their minds against organized labor. Racial exclusiveness, tradition and inexperience, kept them out of industry. Then a strike at the stockyards and the employers miraculously and suddenly discovered their untried genius, while the unions elected to regard them as deliberate miscreants lowering wage standards by design and taking white men's jobs. Smoldering resentment. But with the war and its labor shortage, they came on in torrents. They overran the confines of the old area and spread south in spite of the organized opposition of Hyde Park and Kenwood, where objection was registered with sixty bombs in a period of two years. Passions flamed and broke in a race riot unprecedented for its list of murders and counter-murders, its mutilations and rampant savagery; for the bold resistance of the Negroes to violence. Then gradually passions fired by the first encounter subsided into calm and the industries absorbed 80 per cent of the working members.

Before the deluge, New York City, too, lacked that lusty vigor of increase, apart from migration, which characterized the Negro population as a whole. In sixty years, its increase had been negligible. Time was when that small cluster of descendants of the benevolent old Dutch masters and of the free Negroes moved with freedom and complacent importance about the intimate fringe of the city's active life. These Negroes were the barbers, caterers, bakers, restaurateurs, coachmen—all highly elaborated personal service positions. The crafts had permitted them wide freedom; they were skilled artisans. They owned businesses which were independent of Negro patronage. But that was long ago. This group in 1917 was rapidly passing, its splendor shorn. The rapid evolution of business, blind to the amenities on which they flourished, had devoured their establishments, unsupported and weak in capital resources; the incoming hordes of Europeans had edged them out of their inheritance of personal service businesses, clashed with them in competition for the rough muscle jobs and driven them back into the obscurity of individual personal service.

For forty years, moreover, there have been dribbling in from the South, the West Indies and South America, small increments of population which through imperceptible gradations had changed the whole complexion and outlook of the Negro New Yorker. New blood and diverse cultures these brought—and each a separate problem of assimilation. As the years passed, the old migrants "rubbed off the green," adopted the slant and sophistication of the city, mingled and married, and their children are now the native-born New Yorkers. For fifty years scattered families have been uniting in the hectic metropolis from every state in the union and every province of the West Indies. There have always been undigested colonies—the Sons and Daughters of North Carolina, the Virginia Society, the Southern Beneficial League—these are survivals of self-conscious, intimate bodies. But the mass is in the melting pot of the city.

There were in New York City in 1920, by the census count, 152,467 Negroes. Of these 39,233 are reported as born in New York State, 30,436 in foreign countries, principally the West Indies, and 78,242 in other states, principally the South. Since 1920 about 50,000 more Southerners have been added to the population, bulging the narrow strip of Harlem in which it had lived and spilling over the old boundaries. There are no less than 25,000 Virginians in New York City, more than 20,000 North and South Carolinians, and 10,000 Georgians. Every Southern state has contributed its quota to a heterogeneity which matches that of cosmopolitan New York. If the present Negro New Yorker were analyzed, he would be found to be composed of one part native, one part West Indian and about three parts Southern. If the tests of the army psychologists could work with the precision and certainty with which they are accredited, the Negroes who make up the present population of New York City would be declared to represent different races, for the differences between South and North by actual measurement are greater than the difference between whites and Negroes.

III

A NEW TYPE OF NEGRO is evolving—a city Negro. He is being evolved out of those strangely divergent elements of the general background. And this is a fact overlooked by those students of human behavior, who with such quick comprehension detect the influence of the city in the nervousness of the Jew, the growing nervous disorders of city dwellers in general to the tension of city life. In ten years, Negroes have been actually transplanted from one culture to another.

Where once there were personal and intimate relations, in which individuals were in contact at practically all points of their lives, there are now group relations in which the whole structure is broken up and reassorted, casting them in contact at only one or two points of their lives. The old controls are no longer expected to operate. Whether apparent or not, the newcomers are forced to reorganize their lives, to enter a new status and adjust to it that eager restlessness which prompted them to leave home. Church, lodge, gossip, respect of friends, established customs, social and racial, exercise controls in the small Southern community. The church is the center for face-to-face relations. The pastor is the leader. The rôle of the pastor and the social utility of the church are obvious in this letter sent home:

> Dear pastor
> I find it my duty to write you my whereabouts, also family. . . I shall send my church money in a few days. I am trying to influence our members here to do the same. I received notice printed in a R.R. car (Get right with God). O, I had nothing so striking as the above mottoe. Let me no how is our church I am so anxious to no. My wife always talking about her seat in the church want to no who occupies it.
>
> Yours in Christ

Religion affords an outlet for the emotional energies thwarted in other directions. The psychologists will find rich material for speculation on the emotional nature of some of the Negroes set into the New York pattern in this confession:

> "I got here in time to attend one of the greatest revivals in the history of my life—over 500 people join the church. We had a Holy Ghost shower. You know I like to have run wild."

In the new environment there are many and varied substitutes which answer more or less directly the myriad desires indiscriminately comprehended by the church. The complaint of the ministers that these "emancipated" souls "stray away from God" when they reach the city is perhaps warranted on the basis of the fixed status of the church in the South, but it is not an accurate interpretation of what has happened. When the old ties are broken new satisfactions are sought. Sometimes the Young Men's Christian Association functions. This has in some cities made rivalry between the churches and the Associations. More often the demands of the young exceed the "sterilized" amusements of Christian organizations. It is not uncommon to find groups who faithfully attend church Sunday evenings and as faithfully seek further stimulation in a cabaret afterwards. Many have been helped to find themselves, no doubt, by having their old churches and pastors reappear in the new home and resume control. But too often, as with European immigrants, the family loses control over the children who become assimilated more rapidly than their parents. Tragic evidences of this appear coldly detailed in the records of delinquency.

Social customs must change slowly if excesses and waste would be avoided. Growth of a new custom on a town will be slow; introduction of a foreigner to a new custom in its maturity necessitates rapid accommodation. It cannot be fully comprehended at first sight. The innumerable safeguards which surround these departures from social customs are lacking. There is a different social meaning in Ophelia, Mississippi, when one does not go to church, or a woman smokes or bobs her hair; Palatka's star elocutionist does not always take Chicago's dramatic circles by storm; neither does Noah Brown, the local potentate of fraternal circles wield the same influence in New York. There are new leaders and new objectives, which for many moons remain incomprehensible to the newcomer.

There is a reorganization of attitudes. There is a racial as well as a social disorientation. For those who fed their hopes and expectations on a new status which would afford an escape from unrighteous and oppressive limitations of the South, there is a sensitiveness about any reminder of the station from which they have been so recently emancipated—a hair-trigger resentment, a furious revolt against the years of training in the precise boundaries of their place, a fear of disclosing the weakness of submission where it is not expected, an expansiveness and pretense at ease in unaccustomed situations. Exact balance is difficult. Here are some of the things that register: John Diggs writes home to his friend this letter:

Dear Partner

. . . I am all fixed now and living well, I don't have to work hard. Don't have to mister every little boy comes along. I haven't heard a white man call a colored a nigger you know how—since I been here. I can ride in the street or steam car anywhere I get a seat. I don't care to mix with white what I mean I am not crazy about being with white folks, but if I have to pay the same fare I have learn to want the same acomidation and if you are first in a place here shoping you don't have to wait till all the white folks get thro tradeing yet amid all this I love the good old south and am praying that God may give every well wisher a chance to be a man regardless of color. . ."

If the Negroes in Harlem show at times less courtesy toward white visitors than is required by the canons of good taste, this is bad, but understandable. It was remarked shortly after the first migration that the newcomers on boarding street cars invariably strode to the front even if there were seats in the rear. This is, perhaps, a mild example of tendencies expressed more strikingly in other directions, for with but few exceptions they are forced to sit in the rear of street cars throughout the South.

The difference between the background of northern and southern Negroes is even wider than it seems. In the two there are utterly different packets of stored up memories marking out channels of conduct. The southern Negro directs his ambitions at those amenities of which the northern Negro boasts and, until the first wonderment and envy subside, ignores his reservations. This is the hectic period of transition, so noticeable after huge accessions—inevitably in the wake of the newcomers north, whether the numbers are large or small. There comes the testing of long cherished desires, the thirst for forbidden fruit—and disillusionment, partial or complete, almost as inevitably.

IV

CITIES HAVE PERSONALITIES. THEIR CHIEF industries are likely to determine not only their respective characters, but the type of persons they attract and hold. Detroit manufactures automobiles, Chicago slaughters cattle, Pittsburgh smelts iron and steel—these three communities draw different types of workers whose industrial habits are interlaced with correspondingly different cultural backgrounds. One might look to this factor as having significance in the selection of Negro workers and indeed in the relations of the Negro population with the community. The technical intricacy of the automobile industry, like the army intelligence tests, sifts out the heavy-handed worker who fits admirably into the economy of the steel industries, where 80 per cent of the operations are unskilled. A temperamental equipment easily adapted to the knife-play and stench of killing and preserving cattle is not readily interchangeable either with the elaborated technique of the factory or the sheer muscle play and endurance required by the mill. These communities draw different types of workers.

Similar differences between cities account for the curiously varied directions of growth which the Negro populations take. They help to explain the furious striving after commercial glory in Chicago, and the chasing of the will-o'-the-wisp of culture in New York; the objective of an unshakable berth in a skilled job at $10 a day in Detroit, and a near future of benign comfort in Philadelphia. The Negro workers can no more become a fixed racial concept than can white workers. Conceived in terms either of capacity or opportunity, their employment gives rise to the most perplexing paradoxes. If it is a question of what Negroes are mentally or physically able to do, there are as many affirmations of competence as denials of it.

In skilled work requiring membership in unions they are employed only in small numbers, and membership is rarely encouraged unless the union is threatened. Since the apprentice-recruits for these jobs are discouraged, and the numbers sparse, the safety of the union is rarely threatened by an unorganized Negro minority. In certain responsible skilled positions, such as locomotive engineers, street cars and subway motormen, Negroes are never employed.

The distinctions are irrational. A Negro worker may not be a street or subway conductor because of the possibility of public objection to contact—but he may be a ticket chopper. He may not be a money changer in a subway station because honesty is required—yet he may be entrusted, as a messenger, with thousands of dollars daily. He may not sell goods over a counter—but he may deliver the goods after they have been sold. He may be a porter in charge of a sleeping car without a conductor, but never a conductor; he may be a policeman but not a fireman; a linotyper, but not a motion picture operator; a glass annealer, but not a glass blower, a deck hand, but not a sailor. The list could be continued indefinitely.

Between the principal northern cities there is a simple but vital difference to be observed. While New York City, for example, offers a diversity of employment, the city has not such basic industries as may be found in the automobile plants of Detroit, or the iron and steel works and gigantic meat slaughtering industries of Chicago. In Chicago, there is diversified employment, to be sure, but there is a significantly heavier concentration in the basic industries; more than that, there are gradations of work from unskilled to skilled. In certain plants skilled workers increased from 3.5 per cent of the Negro working population in 1910 to 13.5 per cent in 1920 in Chicago. In the slaughtering houses there are actually more semi-skilled Negro workers than laborers. The number of iron molders increased from 31 in 1910 to 520 in 1920 and this latter number represents 10 per cent of all the iron molders.

In the working age groups of New York there are more women than men. For every hundred Negro men there are 110 Negro women. This is abnormal and would be a distinct anomaly in an industrial center. The surplus women are doubtless the residue from the general wash and ebb of migrants who found a demand for their services. The city actually attracts more women than men. But surplus women bring on other problems, as the social agencies will testify. "Where women preponderate in large numbers there is proportionate increase in immorality because women are cheap." . . . The situation does not permit normal relations. What is most likely to happen, and does happen, is that women soon find it an added personal attraction to contribute to the support of a man. Demoralization may follow this— and does. Moreover, the proportion of Negro women at work in Manhattan (60.6) is twice that of any corresponding group, and one of the highest proportions registered anywhere.

The nature of the work of at least 40 per cent of the men suggests a relationship, even if indirectly, with the tensely active night life by which Harlem is known. The dull, unarduous routine of a porter's job or that of an elevator tender, does not provide enough stimulation to consume the normal supply of nervous energy. It is unthinkable that the restlessness which drove migrants to New York from dull small towns would allow them to be content with the same dullness in the new environment, when a supply of garish excitements is so richly available.

With all the "front" of pretending to live, the aspect of complacent wantlessness, it is clear that the Negroes are in a predicament. The moment holds tolerance but no great promise. Just as the wave of immigration once swept these Negroes out of old strongholds, a change of circumstances may disrupt them again. The slow moving black masses, with their assorted heritages and old loyalties, face the same stern barriers in the new environment. They are the black workers.

V

ENTERING GRADUALLY AN ERA OF industrial contact and competition with white workers of greater experience and numerical superiority, antagonisms loom up. Emotions have a way of re-enforcing themselves. The fierce economic fears of men in competition can supplement or be supplemented by the sentiments engendered by racial difference. Beneath the disastrous East St. Louis conflict was a boiling anger toward southern Negroes coming in to "take white men's jobs." The same antagonisms, first provoked sixty years ago in the draft riots of New York during the Civil War, flared again in the shameful battle of "San Juan Hill" in the Columbus Hill District. These outbreaks were distinctly more economic than racial.

Herein lies one of the points of highest tension in race relations. Negro workers potentially menace organized labor and the leaders of the movement recognize this. But racial sentiments are not easily destroyed by abstract principles. The white, workers have not, except in few instances, conquered the antagonisms founded on race to the extent of accepting the rights of Negro workers to the privileges which they enjoy. While denying them admission to their crafts, they grow furious over their dangerous borings from the outside. "The Negroes are scabs." "They hold down the living standards of workers by cutting under!" "Negroes are professional strike breakers!" These sentiments are a good nucleus for elaboration into the most furious fears and hatreds.

It is believed variously that Negro workers are as a matter of policy opposed to unions or as a matter of ignorance incapable of appreciating them. From some unions they are definitely barred; some insist on separate Negro locals; some limit them to qualified membership; some accept them freely with white workers. The situation of the Negroes, on the surface, is, to say the least, compromising. Their shorter industrial experience and almost complete isolation from the educative influence of organized trade unions contribute to some of the inertia encountered in organizing them. Their traditional positions have been those of personal loyalty, and this has aided the habit of individual bargaining for jobs in industry. They have been, as was pointed out, under the comprehensive leadership of the church in practically all aspects of their lives including their labor. No effective new leadership has developed to supplant this old fealty. The attitude of white workers has sternly opposed the use of Negroes as apprentices through fear of subsequent competition in the skilled trades. This has limited the number of skilled Negroes trained on the job. But despite this denial, Negroes have gained skill.

This disposition violently to protest the employment of Negroes in certain lines because they are not members of the union and the equally violent protest against the admission of Negroes to the unions, created in the Negroes, desperate for work, an attitude of indifference to abstract pleas. In 1910 they were used in New York City to break the teamsters' strike and six years later they were organized. In 1919 they were used in a strike of the building trades. Strained feelings resulted, but they were finally included in the unions of this trade. During the outlaw strike of the railway and steamship clerks, freight handlers, expressmen and station employees, they were used to replace the striking whites and were given preference over the men whose places they had taken. During the shopmen's strike they were promoted into new positions and thus made themselves eligible for skilled jobs as machinists. In fact, their most definite gains have been at the hands of employers and over the tactics of labor union exclusionists.

Where the crafts are freely open to them they have joined with the general movement of the workers. Of the 5,386 Negro longshoremen, about 5,000 are organized. Of the 735 Negro carpenters, 400 are members of the United Brotherhood of Carpenters and Joiners. Of the 2,275 semi-skilled clothing workers practically all are members of the International Ladies Garment Workers Union. The musicians are 50 per cent organized. The difficulty is that the great preponderance of Negro jobs is still in lines which are not organized. The porters, laundresses (outside of laundries) and servants have no organization. The Negroes listed as painters are not in the painters' union, many of them being merely whitewashers. The tailors are in large part cleaners and pressers. The waiters, elevator tenders (except female) are poorly organized.

The end of the Negro's troubles, however, does not come with organization. There is still the question of employers, for it is a certain fact that preference is frequently given white workers when they can be secured, if high wages are to be paid. A vicious circle indeed! One Negro editor has suggested a United Negro Trades Union built on the plan of the United Hebrew Trades and the Italian Chamber of Labor. The unions are lethargic; the Negroes skeptical, untrained and individualistic. Meanwhile they drift, a disordered mass, self-conscious, but with their aims unrationalized, into the face of new problems.

Out of this medley of strains in reaction to totally new experiences, a strange product is evolving, and with it new wishes, habits and expectations. Negro workers have discovered an unsuspected strength even though they are as yet incapable of integrating it. Black labor, now sensitive and insistent, will have the protection of workers' organizations or by the strength of their menace keep these organizations futile and ineffective.

With the shift toward industry now beginning, and a subsequent new status already foreshadowed, some sounder economic policy is imperative. The traditional hold of domestic service vocations is already broken: witness the sudden halt in the increase of Negro male servants and elevator men. The enormous growth of certain New York industries has been out of proportion to the normal native production of workers. The immigration on which these formerly depended has been cut down and the prospects are that this curtailment will continue. For the first time, as a result of promotion, retirement and death, gaps are appearing which the limited recruits cannot fill. Note the clothing industry, one of the largest in New York. There is a persistent lament that the second generation of immigrants do not continue in the trade. Already Negro workers have been sought to supplement the deficiencies in the first generation recruits. This sort of thing will certainly be felt in other lines. The black masses are on the verge of induction from their unenviable status as servants into the forces of the industrial workers, a more arduous, but less dependent rank. They require a new leadership, training in the principles of collective action, a new orientation with their white fellow workers for the sake of a future peace, a reorganization of the physical and mental habits which are a legacy of their old experiences, and deliberate training for the new work to come. It is this rehabilitation of the worker that the Urban Leagues have tried to accomplish, accompanying this effort with a campaign against the barriers to the entrance of Negro workers into industry. Conceiving these workers as inherently capable of an infinite range of employment, this organization insists merely upon an openness which permits opportunity, an objective experiment uncluttered by old theories of racial incompetence and racial dogmas.

The workers of the South and the West Indies who have come to the cities of the North with vagrant desires and impulses, their endowments of skill and strength, their repressions and the telltale marks of backward cultures, with all the human wastes of the process, have directed shafts of their native energy into the cities' life and growth. They are becoming a part of it. The restive spirit which brought them has been neither all absorbed nor wasted. Over two-thirds of all the businesses operated by Negroes in New York are conducted by migrant Negroes. They are in the schools—they are the radicals and this is hopeful. The city Negro—an unpredictable mixture of all possible temperaments—is yet in evolution.

VI

THE VIOLENT SUB-CURRENTS OF RECENT years, which have shifted the economic base of Negro life—as indeed they have affected all other groups—have brought about a new orientation throughout, and have accentuated group attitudes among both black and white, sometimes favorably, sometimes unfavorably; here in a spurt of progress, there in a backwash of reaction.

Take the case of Negro business. It is only within recent years that a coldly practical eye has been turned to the capital created by that body of black workers; to the very obvious fact that a certain affluence breeds a certain respect; that where the pressure is heaviest, and unjust restrictions imposed, there is a politely effective boycott possible in "racial solidarity" which diverts Negro capital from disinterested hands into the coffers of "race institutions." Instance the Negro insurance companies, of which there are now sixty-seven, with over $250,000,000 worth of insurance in force, flourishing out of the situation of special premium rates for Negroes instituted by some companies, and a policy of total exclusion practiced by others. No work for young Negro men and women in general business? Then they will establish their own businesses and borrow from the sentimental doctrine of "race pride" enough propulsion to compensate for the initial deficiencies of capital. But is this entirely representative of the new Negro thought? It is not. This increased activity is largely an opportunistic policy, with its firmest foothold in the South. Where it exists in the North it has been almost wholly transplanted by southern Negroes. The cities of the North where conditions tend most, in special instances to approach the restrictions of the South, become the most active business centers. The greater the isolation, the more pronounced and successful this intensive group commercialism.

Or, to take another angle of this picture: Mr. Marcus Garvey has been accused of inspiring and leading a movement for the "re-exaltation" of things black, for the exploitation of Negro resources for the profit of Negroes, and for the re-establishment of prestige to things Negro. As a fact, he has merely had the clairvoyance to place himself at the head of a docile sector of a whole population which, in different degrees, has been expressing an indefinable restlessness and broadening of spirit. The Garvey movement itself is an exaggeration of this current mood which attempts to reduce these vague longings to concrete symbols of faith. In this great sweep of the Negro population are comprehended the awkward gestures of the awakening black peasantry, the new desire of Negroes for an independent status, the revolt against a culture which has but partially (and again unevenly) digested the Negro masses—the black peasants least of all. It finds a middle ground in the feelings of kinship with all oppressed dark peoples, as articulated so forcefully by the Negro press, and takes, perhaps, its highest expression in the objectives of the Pan-African Congress.

New emotions accompany these new objectives. Where there is ferment and unrest, there is change. Old traditions are being shaken and rooted up by the percussion of new ideas. In this the year of our Lord, 1925, extending across the entire country are seventeen cities in violent agitation over Negro residence areas, and where once there was acquiescence, silent or ineffectually grumbly, there are now in evidence new convictions which more often prompt to resistance. It is this spirit, aided by increased living standards and refined tastes, that has resulted in actual housing clashes, the most notorious of which have been occurring in Detroit, Michigan, where, with a Negro population increase of more than 500 per cent in the past ten years, this new resistance has clashed with the spirit of the South, likewise drawn there by the same economic forces luring and pushing the Negroes. This same spirit was evidenced in the serious racial clashes which flared up in a dozen cities after the first huge migration of Negroes northward, and which took a sad toll in lives. Claude McKay, the young Negro poet, caught the mood of the new Negro in this, and molded it into fiery verse which Negro newspapers copied and recopied:

> *If we must die, let it not be like hogs,*
> *Hunted and penned in an inglorious spot...*

Nor does this embrace all of the ragged pattern: Silently and yet with such steady persistence that it has the aspect of an utterly distinct movement, the newer spirits are beginning to free themselves from the slough of that servile feeling (now happily classified by the psychologists as the "inferiority complex") inherited from slavery and passed along with virulence for over fifty years. The generation in whom lingered memories of the painful degradation of slavery could not be expected to cherish even those pearls of song and poetry born of suffering. They would be expected to do just as they did: rule out the Sorrow Songs as the product of ignorant slaves, taboo dialect as incorrect English, and the priceless folk lore as the uncultured expression of illiterates,—an utterly conscious effort to forget the past, and take over, suddenly, the symbols of that culture which had so long ground their bodies and spirits in the dirt. The newer voices, at a more comfortable distance, are beginning to find a new beauty in these heritages, and new values in their own lives.

Less is heard of the two historic "schools of thought" clashing ceaselessly and loud over the question of industrial and higher education for the Negro. Both schools are, sensibly, now taken for granted as quite necessary. The new questions of the industrial schools are concerned with adjusting their curricula to the new fields of industry in which Negro workers will play an ever mounting rôle, and with expanding their academic and college courses; while the new question of the universities is that of meeting the demand for trained Negroes for business, the professions, and the arts. The level of education has been lifted through the work of both, and the new level, in itself, is taking care of the sentiment about the division.

Thus the new frontier of Negro life is flung out in a jagged, uneven but progressive pattern. For a group historically retarded and not readily assimilated, contact with its surrounding culture breeds quite uneven results. There is no fixed racial level of culture. The lines cut both vertically and horizontally. There are as great differences, with reference to culture, education, sophistication, among Negroes as between the races. (This overlapping is probably what the new psychologists have been trying to point out with their elaborately documented intelligence measurements.) And just as these currents move down and across and intersect, so may one find an utter maze of those rationalizations of attitudes of differently placed Negro groups toward life in general, and their status in particular. But a common purpose is integrating these energies born of new conflicts, and it is not at all improbable that the culture which has both nourished and abused these strivings will, in the end, be enriched by them.

THE NEW SCENE

Harlem: The Culture Capital

James Weldon Johnson

In the history of New York, the significance of the name Harlem has changed from Dutch to Irish to Jewish to Negro. Of these changes, the last has come most swiftly. Throughout colored America, from Massachusetts to Mississippi, and across the continent to Los Angeles and Seattle, its name, which as late as fifteen years ago had scarcely been heard, now stands for the Negro metropolis. Harlem is indeed the great Mecca for the sight-seer, the pleasure-seeker, the curious, the adventurous, the enterprising, the ambitious and the talented of the whole Negro world; for the lure of it has reached down to every island of the Carib Sea and has penetrated even into Africa.

In the make-up of New York, Harlem is not merely a Negro colony or community, it is a city within a city, the greatest Negro city in the world. It is not a slum or a fringe, it is located in the heart of Manhattan and occupies one of the most beautiful and healthful sections, of the city. It is not a "quarter" of dilapidated tenements, but is made up of new-law apartments and handsome dwellings, with well-paved and well-lighted streets. It has its own churches, social and civic centers, shops, theaters and other places of amusement. And it contains more Negroes to the square mile than any other spot on earth. A stranger who rides up magnificent Seventh Avenue on a bus or in an automobile must be struck with surprise at the transformation which takes place after he crosses One Hundred and Twenty-fifth Street. Beginning there, the population suddenly darkens and he rides through twenty-five solid blocks where the passers-by, the shoppers, those sitting in restaurants, coming out of theaters, standing in doorways and looking out of windows are practically all Negroes; and then he emerges where the population as suddenly becomes white again. There is nothing just like it in any other city in the country, for there is no preparation for it; no change in the character of the houses and streets; no change, indeed, in the appearance of the people, except their color.

Negro Harlem is practically a development of the past decade, but the story behind it goes back a long way. There have always been colored people in New York. In the middle of the last century they lived in the vicinity of Lispenard, Broome and Spring Streets. When Washington

Square and lower Fifth Avenue was the center of aristocratic life, the colored people, whose chief occupation was domestic service in the homes of the rich, lived in a fringe and were scattered in nests to the south, east and west of the square. As late as the '80's the major part of the colored population lived in Sullivan, Thompson, Bleecker, Grove, Minetta Lane and adjacent streets. It is curious to note that some of these nests still persist. In a number of the blocks of Greenwich Village and Little Italy may be found small groups of Negroes who have never lived in any other section of the city. By about 1890 the center of colored population had shifted to the upper Twenties and lower Thirties west of Sixth Avenue. Ten years later another considerable shift northward had been made to West Fifty-third Street.

The West Fifty-third Street settlement deserves some special mention because it ushered in a new phase of life among colored New Yorkers. Three rather well-appointed hotels were opened in the street and they quickly became the centers of a sort of fashionable life that hitherto had not existed. On Sunday evenings these hotels served dinner to music and attracted crowds of well-dressed diners. One of these hotels, The Marshall, became famous as the headquarters of Negro talent. There gathered the actors, the musicians, the composers, the writers, the singers, dancers and vaudevillians. There one went to get a close-up of Williams and Walker, Cole and Johnson, Ernest Hogan, Will Marion Cook, Jim Europe, Aida Overton, and of others equally and less known. Paul Laurence Dunbar was frequently there whenever he was in New York. Numbers of those who love to shine by the light reflected from celebrities were always to be found. The first modern jazz band ever heard in New York, or, perhaps anywhere, was organized at The Marshall. It was a playing-singing-dancing orchestra, making the first dominant use of banjos, saxophones, clarinets and trap drums in combination, and was called The Memphis Students. Jim Europe was a member of that band, and out of it grew the famous Clef Club, of which he was the noted leader, and which for a long time monopolized the business of "entertaining" private parties and furnishing music for the new dance craze. Also in the Clef Club was "Buddy" Gilmore who originated trap drumming as it is now practised, and set hundreds of white men to juggling their sticks and doing acrobatic stunts while they manipulated a dozen other noise-making devices aside from their drums. A good many well-known white performers frequented The Marshall and for seven or eight years the place was one of the sights of New York.

The move to Fifty-third Street was the result of the opportunity to get into newer and better houses. About 1900 the move to Harlem began, and for the same reason. Harlem had been overbuilt with large, new-law apartment houses, but rapid transportation to that section was very inadequate—the Lenox Avenue Subway had not yet been built—and landlords were finding difficulty in keeping houses on the east side of the section filled. Residents along and near Seventh Avenue were fairly well served by the Eighth Avenue Elevated. A colored man, in the real estate business at this time, Philip A. Payton, approached several of these landlords with the proposition that he would fill their empty or partially empty houses with steady colored tenants. The suggestion was accepted, and one or two houses on One Hundred and Thirty-fourth Street east of Lenox Avenue were taken over. Gradually other houses were filled. The whites paid little attention to the movement until it began to spread west of Lenox Avenue; they then took steps to check it. They proposed through a financial organization, the Hudson Realty Company, to buy in all properties occupied by colored people and evict the tenants. The Negroes countered by similar methods. Payton formed the Afro-American Realty Company, a Negro corporation organized for the purpose of buying and leasing houses for occupancy by colored people. Under this counter stroke the opposition subsided for several years.

But the continually increasing pressure of colored people to the west over the Lenox Avenue dead line caused the opposition to break out again, but in a new and more menacing form. Several white men undertook to organize all the white people of the community for the purpose of inducing financial institutions not to lend money or renew mortgages on properties occupied by colored people. In this effort they had considerable success, and created a situation which has not yet been completely overcome, a situation which is one of the hardest and most unjustifiable the Negro property owner in Harlem has to contend with. The Afro-American Realty Company was now defunct, but two or three colored men of means stepped into the breach. Philip A. Payton and J. C. Thomas bought two five-story apartments, dispossessed the white tenants and put in colored. J. B. Nail bought a row of five apartments and did the same thing. St. Philip's Church bought a row of thirteen apartment houses on One Hundred and Thirty-fifth Street, running from Seventh Avenue almost to Lenox.

The situation now resolved itself into an actual contest. Negroes not only continued to occupy available apartment houses, but began to purchase private dwellings between Lenox and Seventh Avenues. Then the whole movement, in the eyes of the whites, took on the aspect of an "invasion"; they became panic-stricken and began fleeing as from a plague. The presence of one colored family in a block, no matter how well bred and orderly, was sufficient to precipitate a flight. House after house and block after block was actually deserted. It was a great demonstration of human beings running amuck. None of them stopped to reason why they were doing it or what would happen if they didn't. The banks and lending companies holding mortgages on these deserted houses were compelled to take them over. For some time they held these houses vacant, preferring to do that and carry the charges than to rent or sell them to colored people. But values dropped and continued to drop until at the outbreak of the war in Europe property in the northern part of Harlem had reached the nadir.

In the meantime the Negro colony was becoming more stable; the churches were being moved from the lower part of the city; social and civic centers were being formed; and gradually a community was being evolved. Following the outbreak of the war in Europe Negro Harlem received a new and tremendous impetus. Because of the war thousands of aliens in the United States rushed back to their native lands to join the colors and immigration practically ceased. The result was a critical shortage in labor. This shortage was rapidly increased as the United States went more and more largely into the business of furnishing munitions and supplies to the warring countries. To help meet this shortage of common labor Negroes were brought up from the South. The government itself took the first steps, following the practice in vogue in Germany of shifting labor according to the supply and demand in various parts of the country. The example of the government was promptly taken up by the big industrial concerns, which sent hundreds, perhaps thousands, of labor agents into the South who recruited Negroes by wholesale. I was in Jacksonville, Fla., for a while at that time, and I sat one day and watched the stream of migrants passing to take the train. For hours they passed steadily, carrying flimsy suit cases, new and shiny, rusty old ones, bursting at the seams, boxes and bundles and impedimenta of all sorts, including banjos, guitars, birds in cages and what not. Similar scenes were being enacted in cities and towns all over that region. The first wave of the great exodus of Negroes from the South was on. Great numbers of these migrants headed for New York or eventually got there, and naturally the majority went up into Harlem.

But the Negro population of Harlem was not swollen by migrants from the South alone; the opportunity for Negro labor exerted its pull upon the Negroes of the West Indies, and those islanders in the course of time poured into Harlem to the number of twenty-five thousand or more.

These new-comers did not have to look for work; work looked for them, and at wages of which they had never even dreamed. And here is where the unlooked for, the unprecedented, the miraculous happened. According to all preconceived notions, these Negroes suddenly earning large sums of money for the first time in their lives should have had their heads turned; they should have squandered it in the most silly and absurd manners imaginable. Later, after the United States had entered the war and even Negroes in the South were making money fast, many stories in accord with the tradition came out of that section. There was the one about the colored man who went into a general store and on hearing a phonograph for the first time promptly ordered six of them, one for each child in the house. I shall not stop to discuss whether Negroes in the South did that sort of thing or not, but I do know that those who got to New York didn't. The Negroes of Harlem, for the greater part, worked and saved their money. Nobody knew how much they had saved until congestion made expansion necessary for tenants and ownership profitable for landlords, and they began to buy property. Persons who would never be suspected of having money bought property. The Rev. W. W. Brown, pastor of the Metropolitan Baptist Church, repeatedly made "Buy Property" the text of his sermons. A large part of his congregation carried out the injunction. The church itself set an example by purchasing a magnificent brownstone church building on Seventh Avenue from a white congregation. Buying property became a fever. At the height of this activity, that is, 1920–21, it was not an uncommon thing for a colored washerwoman or cook to go into a real estate office and lay down from one thousand to five thousand dollars on a house. "Pig Foot Mary" is a character in Harlem. Everybody who knows the corner of Lenox Avenue and One Hundred and Thirty-fifth Street knows "Mary" and her stand, and has been tempted by the smell of her pigsfeet, fried chicken and hot corn, even if he has not been a customer. "Mary," whose real name is Mrs. Mary Dean, bought the five-story apartment house at the corner of Seventh Avenue and One Hundred and Thirty-seventh Street at a price of $42,000. Later she sold it to the Y. W. C. A. for dormitory purposes. The Y. W. C. A. sold it recently to Adolph Howell, a leading colored undertaker, the price given being $72,000. Often companies of a half dozen men combined to buy a house—these combinations were and still are generally made up of West Indians—and would produce five or ten thousand dollars to put through the deal.

When the buying activity began to make itself felt, the lending companies that had been holding vacant the handsome dwellings on and abutting Seventh Avenue decided to put them on the market. The values on these houses had dropped to the lowest mark possible and they were put up at astonishingly low prices. Houses that had been bought at from $15,000 to $20,000 were sold at one-third those figures. They were quickly gobbled up. The Equitable Life Assurance Company held 106 model private houses that were designed by Stanford White. They are built with courts running straight through the block and closed off by wrought-iron gates. Every one of these houses was sold within eleven months at an aggregate price of about two million dollars. To-day they are probably worth about 100 per cent more. And not only have private dwellings and similar apartments been bought but big elevator apartments have been taken over. Corporations have been organized for this purpose. Two of these, The Antillian Realty Company, composed of West Indian Negroes, and the Sphinx Securities Company, composed of American and West Indian Negroes, represent holdings amounting to approximately $750,000. Individual Negroes and companies in the South have invested in Harlem real estate. About two years ago a Negro institution of Savannah, Ga., bought a parcel for $115,000 which it sold a month or so ago at a profit of $110,000.

I am informed by John E. Nail, a successful colored real estate dealer of Harlem and a reliable authority, that the total value of property in Harlem owned and controlled by colored people would at a conservative estimate amount to more than sixty million dollars. These figures are amazing, especially when we take into account the short time in which they have been piled up. Twenty years ago Negroes were begging for the privilege of renting a flat in Harlem. Fifteen years ago barely a half dozen colored men owned real property in all Manhattan. And down to ten years ago the amount that had been acquired in Harlem was comparatively negligible. Today Negro Harlem is practically owned by Negroes.

The question naturally arises, "Are the Negroes going to be able to hold Harlem?" If they have been steadily driven northward for the past hundred years and out of less desirable sections, can they hold this choice bit of Manhattan Island? It is hardly probable that Negroes will hold Harlem indefinitely, but when they are forced out it will not be for the same reasons that forced them out of former quarters in New York City. The situation is entirely different and without precedent. When colored people do leave Harlem, their homes, their churches, their investments and their businesses, it will be because the land has bcome so valuable they can no longer afford to live on it. But the date of another move northward is very far in the future. What will Harlem be and become in the meantime? Is there danger that the Negro may lose his economic status in New York and be unable to hold his property? Will Harlem become merely a famous ghetto, or will it be a center of intellectual, cultural and economic forces exerting an influence throughout the world, especially upon Negro peoples? Will it become a point of friction between the races in New York?

I think there is less danger to the Negroes of New York of losing out economically and industrially than to the Negroes of any large city in the North. In most of the big industrial centers Negroes are engaged in gang labor. They are employed by thousands in the stockyards in Chicago, by thousands in the automobile plants in Detroit; and in those cities they are likely to be the first to be let go, and in thousands, with every business depression. In New York there is hardly such a thing as gang labor among Negroes, except among the longshoremen, and it is in the longshoremen's unions, above all others, that Negroes stand on an equal footing. Employment among Negroes in New York is highly diversified; in the main they are employed more as individuals than as non-integral parts of a gang. Furthermore, Harlem is gradually becoming more and more a self-supporting community. Negroes there are steadily branching out into new businesses and enterprises in which Negroes are employed. So the danger of great numbers of Negroes being thrown out of work at once, with a resulting economic crisis among them, is less in New York than in most of the large cities of the North to which Southern migrants have come.

These facts have an effect which goes beyond the economic and industrial situation. They have a direct bearing on the future character of Harlem and on the question as to whether Harlem will be a point of friction between the races in New York. It is true that Harlem is a Negro community, well defined and stable; anchored to its fixed homes, churches, institutions, business and amusement places; having its own working, business and professional classes. It is experiencing a constant growth of group consciousness and community feeling. Harlem is, therefore, in many respects, typically Negro. It has many unique characteristics. It has movement, color, gayety, singing, dancing, boisterous laughter and loud talk. One of its outstanding features is brass band parades. Hardly a Sunday passes but that there are several of these parades of which many are gorgeous with regalia and insignia. Almost any excuse will do—the death of an humble member of the Elks, the laying of a cornerstone, the "turning out" of the order of this or that. In many of these characteristics it is similar to the Italian colony. But withal, Harlem grows more metropolitan and more a part of New York all the while. Why is it then that its tendency is not to become a mere "quarter"?

I shall give three reasons that seem to me to be important in their order. First, the language of Harlem is not alien; it is not Italian or Yiddish; it is English. Harlem talks American, reads American, thinks American. Second, Harlem is not physically a "quarter." It is not a section cut off. It is merely a zone through which four main arteries of the city run. Third, the fact that there is little or no gang labor gives Harlem Negroes the opportunity for individual expansion and individual contacts with the life and spirit of New York. A thousand Negroes from Mississippi put to work as a gang in a Pittsburgh steel mill will for a long time remain a thousand Negroes from Mississippi. Under the conditions that prevail in New York they would all within six months become New Yorkers. The rapidity with which Negroes become good New Yorkers is one of the marvels to observers.

These three reasons form a single reason why there is small probability that Harlem will ever be a point of race friction between the races in New York. One of the principal factors in the race riot in Chicago in 1919 was the fact that at that time there were 12,000 Negroes employed in gangs in the stockyards. There was considerable race feeling in Harlem at the time of the hegira of white residents due to the "invasion," but that feeling, of course, is no more. Indeed, a number of the old white residents who didn't go or could not get away before the housing shortage struck New York are now living peacefully side by side with colored residents. In fact, in some cases white and colored tenants occupy apartments in the same house. Many white merchants still do business in thickest Harlem. On the whole, I know of no place in the country where the feeling between the races is so cordial and at the same time so matter-of-fact and taken for granted. One of the surest safeguards against an outbreak in New York such as took place in so many Northern cities in the summer of 1919 is the large proportion of Negro police on duty in Harlem.

To my mind, Harlem is more than a Negro community; it is a large scale laboratory experiment in the race problem. The statement has often been made that if Negroes were transported to the North in large numbers the race problem with all of its acuteness and with new aspects would be transferred with them. Well, 175,000 Negroes live closely together in Harlem, in the heart of New York—75,000 more than live in any Southern city—and do so without any race friction. Nor is there any unusual record of crime. I once heard a captain of the 38th Police Precinct (the Harlem precinct) say that on the whole it was the most law-abiding precinct in the city. New York guarantees its Negro citizens the fundamental rights of American citizenship and protects them in the exercise of those rights. In return the Negro loves New York and is proud of it, and contributes in his way to its greatness. He still meets with discriminations, but possessing the basic rights, he knows that these discriminations will be abolished.

I believe that the Negro's advantages and opportunities are greater in Harlem than in any other place in the country, and that Harlem will become the intellectual, the cultural and the financial center for Negroes of the United States, and will exert a vital influence upon all Negro peoples.

HOWARD: THE NATIONAL NEGRO UNIVERSITY

Kelly Miller

Howard University shares with Fisk, Atlanta and Wilberforce the proud tradition of over half a century of service in the liberal education of Negro youth. To-day, after years of painstaking advance, it shares with a dozen or more such Negro colleges the rank and standing of an institution of standard and certified collegiate grade. But just as surely as there is a need and place for each,—and for that matter more, of these institutions, just so certain is it that one of them must eventually become the conscious and recognized center of the higher life and cultural inspiration and aspiration of the race. Such by reason of its origin, location, constituency, maintenance and objective, Howard Unversity aspires to be. Largest, oldest as an avowed university in plan and pattern, national in scope and support, Howard University already has advantages that make plausible its claim to be "the Capstone of Negro Education." But with the rapid development and maturing of the race life of the Negro to-day, and the almost floodlike surge of race consciousness and purpose, the competition for primacy among Negro institutions of learning is swift and will be to the swift. The title and prestige must eventually go to that institution that incorporates most readily the progressive spirit of the new generation, best focuses the racial mind, and becomes the center radiating the special influence of leadership and enlightenment which a culturally organized people needs.

The Negro in America constitutes a community far more separate and distinct in needs, aims, and aspirations than any other racial or sectarian element of our national life. The Catholic, Jewish and Protestant denominations develop their own local, and national institutions to foster the peculiar genius and aspirations of their several communions, apart from the general educational life of the nation as a whole, in which they share on equal terms with the rest. In a much deeper sense, under the present conditions of his group life, does the Negro stand in need of local schools and colleges with a national university as a capstone devoted to racial aims and objectives. Howard University assumes the title and function of the national Negro University without egotism or vain boasting, and with the appreciation of the place and

ALAIN LOCKE

importance and special spheres of influence of other worthy institutions of learning and service in the same field. Chartered in 1867 by the Congress of the United States, it is located at the National Capital, and is supported in large part by government appropriations. The current catalogue carries an enrollment of 2,046 students of the colored race drawn from thirty-six states and eleven foreign countries. Its essential objective from the beginning has been to develop a leadership for the reclamation and uplift of the Negro race through the influence of the higher culture. Further, Howard University can modestly claim that it is the only institution of its class that maintains the full complement of standardized academic and professional departments which go to make up the normal American university. With over two thousand students in its collegiate and professional schools, it does not operate any courses below the collegiate level. This would easily duplicate the enrollment in all the other Negro institutions combined in courses of like grade and character. Advantage and opportunity confer obligation. Howard University must, therefore, by sheer force of circumstances, assume first place in the higher learning and life of the Negro peoples or fall below the level of its opportunity and popular expectation.

All Negro schools and colleges are emergencies from the same background. They grew out of the smoke and fire of the Civil War, and the patriotic missionarism of emancipation. General O. O. Howard, a well-known hero of the Civil War, was the founder and first President of this University which bears his name as well as the impress of his spirit. He was at the time Commissioner of the Freedmen's Bureau, and focussed upon the task of Negro education the patriotic, religious, and philanthropic sentiment of the American people. It might be said that the University was reared on these three pillars. The fundamental aim of the founders was to build up an enlightened leadership within the race. To do this it was necessary to refute derogatory dogmas hoary with age and tradition. An enslaved people had not been permitted to taste of the tree of knowledge, which is the tree of good and evil. This coveted tree has been zealously and jealously guarded by the flaming sword of prejudice, kept keen and bright by avarice and cupidity. It was said that the Negro could not be educated. The missionaries refuted the charge by educating him. Phyllis Wheatley, Benjamin Banneker and Frederick Douglass were looked upon as freaks of nature. Experience soon showed that Negro youth fresh from the yoke of slavery could master the white man's knowledge, so-called, in the same length of time and with comparable degree of thoroughness, as the most favored youth of the most favored race.

Nowhere in all history has education so fully vindicated its claim as the process of unlocking and releasing the higher powers and faculties of human nature. The circumstances amid which this work had its inception read like the swiftly moving scenes of a mighty drama. In track of the victorious army of the North there followed a valiant band of heroes and heroines to do battle in a worthier cause. Theirs was no carnal warfare; it was the battle against the powers of darkness entrenched in the ignorance and poverty of an imbruted race. A worthier or more heroic band has never furnished theme for sage or bard. They were sustained by an unbounded zeal amounting almost to fanaticism, and were drunk with the new wine of human enthusiasm. They gave the highest proof that the nineteenth century furnished, that the religion of the Christ was not a dead formula of barren abstract moralism, but a living vital power. The pen of the beneficiary never tires portraying the virtues of the benefactor. Their monument is builded in the hearts and hopes of a race struggling upward from ignorance to enlightenment, from incompetence to efficiency. It was in this wise that Howard University and its sister institutions were born.

Howard University assumed the name and rank of a university from the beginning. To project an institution of learning on the highest intellectual standards for a race that had not yet learned the use of letters was an astounding feat of faith. But the faith of the founders has been abundantly vindicated by the fruits of their foundation. Howard University not only assumed the name, but the several departments with range and reaches of studies which justified the title of university according to the prevailing standards of American institutions of learning. In addition to the regular collegiate courses, it carried departments of agriculture, theology, law and medicine. These have been continued practically as projected down to the present time. This institution, like all others of its class, had to begin with the primary grades of instruction, as it was intended to meet the needs of a race at the zero point of culture. But by reason of the rapid progress of the education of the Negro race at large, it soon found it expedient to eliminate the lower grades one by one, until it now operates only degree courses of a collegiate and professional character.

Howard University has thus modernized and extended its curriculum until it now has a recognized place in the sisterhood of American colleges. It is on the accredited list of the Association of Schools and Colleges of the Middle States and Maryland, which includes such nationally known institutions as Columbia, Cornell, Princeton and the University of Pennsylvania.

Howard University was chartered as a university for the education of youth in the liberal arts and sciences. At that time education was extolled chiefly in its cultural and humanitarian aspects. The stress of emphasis was laid on manhood rather than mechanism. The man was educated for his worth rather than his work. To be somebody counted for more than to do something. Produce the man, the rest will follow. The chief aim of the founders of Howard University as of other Negro institutions of like character was to develop a body of Negro men and women with disciplined faculties and liberalized powers with the hope and expectation that they would quickly assume their place as leaders of the life of the masses by virtue of the rightful claim and authority of the higher culture. There has been a great change in educational thought and opinion since that day. The older advocacy was much more complimentary to the inherent claims and dignity of humanity than the modern vocational point of view. The vocational objective of education, however, has proved the more persuasive, so that our entire educational fabric is more or less dominated by the modern bias. Howard University, along with the rest, has had to shift the basis of its plea in harmony with the newer demand. But the motive, reason, end in view remain the same. Its new objective as the old is to develop leaders for the wise guidance and direction of the masses of the Negro race. Wherever the blind lead the blind, the whole procession is headed for the inevitable ditch. For want of vision the people still perish. Howard University merely interprets the old ideal in terms of the modern day requirements. The Negro race has as yet no leisure class. There are no scholars or *literati* devoted to the pure love of learning whose ulterior aim is to influence public thought and opinion through the subtle influence of letters. By reason of the material poverty of the race every educated Negro must first make a living for himself. The necessities of a livelihood absorb a large part of his energies. He must exert his leadership in connection with his vocation. On scanning the last catalogue one might be disposed to look upon Howard University as a purely vocational school. Its departments comprise the College of Liberal Arts, the College of Education, the College of Applied Sciences, the School of Commerce and Finance, the School of Music, the School of Public Health, the School of Religion, the School of Law, the School of Medicine, the School of Dentistry and the School of Pharmacy. The vocational aim is connoted in the very captions of the departments into which the work is divided. Perhaps not a single one of those who receive the pure arts degree will devote himself to non-vocational scholarship but will enter immediately upon the study of one of the professions or upon some practical pursuit.

The last commencement program contains the list of 330 graduates, distributed as follows: Bachelor of Arts, 52; Bachelor of Science, 43; Bachelor of Science in Commerce, 9; Bachelor of Music, 6; Bachelor of Science in Architecture, 1; Bachelor of Science in Civil Engineering, 2; Bachelor of Science in Electrical Engineering, 1; Bachelor of Science in Architecture, 1; Bachelor of Theology, 4; Diplomas in Theology, 4; Master of Law, 1; Bachelor of Law, 26; Doctor of Medicine, 72; Doctor of Dentistry, 26; Pharmaceutical Chemists, 11; Master of Arts, 3; Master of Science, 2; Second Lieutenants, U. S. R. C., 34. Of the three hundred and thirty graduates who completed their courses last June, 234 were prepared to enter immediately upon their profession or practical pursuit while the other ninety-six are making ready to follow in their train. The leadership of the Negro race must be found in professions which furnish the leader a livelihood in the meantime.

The great responsibilities that devolve upon the Negro professional man and woman make it all the more imperative, however, that their preparation should be laid upon a double basis of exact knowledge and liberal culture. Howard University does not insist less now than formerly upon the cultural idea in education, but rather that this culture should reach and ramify the professional and practical vocations. The ideal of Howard University, as the writer has interpreted it through the years, is to inculcate upon the mind of Negro youth a conscious sense of manhood through the influence of the higher culture. This aroused sense of the highest human values will manifest itself in whatever mode of service the world for the time may need. The writer in this connection may be permitted to quote what he has said in another place. "Man is more than industry, trade, commerce, politics, government, science, art, literature or religion; all of which grow out of his inherent needs and necessities. The fundamental aim of education, therefore, should be manhood rather than mechanism. The ideal is not a working man, but a man working; not a business man, but a man doing business; not a school man, but a man teaching school; not a statesman, but a man handling the affairs of state; not a medicine man, but a man practicing medicine; not a clergyman, but a man devoted to the things of the soul." Only upon such a platform, the writer submits, could Howard University justify its claims as the national University of the colored race.

A university which claims to embody, express and impart the aims and aspirations of any group must necessarily be a social institution. It must assemble on its staff those who embody in their own personality the traditions, aims and aspirations of the community for which it is established. The Catholic University of America must be under the leadership and direction of Catholic sages, statesmen and scholars. The Jewish University whether in America or Palestine must derive its genius and inspiration from the elders of Israel. But here, as elsewhere, the anomaly of the Negro situation obtrudes itself. At the time of the foundation of Howard University and other institutions of its character the Negro race had to depend upon vicarious leadership, because it had not at that time produced a competent body of men in its own ranks with developed capacities for competent and efficient self-expression and wise self-direction. Then came the missionaries from the North with the love for God in their hearts and with the Bible in the right hand and the school books in the left. They regarded themselves, not as superior creatures, but as elder brothers. They voluntarily divested themselves of all superior claims and pretensions in order that they might the more effectually serve those who needed their help. They planted Howard University and projected it as the national institution for the training of leaders of the benefited race. They understood that their tenure was temporary.

The members of one group cannot furnish ideals for another, if they must needs live a life apart from those whom they would serve. The sentiment of the times has changed. Crystallized laws and customs, in sections where the Negro colleges are located, now make it impossible for the white man to identify his life and interests with the colored race, even if he desires so to do. The two races cannot ride in the same car, send their children to the same school, or attend the same church, and must perforce walk the streets apart. Under such circumstances a perfect meeting of minds is impossible. Any national Negro enterprise must derive its future leadership and guidance from within the race.

A national enterprise for any group is ordinarily supposed to derive its support from internal sources. There can be no stable equilibrium so long as the center of gravity falls outside. Interestingly enough, Howard University, almost from the beginning, has rested on the material maintenance of the Negro race, through its own contributions by way of tuition, and through governmental grants based upon the just dues of the Negro from the public treasury. Quite unfortunately, as the writer feels, general philanthropy that has done so much for other institutions has all but neglected the claims of this institution. The last report of the treasurer shows that for the fiscal year 1923–4, the students contributed in tuition and in other fees, $179,000. Congress appropriated $190,000, while donations from all other sources amounted to only $27,000. During the past two years, the Negro race has contributed $250,000 for the endowment of the Medical School to meet a like contribution from the General Education Board. And yet Howard University makes the strongest possible appeal, not merely to the self-support of the Negro himself, but for the vicarious help of American statesmanship, philanthropy and religion combined. The great objective of philanthropy in this field is to help the Negro to help himself, and to relieve the national tension around the issue of race. There is no institution in the land that is so well calculated to deal effectually with the Negro problem as a national issue as is Howard University. The right type of leadership is essential to any attempt at solution. Howard University, as we have seen, furnishes in very large part the leadership for the race.

In 1879, the President of Howard University persuaded Congress to vote a grant of $10,000 to aid Howard University because of the national character of the type of work it was doing. From that time to the present the annual congressional grants have gradually increased, until the fiscal year 1924, the allotment amounted to $365,000. The total sum appropriated during the forty-six years amounts to the magnificent sum of $3,568,815. As result the University has sent into the field already white unto harvest over six thousand graduates who are distributed over the entire range of the professional and practical callings and are scattered over the entire area wherever any considerable number of Negroes reside. Congress is challenged to isolate a like sum that has resulted in so much national service and advantage as the amount devoted to this national University of the Negro race.

But a national Negro university must be a conscious and recognized center of the higher life and cultural interests of the race. Howard University has gathered about itself more than a hundred Negro

ALAIN LOCKE

educators, who are filling its various chairs of instruction. There cannot be duplicated anywhere in the world such an aggregation of Negro educators, scholars and thinkers. With such a nucleus, Howard must become in due time the recognized center of Negro scholarship, especially for the fostering and development of those special studies of race history and of the pressing contemporary problems of race relations which are, in last analysis, the special field and functions of such an institution. There exists as yet no such center in spite of the obvious need for one. Every group, coming into cultural maturity, needs its Forum and its Acropolis. A national Negro university must shed the light of reason on the particular issues of Negro life and add the guidance of science to the tangled issues of race adjustment. A body of intellectual, moral and spiritual élite, consecrated to these ideals and co-operating in this aim, is calculated to put a new front on the whole scheme of racial life and aspiration. Under the stimulus of such a conception of its mission, Howard University, or the institution that most zealously undertakes it, will become the Mecca of ambitious Negro youth from all parts of the land and from all lands.

It is the internal urge of this service, racial and national, that more than any external pressure or urgency of educational segregation gives the Negro college of the present its truest reason for being. What is the need of Howard University, one might ask, when every first-class university in the North and West is open to any candidate qualified to meet its requirements without regard to race or color? The very fact that an institution would exclude a candidate who measures up to its intellectual, moral and financial standards, merely on the basis of race, is ample proof that it is not first class. Few institutions that are zealous to maintain good repute in the eyes of the world would have the candor to acknowledge such basis of exclusion without apology. Colored youth in increasing numbers are entering Northern institutions and are gaining distinction in both the intellectual and in the athletic arenas. Some go so far as to deprecate the existence of distinctively Negro colleges and universities, claiming that capable colored youth can find accommodation in institutions, which can furnish superior advantages and facilities to those any Negro school is likely to possess. It would be absurd for Howard University or any other Negro school to claim that it can match the material and intellectual facilities of those great educational establishments with millions of wealth and centuries of tradition. One might as well ask, or had better ask, the rationale of Jewish

Seminaries or of Methodist colleges and universities. These racial and denominational schools impart to the membership of their community something which the general educational institution is wholly unable to inculcate. But for the Negro college, Negro scholarship would decay, and Negro leadership would be wanting in effectiveness and zeal. The Negro college must furnish stimulus to hesitant Negro scholarship, garner, treasure and nourish group tradition, enlighten both races with a sense of the cultural worth and achievement of the constituency it represents, and supply the cultural guidance of the race.

The insurgence of race consciousness is indeed the most noticeable feature in the trend of modern day tendencies. With it, the place of the Negro in the general scheme of things is growing more defined. The primary need of the race is a philosophy of life, whereby hope, courage and ambition can be maintained amidst an environment which seems hostile and crushing. This philosophy must be based upon the fundamental principles of democracy and human brotherhood, yet it must reckon with those existing circumstances and conditions which would frustrate these great ideals. The Negro race must live and move and have its being amidst the difficulties and vicissitudes of the tangled issues of race adjustment. Ambitious and high-minded Negro youth must preserve the spirit of optimism and hope. Pessimism enfeebles the faculties, paralyzes the energies and sours the soul. The race must be redeemed from the fatuity of supine self-surrender and the impotency of despair. The national Negro University should supply this defensive philosophy. Every minor and suppressed group in the world looks to its central seat of learning for the emission of that kindly light by which they are to be led to the goal after which they strive. Howard University must keep the race spirit courageous and firm, and direct it in harmony with ideals of God, country and truth.

Howard University, located at the seat of government by which it is fostered and encouraged, deriving its student body from thirty-six states and eleven foreign countries, justifying its claim for patriotic and philanthropic support, appealing to all right-minded Americans for sympathy and co-operation in carrying out its great mission, is destined to become in truth and deed the National Negro University. From this unique center of advantage and opportunity its lines reach to the remotest ramification of our national domain. From this wide area it draws the picked youth of an awakening race and sends them forth to recruit the high places of racial service and leadership.

Such is the function and mission of Howard University. To this end it appeals to the interest, encouragement and support of all who believe that in the scheme of human development, the mind must quicken, stimulate, uplift and sustain the masses.

HAMPTON-TUSKEGEE: MISSIONERS
OF THE MASS

Robert R. Moton

H ampton and Tuskegee and Points North! A call like this has been sounding in every important railroad center in the South since 1915, varying according to location whether in Alabama, Georgia, Mississippi, South Carolina or Louisiana. It has been the signal for thousands of Negroes to gather their bundles, dress-suit cases and lunch boxes, and board the trains for the great industrial centers of the North—Detroit, Chicago, Akron, Pittsburgh, Newark, New York, Springfield, Cleveland and Buffalo. Some have been content to take a shorter flight and have stopped off at Birmingham, Chattanooga, Newport News and Norfolk; but all of them have been impelled by a vision, sometimes vague and dim, sometimes sharp and clear, of better wages, better living conditions and better opportunities than have been theirs on the farms and plantations of the South.

Estimates of the numbers who have joined in this migration have varied all the way from 350,000 to 1,000,000 but all have agreed that there has been a steady exodus from the country to the city, from the soil to the factory. The consequences have aroused attention both in the section from which they have come and in the section to which they have moved. The movement itself has altered conditions which they left behind and is altering the very conditions which they hoped to find. For a time the agricultural program of certain sections of the South was completely upset. In some places there was an almost complete stagnation of farming operations. Negro farm laborers left at all seasons of the year, and many a crop was left ungathered because there were no hands to take it in.

Had such a movement occurred a generation earlier the result might have been very different not alone for the Negro, but for the South whose economic system is so largely dependent upon Negro labor, and the North would have been utterly unable to absorb so great an access to its population. But two conditions operated simultaneously with this movement of the Negroes. One was the expansion of industry in the North consequent on the war, coupled with the depletion of the ranks of immigrant labor by those returning home to fight. The other was the fact that for nearly fifty years strong influences had been at work among Negroes which enabled them to adapt themselves more quickly to the change from rural to urban life and from agricultural to industrial pursuits.

This vast movement of the Negro population was the result of a wartime demand for labor in the industrial centers North and South. Negroes had long felt the restraint of restricted opportunities in the South. Individuals and small groups had all along been finding release in various sections of the North, but the great masses were compelled to remain where they were, as there was at that time no disposition to exploit the labor supplies of the South. During the same period there was a mighty influence at work below Mason and Dixon's Line enlarging the outlook of the Negro and preparing the race not only to take advantage of new opportunities but to create opportunities for themselves in the midst of surrounding conditions.

This influence was the Hampton-Tuskegee movement inaugurated by General Samuel Chapman Armstrong at Hampton, Virginia, in 1868 and expanded by his pupil, Booker T. Washington, at Tuskegee, in the years succeeding through the remarkable spread of his gospel of industry and self-reliance throughout the whole of the Negro race. In its early development it was called industrial education, but thoughtful observers have long since come to see that the work of Hampton and Tuskegee is not the training of men and women as mere units of industry, but rather the training of the individual, indeed to be self-supporting, but at the same time to be a contributing element to community life—to be conscious factors in every community for establishing the highest ideals of American life and inspiring all whom they touch to win salvation for themselves and to create by their own efforts that new and better order of things which it had been vainly hoped would come from the hands of others.

Hampton was the pioneer in this movement. Down in the Tidewater section, General Armstrong at the close of the Civil War took refugees that had gathered from the plantations of that section and began the solution of their problems by teaching them to work with their hands while they trained their minds, and developed the fundamental attributes of industry, thrift, self-reliance and self-respect. He worked, of course, with those who came to him, establishing a school to combine labor with books in the process of education; developing the head, the hand and the heart at the same time. But he did not stop there. He reached out to the homes and communities from which his students came and set up there for fathers and mothers the same standards and ideals of home surroundings and character development that he was creating for the young men and women who came to him as students. Home and community became the ultimate objectives of his labors. Boys and girls that came to him as students were impressed with the idea that their training was not merely for their individual success, but rather that they should be positive factors in improving life and conditions wherever they might locate.

Of all who came to him, the one pupil most apt to catch this vision was Booker T. Washington. Out he went from Hampton to translate his inspiration into deeds. Called to Alabama to take charge of a projected school, he immediately set himself to work out in terms of local conditions the ideas that were instilled in him at Hampton. From the very beginning he conceived of the whole South as his schoolroom and the entire Negro race as his class. The one subject which he taught was life. Arithmetic, reading, geography, history, were all interpreted in terms of the life surroundings of his students. He talked of the life they lived. Every day he put them to work creating life for themselves, building their own buildings, making their own tools, producing their own food, making their own clothes and in a hundred other ways supplying their own needs. These were the things they talked about in their classrooms. These were the problems they figured out and then he talked of conditions as they had just left them at home. He went out to visit their parents. He went into their homes, into their churches, into their school-houses; having found the better way of life himself he carried his vision to his people, inspiring them to have things better for themselves and for their children and to win those things by their own industry and worth.

Those two institutions have thus become vastly more than the conventional schools. They have their class-room work as do others, they study books, they write essays and deliver orations, but there is a character and a quality to it all that is unique. That is to say, that *was* unique, for the idea has spread abroad, and though Hampton and Tuskegee are unique exemplars of this larger conception and interpretation of education, yet the idea which they have developed has been appropriated by others. Not only those that style themselves industrial schools, but colleges also are grasping the importance of making their instruction touch life beyond the college walls, thus making their institutions centers of inspiration and elevation for that larger clientele which includes the households from which the students come and communities to which they go for service.

The influence of this gospel of larger and better living has not been without its effect upon the Negro race as a whole. These institutions have maintained specific agencies for reaching out into the body of the Negro race—farmers' conferences, educational tours, extension departments in all of their ramifications, are an essential part of the work of Hampton and Tuskegee. While the boys and girls were being taught in the class-rooms, the fathers and mothers were being reached in the field and in the home; education was carried to them in simple direct terms made plain by demonstrations, with witnesses to testify how the plan had worked with them. The effect was as inspiring as a revival.

Booker Washington made a religion out of life for his people and few indeed were those who heard one of his talks who came away without getting this kind of religion. Everywhere in the South are to be found evidences of its influence. Negroes have been buying land for a generation till to-day about one-fourth of them own their homes. This is probably not true so largely of any other racial group in America. School facilities have been improved by leaps and bounds, because these institutions have inspired Negroes to undertake the solution of their own educational problems, building their own schools if necessary, supplementing directly out of their own pockets the salaries provided by the state and adding to the school term on their own initiative if the authorized school term was not long enough.

This impulse was extended even to business. A generation ago Negroes were the consumers, other races were the producers and distributors. The idea was set afloat that Negroes could profit by catering to the needs of their own people, that such profit would operate to create larger opportunities for their own race with a corresponding benefit both to the proprietor and to his patrons. To-day Negroes are found in all lines of business with many outstanding examples of success, as well as their own share of failures. In one of the Founder's Day addresses at Tuskegee Institute, a prominent member of his own race said that Booker Washington had "changed a *crying* race into a *trying* race." This phrase epitomizes the idea behind Hampton and Tuskegee. General Armstrong gave to the Negro race its first lessons in this sort of self-reliance. Booker Washington inspired the whole race with his confidence which is now being felt in the rapid strides with which the race is advancing.

For a time the South was hesitant as to the effect of this new gospel on the Negro. It welcomed the idea of teaching the Negro to work if that was what was meant by the "dignity of labor"—but for a time there was some apprehension lest behind this idea there should be a subtle force inspiring Negroes to rebel against unsatisfactory conditions and to resist the domination of the Anglo-Saxon who was in control of economic as well as political life in this section. But the years have proved these suspicions unfounded. The South has seen a great change come over the Negro. Education has been found to be profitable not only for the black man but for the white man too. To-day the South is more zealous for the improvement of educational conditions for both races than any other section of our country. What was heralded as good for the Negro has been accepted as equally good for white people. As "industrial education" it was accepted for the solution of Negro problems: as "vocational education" it has been adopted by state and federal governments as the solution of economic and social problems for both races. On this point Dr. Washington very early found a platform where both races could stand side by side with respect for themselves and for each other. Almost in spite of himself he became through this means a messenger of good will to both races and to both sections.

Through Hampton Institute large-minded men and women of the North expressed their interest in the Negro. Through Tuskegee Institute forward-looking men and women of the South found a way for renewing contacts with the Negro race. When Hollis Burke Frissell appeared on the scene at Hampton, the time was ripe for these three elements to join hands in inaugurating a new program for race relations in the South. To-day we hear much talk of inter-racial co-operation, but it began years ago. What was then the faith of a few has become the conviction of many. The confidence sown then is bringing forth a harvest of good-will now, and the field is being enlarged continually.

A great many unexpected results came out of the war. One of the earliest and most encouraging was the opening up of industrial opportunities for the Negro in the North. Then came the migration. In the wake of this movement many problems developed in both the North and the South. It became necessary to reconstruct the agricultural program of the South. The North was introduced to a new social program. A new bond of sympathy has been established between the two sections. What was considered a sectional problem has become a national problem. What has been considered a racial problem is coming more and more to be recognized as a purely human problem. These problems, however, are not as acute as they might have been because of the influence of Hampton and Tuskegee and of the other institutions like Howard, Virginia Union, Atlanta, Fisk, Morehouse, Clark and Biddle which have been exerting the same influence on the Negro race.

Negroes who went North were not all raw, unskilled laborers. Out of the industrial schools had come Negroes trained for the requirements of industry—blacksmiths, carpenters, brickmasons, plumbers, steam-fitters, auto-mechanics. When the opportunity came these men were ready for the test to which they were to be subjected. Though the great bulk of those who migrated had had no specific training in these lines, there were enough trained at Tuskegee and Hampton, and other industrial schools as well as in industrial plants in the South to make it feasible for Northern manufacturers to experiment with Negro mechanics. In all the industrial centers of the North and South graduates of these schools can be found, and it is a source of satisfaction that they have so far justified the experiment as to remove practically all doubt as to their availability for skilled work in whatever lines are open to them.

These laborers did not go alone, however, so broad was the current of migration that it carried along with it professional men and leaders in business and other lines of activity, trained in the schools of the South. Lawyers, doctors, dentists found it desirable to change their location to the new centers to which their clients had migrated. Even ministers, finding their congregations depleted by the movement, found it possible in not a few instances to establish churches in the North whose memberships were in a large measure composed of their former parishioners in the South.

The initial effect of this on the North was to create a housing problem. Residential sections inhabited formerly by whites were invaded by Negroes under the pressure of expanding population. One reaction to this was the riots in Washington, Chicago and Omaha. Not every city, however, witnessed such violent eruption; Springfield, Cleveland, Akron, Detroit, proceeded to absorb the influx of Negro population without apparent friction. This was nowhere better done than in New York City. Already densely populated, the metropolitan center proceeded to readjustments that have given it the largest Negro population of any city in the country and probably the world. The coming of this excess population presented to the real estate dealers an opportunity for increased profits of which they proceeded immediately to take advantage. Whole blocks of tenements and apartment houses were bought by speculators and turned over to Negro tenants, the former white occupants moving farther uptown. By accommodating themselves to limited quarters, many Negro families found comfortable residence in well-appointed modern livings, and that, too, without the annoyance or embarrassment of legal residence restrictions.

Harlem is recognized as the Negro section of New York without any requirement of law. Here Negroes have their own theaters, their own newspaper establishments, restaurants, stores, barber shops, offices, and all the other accessories and necessities of community life. White merchants still accommodate the bulk of the trade, and it is interesting to observe that groceries and meat markets have made it a point to cater to the tastes and habits that the Negro population have brought from the South. Restaurants serve those dishes to which Negroes have become accustomed, and the markets put in large supplies of these staple products, many of them specially imported from the Southern States.

In New York, as in other cities, there was no great difficulty for the newcomer to find work, but in this city a large proportion of these migrants went into personal service, whereas in other cities like Pittsburgh, Cleveland, Detroit, Youngstown, employment was found in the industries such as steel mills, automobile factories, and in Chicago the packing plants.

The important thing to observe in all this is that contrary to predictions and many expectations the Negro has found a real place for himself in the North, and has been able with surprising facility to adapt himself to the new conditions. In truth, it is a matter of pride to Negroes themselves to take on the manners and follow the customs that are characteristic of the North. It is surprising, also, to note the cordial and genuinely sympathetic attitude taken towards these newcomers by the older residents, colored and white, not the welfare workers merely, but many of the leading citizens. Newcomers are not infrequently carefully admonished by those who have preceded them as to their dress, manners and habits of speech lest they be ridiculed as having recently come from some Southern plantation.

Much of the easy solution of the housing problem in Northern cities, notably in Harlem, is due to the enterprise of Negro real estate men

ALAIN LOCKE

who have taken the initiative in finding homes for their people. In one city, Springfield, Massachusetts, it is a church that has taken the lead in solving this problem. In many places the Urban League, with other welfare movements, has taken the lead.

New lines of business have opened up with Negro proprietors where formerly no such business existed. It has very often been a surprise to Northern Negroes to witness the energy with which their brethren from the South have taken the leadership in community enterprise.

In the majority of cases the migrants have been quick to take advantage of the improved educational facilities of the North, and have sometimes precipitated the question of segregated schools, itself a tribute to the Negro's eager desire for education. In time this must raise the question of an educational program which will enable the Negro youth to prepare themselves in advance for these new places in industry that are being opened to them. So long as the trade unions exclude Negroes from the opportunities of apprenticeship, it will be necessary for Negro youth to look elsewhere for their training. Some of these are already returning South to the industrial schools there, but these schools find it impossible even now to adequately accommodate their local applicants.

The factor in all this is the leadership of Negro men and women who have received their training in most cases in schools in the South, such as Hampton, Tuskegee, Howard, Fisk, Atlanta, Morehouse, Wiley; these will be found in the professions, in business, in social work, helping their people to take advantage of new opportunities and adjust themselves to new and sometimes hostile conditions.

These are but some of the indications that the leaven of Hampton and Tuskegee is working with increased force throughout the Negro race. It is a matter of common observation within the race that men and women who have been trained in these schools enter into community life with a zeal and enthusiasm which are characteristic. They ally themselves with the churches, literary societies, welfare movements, fraternal organizations and other activities that have for their object the improvement of the Negro race. They are demonstrating that Negroes can succeed where others have succeeded, that Negroes are capable of the same development which other races have manifested when given the same opportunity. In the pursuit of these aims they are developing a race consciousness—a pride, that is really inspiring. For the good name of their people they want to prove themselves worthy of every opportunity that is open to them and have every privilege that is their due as American citizens, and in proportion as they prove themselves capable they win the confidence and respect of the people of both races, and are counted as an asset to the industry, the organization and community with which they are identified. After all, the strongest recommendation that Hampton and Tuskegee have is the character and service of the men and women whom they have trained for the leadership of their people. It not infrequently happens that men and women have caught this same spirit and outlook in other schools—for there are other schools doing the same thing for their students—it generally happens that there is a most happy and effective co-operation between the men and women from all these schools for the highest development of their communities.

Durham: Capital of the Black Middle Class

E. Franklin Frazier

Durham offers none of the color and creative life we find among Negroes in New York City. It is a city of fine homes, exquisite churches, and middle class respectability. It is not the place where men write and dream; but a place where black men calculate and work. No longer can men say that the Negro is lazy and shiftless and a consumer. He has gone to work. He is a producer. He is respectable. He has a middle class.

Many who have been interested in the Negro's progress, and especially his critics, have bemoaned the fact that the Negro has had no middle class. Negro society has been divided chiefly into the professional and the working classes. The working class has not consisted of skilled artisans but unskilled laborers and domestic servants. While the professional class has imitated many of the traits of the white middle class, they have regarded themselves as essentially an aristocracy. The working classes have been execrated by both white and colored for their love of pleasure. So in neither of these classes have the Negroes developed a middle class economic outlook. We can discount the fanciful schemes for getting rich and the activities of the swindler. Even small retail stores operated by Negroes are conspicuously absent from Negro communities. But the Negro is at last developing a middle class, and its main center is in Durham. As we read the lives of the men in Durham who have established the enterprises there, we find stories parallelling the most amazing accounts of the building of American fortunes. We find them beginning their careers without much formal education and practising the old-fashioned virtues of the old middle class. Their lives are as free from the Negro's native love of leisure and enjoyment of life as Franklin's life. Hard work was their rule. We see them assuming the rôle of promoter and organizer. And finally we find them in the rôle of the modern business man. Consequently, we have in Durham to-day the outstanding group of colored capitalists who have entered the second generation of business enterprise. This is significant, as few Negro enterprises have survived the personal direction and energy of the founders. Moreover, these men have mastered the technique of modern business and acquired the spirit of modern enterprise.

When we trace the history of this development we must begin with the late John Merrick. He was born a slave in 1859 in Sampson County, North Carolina. His early years were spent at work in a brickyard in Chapel Hill. He learned to read and write from the Bible. As he was compelled to support his mother and younger brother, he could not attend school. Although he could not share in the educational advantages which Northern missionaries were offering Negroes during the Reconstruction, he helped as a brickmason to build one of their leading schools, Shaw University in Raleigh. Next we find Mr. Merrick a bootblack and later a barber in the same shop. Full of energy and enterprise, he set out with his wife to work in a new barber shop in Durham, where he was to make his distinguished career. It is a significant fact that Mr. Merrick came to Durham at the time when white men were beginning to devote themselves to the exploitation of the wealth of the South. Of more fundamental influence upon them was the contact with the leading business men such as the Dukes, who were his customers. His biographer, T. McCantsAndrews, remarks: "Mr. Merrick's contact with the leading business men of Durham had as much to do with his success as his own personal gifts." We soon find Mr. Merrick the sole proprietor of the barber shop in which he worked and the owner of his home. The story of the organization and the development of the Royal Knights of King David shows that Mr. Merrick possessed the organizing ability and the spirit of the promoter. When an itinerant Baptist preacher from Georgia offered to sell the ritualistic rights to a group of Durham Negroes, Mr. Merrick was chief among those to buy the entire order. Nor was he satisfied with the usual fraternal features, for he soon made it known that he would not have anything to do with it if it were not a business proposition. Merrick declared: "Well, I ain't no society man." By shrewd advertisement of the payment of death dues the order grew. A few years later, Mr. William Pearson, one of the leading men in the present Durham group, became the guiding spirit in the order. When he took charge, the collections amounted to fourteen dollars a month. Under his skill and management, the order, which is essentially an insurance company, has grown until it numbers 21,000 members in eight states.

We come now to the greatest achievement of the Durham group and no doubt the greatest monument to Negroes' business enterprise in America—the North Carolina Mutual Life Insurance Company. The first organization of this company in 1898 consisted of seven men who paid in fifty dollars each to meet immediate expenses. At first the enterprise did not flourish and some became discouraged. It was then that Mr. Merrick and Dr. Moore bought in the interests of the others and, with the present president, Mr. Spaulding, brought the company to its present development. Space in Dr. Moore's office was rented for the work of the company, which was then known as the North Carolina Mutual and Provident Association. Mr. Merrick took charge of the financial direction; Dr. Moore became medical examiner; and Mr. Spaulding, promoter. The payment of the first death claim of forty dollars caused such a crisis that the promoters had to call a meeting and pay part of the sum from their own pockets. This was heralded abroad. By 1905 it was able to pay salaries after erecting an $8,000 office building in 1904. At this time another man, Mr. John Avery, became associated with the company. He is another example of those Americans who have begun their careers as poor farm boys and in a generation found themselves in managerial chairs of million dollar enterprises. Mr. Avery is now the secretary of this company, having an annual income of over two million dollars.

The growth of the company has been continuous and well founded. It has grown from a collection of $840 in 1899 to over $5,000 a day. It is now operating in eleven states and the District of Columbia, and has over 1,500 employees. In 1914 the company began issuing ordinary policies based upon the American Experience Table of Mortality. In 1919 it became mutualized. To-day it has $42,000,000 of insurance in force and assets amounting to over $2,000,000. The company's office building is one of the ornaments of Durham's business district. In this building there is another enterprise of this group—the Mechanics and Farmers Bank, established in 1908. It handles the bulk of the business of the insurance company and has deposits amounting to $612,700. Its resources amount to $800,000. In 1920 this institution saved more than 500 homes and farms being bought by Negroes by lending the purchasers over $200,000. A branch has been established in Raleigh.

True to the spirit and habits of modern business men, these men have undertaken other forms of enterprises wherever an opportunity to promote some form of productive enterprise appeared. We can count among their projects two drug stores and a real estate firm. A venture into industrial exploitation was the only unsuccessful enterprise of these men. The textile mill which they organized in 1914 was discontinued a year later, fortunately, without loss, because of the lack of technical assistance and the European war. One of the more recent undertakings of this group is the Bankers Fire Insurance Company, which was organized in 1920. This company is now operating in five states and the District of Columbia. After the merger with another concern, this company had over $200,000 in paid in capital. Its strength was demonstrated in 1922 when it paid out $38,000 in the fire in New Bern. The assets of this company amount to $350,000.

The latest project to locate in this prolific center of Negro enterprise is the National Negro Finance Corporation with Dr. Moton as president and Mr. C. C. Spaulding as vice-president. Its purpose is to furnish working capital for individuals, firms and corporations. This corporation hopes by this means to foster the financial and commercial development of Negroes. It is co-operating with the National Negro Business League. As this enterprise was only begun in 1924, it is too soon to estimate its contribution to the development of the middle class economic outlook among Negroes, but it promises a new era in the development of Negro business enterprise.

In interpreting the advent of the new middle class in Negro life, it will be interesting to cast a glance at the educational influences responsible. The men responsible for this phenomenal development in Negro business did not in the majority of instances come up from the uneducated ranks. In the case of Mr. Merrick, we have, it is true, the same story of most Americans who without education have built fortunes in the last century. But Mr. Spaulding was more fortunate. He had a high school education. Probably a more important part of his education for business was his experience as manager of a grocery store. Many have brought the charge against the so-called higher education that it was impractical and did not prepare Negroes for life, for practical success. Yet the promoters of these concerns were for the most part men who had received education in the schools of higher education. Avery, Pearson, and Moore were all from such schools. A factor that must not be overlooked in considering the preparation of the Negro for economic activities, is that Negroes scarcely ever have an opportunity for apprenticeship in business concerns, which is the most valuable form of business education. Consequently it was necessary for men with a larger education who understood the mechanism of credit to establish such businesses as we are considering. They had acquired the true spirit of the modern promoter and a knowledge of his methods. Young Negroes leaving colleges to-day who would ordinarily enter some business institution and work their way up, go to schools to acquire business technique. When a young Negro says he is going into business, he is usually one who has acquired a college education and intends after a business course to get a managerial position. He has little faith in the acquisition of wealth by thrift and the sweat of his brow. Thus we see the colored middle class growing not out of shopkeepers, but from men who have a larger outlook.

With the establishment of a number of Negro enterprises, however, it will be possible for some to find education by apprenticeship. Even here most of them are men of broad education such as will give them an appreciation and understanding of the business. The Durham businesses have begun their second generation. Mr. Edward Merrick, the son of the most distinguished member of the pioneer group, is the treasurer of the insurance company. He came to the work with a good education and learned the business from the bottom. He entered the business just as the second generation in white businesses enter their fathers' business. This younger generation is building upon the firm foundation of the work of the first generation. They are not dreamers attempting to create Negro business out of nothing. It is well to mention here the recent failure in Atlanta. The attempt to establish big business there began in an enterprise—the Standard Life—that was sound in principle. The failure came when the promoters resorted to the practices of the magician and the schemes of speculators. Although the Atlanta group, especially the young men, did not have the business experience of the Durham group, the failure was not due to the young men with technical training but to the older men.

These younger men are truly modern business men. They have adopted the technique of modern business and are saturated with the psychology of the capitalist class. They work hard, not because of necessity, but to expand their businesses and invade new fields. They have the same outlook on life as the middle class everywhere. They support the same theories of government and morality. They have little sympathy with waste of time. Their pleasures are the pleasures of the tired business man who does not know how to enjoy life. They are distinguished laymen in the churches. They endow charities and schools. Middle class respectability is their ideal. Above all they want progress. Like modern business men who have one economy for business and one for private consumption, they maintain fine homes and expensive cars. They spend their vacations in the same manner as the whites at Newport.

In this account of the rise of the black middle class, we have said nothing of its relation to the white world. The founders of these enterprises grew up with the exploitation of the New South. Had it not been for the bar of color some of them would have been counted among the most conspicuous of the new industrial and commercial classes in the South. They were restricted in the field of their activities. Yet they are as typical of the New South as any white business man. Their outlook is the same. John Merrick in a letter commenting on the Wilmington riots enunciated views on government held by the middle class everywhere. Have the men of the white South recognized these brothers under the skin? Yes. They show respect for their achievements. They have been friendly to their enterprises. This is perhaps due to two causes: namely, the lack to a large extent of the savage race prejudice of the lower South and the absence of serious competition. White men have recognized these men as the supporters of property rights. They know these men would no more vote for Debs than they. Yet, there are still Jim Crow cars in North Carolina, and the Negro is denied civil and political rights.

Durham is promise of a transformed Negro. The Negro has been a strange mixture of the peasant and the gentleman in his outlook on life. Because of the Negro's love of leisure and sensuous enjoyment, men have called him lazy and immoral. Because he lacks calculation, white folk have called him shiftless. But two hundred and fifty years of enforced labor, with no incentive in its just rewards, more than any inherent traits, explain why the Negro has for so long been concerned chiefly with consumption rather than production. Peasant virtues are middle-class faults. And so are the gentleman's; and the Negro has come by these in curious but inevitable ways. Some he has absorbed from the master-class of the South that he served and knew so intimately; the rest has come from his artistic nature. The drab way of life that seeks ever to work and pile up wealth and finds its enjoyment in spasmodic intoxications of pleasure has not been the way of the Negro. His desire for color and form has been the cause of mockery. His desire to work for only enough to supply his wants is only the ideal that has motivated economic activities in former ages. Moreover, love of leisure and interest in consumption are aristocratic virtues. But to-day, the Negro has his middle class, and with it his middle-class psychology. More and more certain elements of the race are absorbing the typical spirit and push of modern industrialism in America; in the composite portrait of the New Negro must be put the sharp and forceful features of the Negro man of business. Through his effort and success, the Negro is becoming an integral part of the business life of America, and is sharing particularly in the economic development of the New South, which is perhaps the outstanding economic consequence of the World War on America.

Gift of the Black Tropics

W. A. Domingo

A lmost unobserved, America plays her usual rôle in the meeting, mixing and welding of the colored peoples of the earth. A dusky tribe of destiny seekers, these brown and black and yellow folk, eyes filled with visions of an alien heritage—palm-fringed seashores, murmuring streams, luxuriant hills and vales—have made an epical march from the far corners of the earth to the Port of New York and America. They bring the gift of the black tropics to America and to their kinsmen. With them come vestiges of a quaint folk life, other social traditions, and as for the first time in their lives, colored people of Spanish, French, Dutch, Arabian, Danish, Portuguese, British and native African ancestry meet and move together, there comes into Negro life the stir and leavening that is uniquely American. Despite his inconsiderable numbers, the black foreigner is a considerable factor and figure. It is not merely his picturesqueness that he brings, his lean, sun-burnt features, quaint manners and speech, his tropical incongruities, these as with all folkways rub off in less than a generation—it is his spirit that counts and has counted in the interplay of his life with the native population.

According to the census for 1920 there were in the United States 73,803 foreign-born Negroes; of that number 36,613, or approximately 50 per cent, lived in New York City, 28,184 of them in the Borough of Manhattan. They formed slightly less than 20 per cent of the total Negro population of New York.

Here they have their first contact with each other, with large numbers of American Negroes, and with the American brand of race prejudice. Divided by tradition, culture, historical background and group perspective, these diverse peoples are gradually hammered into a loose unit by the impersonal force of congested residential segregation. Unlike others of the foreign-born, black immigrants find it impossible to segregate themselves into colonies; too dark of complexion to pose as Cubans or some other Negroid but alien-tongued foreigners, they are inevitably swallowed up in black Harlem. Their situation requires an adjustment unlike that of any other class of the immigrant population; and but for the assistance of their kinsfolk they would be capsized almost on the very shores of their haven.

From 1920 to 1923 the foreign-born Negro population of the United States was increased nearly 40 per cent through the entry of 30,849 Africans (black). In 1921 the high-water mark of 9,873 was registered. This increase was not permanent, for in 1923 there was an exit of 1,525 against an entry of 7,554. If the 20 per cent that left that year is an index of the proportion leaving annually, it is safe to estimate a net increase of about 24,000 between 1920 and 1923. If the newcomers are distributed throughout the country in the same proportion as their predecessors, the present foreign-born Negro population of Harlem is about 35,000. These people are, therefore, a formidable minority whose presence cannot be ignored or discounted. It is this large body of foreign-born who contribute those qualities that make New York so unlike Pittsburgh, Washington, Chicago and other cities with large aggregations of American Negroes.

The largest number comes from the British West Indies and are attracted to America mainly by economic reasons: though considerable numbers of the younger generation come for the purposes of education. The next largest group consists of Spanish-speaking Negroes from Latin America. Distinct because of their language, and sufficiently numerous to maintain themselves as a cultural unit, the Spanish element has but little contact with the English-speaking majority. For the most part they keep to themselves and follow in the main certain definite occupational lines. A smaller group, French-speaking, have emigrated from Haiti and the French West Indies. There are also a few Africans, a batch of voluntary pilgrims over the old track of the slave-traders.

Among the English-speaking West Indian population of Harlem are some 8,000 natives of the American Virgin Islands. A considerable part of these people were forced to migrate to the mainland as a consequence of the operation of the Volstead Act which destroyed the lucrative rum industry and helped to reduce the number of foreign vessels that used to call at the former free port of Charlotte Amelia for various stores. Despite their long Danish connection these people are culturally and linguistically English, rather than Danish. Unlike the British Negroes in New York, the Virgin Islanders take an intelligent and aggressive interest in the affairs of their former home, and are organized to co-operate with their brothers there who are valiantly struggling to substitute civil government for the present naval administration of the islands.

To the average American Negro, all English-speaking black foreigners are West Indians, and by that is usually meant British subjects. There is a general assumption that there is everything in common among West Indians, though nothing can be further from the truth. West Indians regard themselves as Antiguans or Jamaicans as the case might be, and a glance at the map will quickly reveal the physical obstacles that militate against homogeneity of population; separations of many sorts, geographical, political and cultural tend everywhere to make and crystallize local characteristics.

This undiscriminating attitude on the part of native Negroes, as well as the friction generated from contact between the two groups, has created an artificial and defensive unity among the islanders which reveals itself in an instinctive closing of their ranks when attacked by outsiders; but among themselves organization along insular lines is the general rule. Their social grouping, however, does not follow insular precedents. Social gradation is determined in the islands by family connections, education, wealth and position. As each island is a complete society in itself, Negroes occupy from the lowliest to the most exalted positions. The barrier separating the colored aristocrat from the laboring class of the same color is as difficult to surmount as a similar barrier between Englishmen. Most of the islanders in New York are from the middle, artisan and laboring classes. Arriving in a country whose every influence is calculated to democratize their race and destroy the distinctions they had been accustomed to, even those West Indians whose stations in life have been of the lowest soon lose whatever servility they brought with them. In its place they substitute all of the self-assertiveness of the classes they formerly paid deference to.

West Indians have been coming to the United States for over a century. The part they have played in Negro progress is conceded to be important. As early as 1827 a Jamaican, John Brown Russwurm, one of the founders of Liberia, was the first colored man to be graduated from an American college and to publish a newspaper in this country; sixteen years later his fellow countryman, Peter Ogden, organized in New York City the first Odd-Fellows Lodge for Negroes. Prior to the Civil War, West Indian contribution to American Negro life was so great that Dr. W. E. B. DuBois, in his *Souls of Black Folk*, credits them with main responsibility for the manhood program presented by the race in the early decades of the last century. Indicative of their tendency to blaze new paths is the achievement of John W. A. Shaw of Antigua who, in the early '90's of the last century, passed the civil service tests and became deputy commissioner of taxes for the County of Queens.

It is probably not realized, indeed, to what extent West Indian Negroes have contributed to the wealth, power and prestige of the United States. Major-General Goethals, chief engineer and builder of the Panama Canal, has testified in glowing language to the fact that when all other labor was tried and failed it was the black men of the Caribbean whose intelligence, skill, muscle and endurance made the union of the Pacific and the Atlantic a reality.

Coming to the United States from countries in which they had experienced no legalized social or occupational disabilities, West Indians very naturally have found it difficult to adapt themselves to the tasks that are, by custom, reserved for Negroes in the North. Skilled at various trades and having a contempt for body service and menial work, many of the immigrants apply for positions that the average American Negro has been schooled to regard as restricted to white men only, with the result that through their persistence and doggedness in fighting white labor, West Indians have in many cases been pioneers and shock troops to open a way for Negroes into new fields of employment.

This freedom from spiritual inertia characterizes the women no less than the men, for it is largely through them that the occupational field has been broadened for colored women in New York. By their determination, sometimes reinforced by a dexterous use of their hatpins, these women have made it possible for members of their race to enter the needle trades freely.

It is safe to say that West Indian representation in the skilled trades is relatively large; this is also true of the professions, especially medicine and dentistry. Like the Jew, they are forever launching out in business, and such retail businesses as are in the hands of Negroes in Harlem are largely in the control of the foreign-born. While American Negroes predominate in forms of business like barber shops and pool rooms in which there is no competition from white men, West Indians turn their efforts almost invariably to fields like grocery stores, tailor shops, jewelry stores and fruit vending in which they meet the fiercest kind of competition. In some of these fields they are the pioneers or the only surviving competitors of white business concerns. In more ambitious business enterprises like real estate and insurance they are relatively numerous. The only Casino and moving picture theatre operated by Negroes in Harlem is in the hands of a native of one of the small islands.

On Seventh Avenue a West Indian woman conducts a millinery store that would be a credit to Fifth Avenue.

The analogy between the West Indian and the Jew may be carried farther; they are both ambitious, eager for education, willing to engage in business, argumentative, aggressive and possessed of great proselytizing zeal for any cause they espouse. West Indians are great contenders for their rights and because of their respect for law are inclined to be litigious. In addition, they are, as a whole, home-loving, hard-working and frugal. Like their English exemplars they are fond of sport, lack a sense of humor (yet the greatest black comedian of America, Bert Williams, was from the Bahamas) and are very serious and intense in their attitude toward life. They save their earnings and are mindful of their folk in the homeland, as the volume of business of the Money Order and Postal Savings Departments of College Station Post Office will attest.

Ten years ago it was possible to distinguish the West Indian in Harlem, especially during the summer months. Accustomed to wearing cool, light-colored garments in the tropics, he would stroll along Lenox Avenue on a hot day resplendent in white shoes and flannel pants, the butt of many a jest from his American brothers who, to-day, have adopted the styles that they formerly derided. This trait of non-conformity manifested by the foreign-born has irritated American Negroes, who resent the implied self-sufficiency, and as a result there is a considerable amount of prejudice against West Indians. It is claimed that they are proud and arrogant; that they think themselves superior to the natives. And although educated Negroes of New York are loudest in publicly decrying the hostility between the two groups, it is nevertheless true that feelings against West Indians is strongest among members of that class. This is explainable on the ground of professional jealousy and competition for leadership. As the islanders press forward and upward they meet the same kind of opposition from the native Negro that the Jew and other ambitious white aliens receive from white Americans. Naturalized West Indians have found from experience that American Negroes are reluctant to concede them the right to political leadership even when qualified intellectually. Unlike their American brothers, the islanders are free from those traditions that bind them to any party and, as a consequence, are independent to the point of being radical. Indeed, it is they who largely compose the few political and economic radicals in Harlem; without them the genuinely radical movement among New York Negroes would be unworthy of attention.

There is a diametrical difference between American and West Indian Negroes in their worship. While large sections of the former are inclined to indulge in displays of emotionalism that border on hysteria, the latter, in their Wesleyan Methodist and Baptist churches maintain in the face of the assumption that people from the tropics are necessarily emotional, all the punctilious emotional restraint characteristic of their English background. In religious radicalism the foreign-born are again pioneers and propagandists. The only modernist church among the thousands of Negroes in New York (and perhaps the country) is led by a West Indian, Rev. E. Ethelred Brown, an ordained Unitarian minister, and is largely supported by his fellow islanders.

In facing the problem of race prejudice, foreign-born Negroes, and West Indians in particular, are forced to undergo considerable adjustment. Forming a racial majority in their own countries and not being accustomed to discrimination expressly felt as racial, they rebel against the "color line" as they find it in America. For while color and caste lines tend to converge in the islands, it is nevertheless true that because of the ratio of population, historical background and traditions of rebellions before and since their emancipation, West Indians of color do not have their activities, social, occupational and otherwise, determined by their race. Color plays a part but it is not the prime determinant of advancement; hence, the deep feeling of resentment when the "color line," legal or customary, is met and found to be a barrier to individual progress. For this reason the West Indian has thrown himself whole-heartedly into the fight against lynching, discrimination and the other disabilities from which Negroes in America suffer.

It must be remembered that the foreign-born black men and women, more so even than other groups of immigrants, are the hardiest and most venturesome of their folk. They were dissatisfied at home, and it is to be expected that they would not be altogether satisfied with limitation of opportunity here when they have staked so much to gain enlargement of opportunity. They do not suffer from the local anesthesia of custom and pride which makes otherwise intolerable situations bearable for the home-staying majorities.

Just as the West Indian has been a sort of leaven in the American loaf, so the American Negro is beginning to play a reciprocal rôle in the life of the foreign Negro communities, as for instance, the recent championing of the rights of Haiti and Liberia and the Virgin Islands, as well as the growing resentment at the treatment of natives in the

African colonial dependencies. This world-wide reaction of the darker races to their common as well as local grievances is one of the most significant facts of recent development. Exchange of views and sympathy, extension and co-operation of race organizations beyond American boundaries, principally in terms of economic and educational projects, but also to a limited extent in political affairs, are bound to develop on a considerable scale in the near future. Formerly, ties have been almost solely through the medium of church missionary enterprises.

It has been asserted that the movement headed by the most-advertised of all West Indians, Marcus Garvey, absentee "president" of the continent of Africa, represents the attempt of West Indian peasants to solve the American race problem. This is no more true than it would be to say that the editorial attitude of *The Crisis* during the war reflected the spirit of American Negroes respecting their grievances or that the late Booker T. Washington successfully delimited the educational aspirations of his people. The support given Garvey by a certain type of his countrymen is partly explained by their group reaction to attacks made upon him because of his nationality. On the other hand, the earliest and most persistent exposures of Garvey's multitudinous schemes were initiated by West Indians in New York like Cyril Briggs and the writer.

Prejudice against West Indians is in direct ratio to their number; hence its strength in New York where they are heavily concentrated. It is not unlike the hostility between Englishmen and Americans of the same racial stock. It is to be expected that the feeling will always be more or less present between the immigrant and the native born. However it does not extend to the children of the two groups, as they are subject to the same environment and develop identity of speech and psychology. Then, too, there has been an appreciable amount of intermarriage, especially between foreign-born men and native women. Not to be ignored is the fact that congestion in Harlem has forced both groups to be less discriminating in accepting lodgers, thus making for reconciling contacts.

The outstanding contribution of West Indians to American Negro life is the insistent assertion of their manhood in an environment that demands too much servility and unprotesting acquiescence from men of African blood. This unwillingness to conform and be standardized, to accept tamely an inferior status and abdicate their humanity, finds an open expression in the activities of the foreign-born Negro in America.

Their dominant characteristic is that of blazing new paths, breaking the bonds that would fetter the feet of a virile people—a spirit eloquently expressed in the defiant lines of the Jamaican poet, Claude McKay:

> *Like men we'll face the murderous, cowardly pack,*
> *Pressed to the wall, dying, but fighting back.*

THE NEGRO AND THE AMERICAN TRADITION

The Negro's Americanism

Melville J. Herskovits

Glimpses of the whirring cycle of life in Harlem leave the visitor bewildered at its complexity. There is constantly before one the tempting invitation to compare and contrast the life there with that of other communities one has had the opportunity of observing. Should I not find there, if anywhere, the anomalous cultural position of the Negro, of which I had heard so much? Should I not be able to discover there his ability, of which we are so often told, to produce unique cultural traits, which might be added to the prevailing white culture, and, as well, to note his equally well-advertised inability to grasp the complex civilization of which he constitutes a part?

And so I went, and what I found was churches and schools, club houses and lodge meeting-places, the library and the newspaper offices and the Y. M. C. A. and busy One Hundred and Thirty-fifth Street and the hospitals and the social service agencies. I met persons who were lawyers and doctors and editors and writers, who were chauffeurs and peddlers and longshoremen and real estate brokers and capitalists, teachers and nurses and students and waiters and cooks. And all Negroes. Cabarets and theaters, drug stores and restaurants just like those everywhere else. And finally, after a time, it occurred to me that what I was seeing was a community just like any other American community. The same pattern, only a different shade!

Where, then, is the "peculiar" community of which I had heard so much? To what extent, if any, has the Negro genius developed a culture peculiar to it in America? I did not find it in the great teeming center of Negro life in Harlem, where, if anywhere, it should be found. May it not then be true that the Negro has become acculturated to the prevailing white culture and has developed the patterns of culture typical of American life?

Let us first view the matter historically. In the days after the liberation of the Negroes from slavery, what was more natural than that they should strive to maintain, as nearly as possible, the standards set up by those whom they had been taught to look up to as arbiters—the white group? And we see, on their part, a strong conscious effort to do just this. They went into business and tried to make money as their white fellows did. They already had adopted the white forms of religious faith and practice, and now they began to borrow other types of organization. Schools sprang up in which they might learn, not the language and technique of their African ancestors, but that of this country, where they lived. The "respected" members of the community were those who lived upright lives such as the "respected" whites lived—they paid their debts, they walked in the paths of sexual morality according to the general pattern of the prevailing Puritanical culture, and they went to church as was right and proper in every American town. The matter went so far that they attempted to alter their hair to conform to the general style, and the fortunes made by those who sold hair-straightening devices and medicines are a matter of record.

In Harlem we have to-day, essentially, a typical American community. You may look at the Negroes on the street. As to dress and deportment, do you find any vast difference between them and the whites among whom they carry on their lives? Notice them as they go about their work—they do almost all of the things the whites do, and in much the same way. The popular newspapers in Harlem are not the Negro papers—there is even no Negro daily—but the city newspapers which everyone reads. And there is the same gossipy reason why the Harlemites read their own weeklies as that which causes the inhabitants of Chelsea, of the Bronx, of Putnam, Connecticut, or of West Liberty, Ohio, to read theirs. When we come to the student groups in Harlem, we find that the same process occurs—the general culture-pattern has taken them horse, foot and artillery. Do the whites organize Greek-letter fraternities and sororities in colleges, with pearl-studded pins and "houses"? You will find a number of Negro fraternities and sororities with just the same kind of insignia and "houses." Negro community centres are attached to the more prosperous churches just as the same sort of institutions are connected with white churches. And they do the same sort of things there; you can see swimming and gymnasium classes and sewing classes and nutrition talks and open forums and all the rest of it that we all know so well.

When I visit the Business Men's Association, the difference between this gathering and that of any Rotary Club is imperceptible. And on the other end of the economic scale that equally applies to Negro and white, and which prevails all over the country, we find the Socialist and labor groups. True, once in a while an element peculiarly Negro does manifest itself; thus I remember vividly the bitter complaints of one group of motion picture operators at the prejudices which prevent them from enjoying the benefits of the white union. And, of course, you will meet with this sort of thing whenever the stream of Negro life conflicts with the more general pattern of the "color line." But even here I noticed that the *form* of the organization of these men was that assumed by their white fellow-workers, and similarly when I attended a Socialist street-meeting in Harlem, I found that the general economic motif comes in for much more attention that the problems which are of interest to the Negro *per se.*

Perhaps the most striking example of complete acceptance of the general pattern is in the field of sex relations. I shall never forget the storm of indignation which I aroused among a group of Negro men and women with whom I chanced to be talking on one occasion, when, *a propos* of the question of the treatment of the Negro woman in literature, I inadvertently remarked that even if the sexual looseness generally attributed to her were true, it was nothing of which to be essentially ashamed, since such a refusal to accept the Puritanical modes of procedure generally considered right and proper might contribute a welcome leaven to the conventionality of current sex *mores.* The reaction, prompt and violent, was such as to show with tremendous clarity the complete acculturation of these men and women to the accepted standards of sex behavior. There was not even a shade of doubt but that sexual rigidity is the ultimate ideal of relations between men and women, and certainly there was no more indication of a leaning toward the customs to be found in ancestral Africa than would be found among a group of whites.

Or, let us consider the position of the Negro intellectuals, the writers and artists. The proudest boast of the modern young Negro writer is that he writes of humans, not of Negroes. His literary ideals are not the African folk-tale and conundrum, but the vivid expressionistic style of the day—he seeks to be a writer, not a Negro writer. It was this point, indeed, which was especially stressed at a dinner recently given in New York City for a group of young Negro writers on the occasion of the publication of a novel by one of their number. Member after member of the group stated this position as his own—not Negro as such, but human—another striking example of the process of acculturation.

The problem then may be presented with greater clarity. Does not the Negro have a mode of life that is essentially similar to that of the general community of which he is a part? Or can it be maintained that he possesses a distinctive, inborn cultural genius which manifests itself even in America? To answer this, we must answer an even more basic question: what is cultural genius? For the Negro came to America endowed, as all people are endowed, with a culture, which had been developed by him through long ages in Africa. Was it innate? Or has it been sloughed off, forgotten, in the generations since he was brought into our culture?

To understand the problem with which we are presented, it may be well to consider what this thing, culture, is, and the extent to which we can say that it falls into patterns. By the word culture I do not mean the refinements of our particular civilization which the word has come to connote, but simply those elements of the environment which are the handiwork of man himself. Thus, among ourselves, we might consider a spinning machine, or the democratic theory of society, or a fork, or the alphabet as much a cultural fact as a symphonic tone-poem, a novel, or an oil painting.

We may best come to an understanding of culture through a consideration of some of the phases of primitive life, where the forces at work are not overshadowed by the great imponderable fact of dense masses of population. As we look over the world, we see that there is no group of men, however simply they may live their lives, without the thing we call culture. And, what is more important, the culture they possess as the result of their own historical background—is an adult affair, developed through long centuries of trial and error, and something constantly changing. Man, it has been said, is a culture-building animal. And he is nowhere without the particular culture which his group have built. It is true that the kinds of culture which he builds are bewilderingly different—to compare the civilization of the Eskimo, the Australian, the Chinese, the African, and of ourselves leaves the student with a keener sense of their differences, both as to form and complexity, rather than with any feeling of resemblances among them. But one thing they do have in common: the cultures, when viewed from the outside, are stable. In their main elements they go along much as they always have gone, unless some great historical accident (like the discovery of the steam engine in our culture or the intrusion of the Western culture on that of the Japanese or the transplanting of Negro slaves from Africa to America) occurs to upset the trend and to direct the development of the culture along new paths. To the persons within the cultures, however, they seem even more than just stable. They seem fixed, rigid, all-enduring—indeed, they are so taken for granted that, until comparatively recent times, they were never studied at all.

But what is it that makes cultures different? There are those, of course, who will maintain that it is the racial factor. They will say that the bewildering differences between the cultures of the Englishman, the Chinaman, the Bantu and the Maya, for example, are the result of differences in innate racial endowment, and that every race has evolved a culture peculiarly fitted to it. All this sounds very convincing until one tries to define the term "race." Certain anthropologists are trying, even now, to discover criteria which will scientifically define the term "Negro." One of the most distinguished of these, Professor T. Wingate Todd, has been working steadily for some years in the attempt, and the net results are certain hypotheses which he himself calls tentative. The efforts of numerous psychological testers to establish racial norms for intelligence are vitiated by the two facts that first, as many of them will admit, it is doubtful just what it is they are testing, and, in the second place, that races are mixed. This is particularly true in the case of the Negroes; in New York City, less than two percent of the group from whom I obtained genealogical material claimed pure Negro ancestry, and while this percentage is undoubtedly low, the fact remains that the vast majority of Negroes in America are of mixed ancestry.

If ability to successfully live in one culture were restricted to persons of one race, how could we account for the fact that we see persons of the most diverse races living together, for example, in this country, quite as though they were naturally endowed with the ability to meet the problems of living here, while again we witness an entire alien people adopting our civilization, to use the Japanese again for illustration?

Our civilization is what it is because of certain historic events which occurred in the course of its development. So we can also say for the civilization of the African, of the Eskimo, of the Australian. And the people who lived in these civilizations like ourselves, view the things they do—as a result of living in them—not as inbred, but as inborn. To the Negro in Africa, it would be incomprehensible for a man to work at a machine all day for a few bits of paper to be given him at the end of his work-day, and in the same way, the white traveller stigmatizes the African as lazy because he will not see the necessity for entering on a gruelling forced march so as to reach a certain point in a given time. And when we turn to our civilization, we find that it has many culture-patterns, as we may term these methods of behavior. They are ingrained in us through long habituation, and their violation evokes a strong emotional response in us, no matter what our racial background. Thus for a person to eat with a knife in place of a fork, or to go about the streets hatless, or for a woman to wear short dresses when long ones are in fashion, are all violations of the patterns we have been brought up to feel right and proper, and we react violently to them. More serious, for a young man not to "settle down" and make as much money as he can is regarded as bordering on the immoral, while, in the régime of sex the rigid patterns have been remarked upon, as has been the unmitigated condemnation which the breaking of these taboos calls forth. The examples which I have given above of the reaction of the Negro to the general cultural patterns of this country might be multiplied to include almost as many social facts as are observable, and yet, wherever we might go, we would find the Negro reacting to the same situations in much the same fashion as his white brother.

What, then, is the particular Negro genius for culture? Is there such a thing? Does he contribute something of his vivid, and yet at the same time softly gracious personality to the general culture in which he lives? What there is to-day in Harlem distinct from the white culture which surrounds it, is, as far as I am able to see, merely a remnant from the peasant days in the South. Of the African culture, not a trace. Even the spirituals are an expression of the emotion of the Negro playing through the typical religious patterns of white America. But from that emotional quality in the Negro, which is to be sensed rather than measured, comes the feeling that, though strongly acculturated to the prevalent pattern of behavior, the Negroes may, at the same time, influence it somewhat eventually through the appeal of that quality.

That they have absorbed the culture of America is too obvious, almost, to be mentioned. They have absorbed it as all great racial and social groups in this country have absorbed it. And they face much the same problems as these groups face. The social ostracism to which they are subjected is only different in extent from that to which the Jew is subjected. The fierce reaction of race-pride is quite the same in both groups. But, whether in Negro or in Jew, the protest avails nothing, apparently. All racial and social elements in our population who live here long enough become acculturated, Americanized in the truest sense of the word, eventually. They learn our culture and react according to its patterns, against which all the protestations of the possession of, or of hot desire for, a peculiar culture mean nothing.

As we turn to Harlem we see its social and economic and political make-up a part of the larger whole of the city—separate from it, it is true, but still essentially not different from any other American community in which the modes of life and of action are determined by the great dicta of "what is done." In other words, it represents, as do all American communities which it resembles, a case of complete acculturation. And so, I return again to my reaction on first seeing this center of Negro activity, as the complete description of it: "Why, it's the same pattern, only a different shade!"

The Paradox of Color

Walter White

The hushed tenseness within the theater was broken only by the excited chattering between the scenes which served as oases of relief. One reassured himself by touching his neighbor or gripping the edge of the bench as a magnificently proportioned Negro on the tiny Provincetown Theatre stage, with a voice of marvellous power and with a finished artistry enacted Eugene O'Neill's epic of human terror, *The Emperor Jones*. For years I had nourished the conceit that nothing in or of the theater could thrill me—I was sure my years of theater-going had made me immune to the tricks and the trappings which managers and actors use to get their tears and smiles and laughs. A few seasons ago my shell of conceit was cracked a little—in that third act of Karel Capek's R. U. R. when Rossum's automatons swarmed over the parapet to wipe out the last human being. But the chills that chased each other up and down my spine then were only pleasurable tingles compared to the sympathetic terror evoked by Paul Robeson as he fled blindly through the impenetrable forest of the "West Indian island not yet self-determined by white marines."

Nor was I alone. When, after remaining in darkness from the second through the eighth and final scene, the house was flooded with light, a concerted sigh of relief welled up from all over the theater. With real joy we heard the reassuring roar of taxicabs and muffled street noises of Greenwich Village and knew we were safe in New York. Wave after wave of applause, almost hysterical with relief, brought Paul Robeson time and time again before the curtain to receive the acclaim his art had merited. Almost shyly he bowed again and again as the storm of handclapping and bravos surged and broke upon the tiny stage. His color—his race—all, all were forgotten by those he had stirred so deeply with his art.

Outside in narrow, noisy Macdougal Street the four of us stood. Mrs. Robeson, alert, intelligent, merry, an expert chemist for years in one of New York's leading hospitals; Paul Robeson, clad now in conventional tweeds in place of the ornate, gold-laced trappings of the Emperor Jones; my wife and I. We wanted supper and a place to talk. All about us blinked invitingly the lights of restaurants and inns of New

York's Bohemia. Place after place was suggested and discarded. Here a colored man and his companion had been made to wait interminably until, disgusted, they had left. There a party of four colored people, all university graduates, had been told flatly by the proprietress, late of North Carolina, she did not serve "niggers." At another, other colored people had been stared at so rudely they had bolted their food and left in confusion. The Civil Rights Act of New York would have protected us—but we were too much under the spell of the theater we had just quitted to want to insist on the rights the law gave us. So we mounted a bus and rode seven miles or more to colored Harlem where we could be served with food without fear of insult or contumely. The man whose art had brought homage to his feet from sophisticated New York could not enter even the cheapest of the eating places of lower New York with the assurance that some unpleasantness might not come to him before he left.

What does race prejudice do to the inner man of him who is the victim of that prejudice? What is the feeling within the breasts of the Paul Robesons, the Roland Hayes's, the Harry Burleighs, as they listen to the applause of those whose kind receive them as artists but refuse to accept them as men? It is of this inner conflict of the black man in America—or, more specifically in New York City, I shall try to speak.

I approach my task with reluctance—it is no easy matter to picture that effect which race or color prejudice has on the Negro of fineness of soul who is its victim. Of wounds to the flesh it is easy to speak. It is not difficult to tell of lynchings and injustices and race proscription. Of wounds to the spirit which are a thousand times more deadly and cruel it is impossible to tell in entirety. On the one hand lies the Scylla of bathos and on the other the Charybdis of insensivity to subtler shadings of the spirit. If I can evoke in your mind a picture of what results proscription has brought, I am content.

With its population made up of peoples from every corner of the earth, New York City is, without doubt, more free from ordinary manifestations of prejudice than any other city in the United States. Its Jewish, Italian, German, French, Greek, Czecho-slovakian, Irish, Hungarian quarters with their teeming thousands and hundreds of thousands form so great a percentage of the city's population that "white, Gentile, Protestant" Nordics have but little opportunity to develop their prejudices as they do, for example, in Mississippi or the District of

Columbia. It was no idle joke when some forgotten wit remarked, "The Jews own New York, the Irish run it and the Negroes enjoy it."

New York's polyglot population, which causes such distress to the Lothrop Stoddards and the Madison Grants, by a curious anomaly, has created more nearly than any other section that democracy which is the proud boast but rarely practised accomplishment of these United States. The Ku Klux Klan has made but little headway in New York City for the very simple reason that the proscribed outnumber the proscribers. Thus race prejudice cannot work its will upon Jew or Catholic—or Negro, as in other more genuinely American centers. This combined with the fact that most people in New York are so busy they haven't time to spend in hating other people, makes New York as nearly ideal a place for colored people as exists in America.

Despite these alleviating causes, however, New York is in the United States where prejudice appears to be indigenous. Its population includes many Southern whites who have brought North with them their hatreds. There are here many whites who are not Southern but whose minds have indelibly fixed upon them the stereotype of a Negro who is either a buffoon or a degenerate beast or a subservient lackey. From these the Negro knows he is ever in danger of insult or injury. This situation creates various attitudes of mind among those who are its victims. Upon most the acquisition of education and culture, of wealth and sensitiveness causes a figurative and literal withdrawal, as far as is humanly possible or as necessity permits, from all contacts with the outside world where unpleasant situations may arise. This naturally means the development of an intensive Negro culture and a definitely bounded city within a city. Doubtless there are some advantages, but it is certain that such voluntary segregation works a greater loss upon those within and those without the circle.

Upon those within, it cuts off to a large extent the world of music, of the theater, of most of those contacts which mean growth and development and which denied, mean stagnation and spiritual atrophy. It develops as well a tendency towards self-pity, towards a fatal conviction that they of all peoples are most oppressed. The harmful effects of such reactions are too obvious to need elaboration.

Upon those without, the results are equally mischievous. First there is the loss of that deep spirituality, that gift of song and art, that indefinable thing which perhaps can best be termed the over-soul of the Negro, which has given America the only genuinely artistic things

ALAIN LOCKE

which the world recognizes as distinctive American contributions to the arts.

More conventional notions as Thomas Dixon and Octavus Roy Cohen and Irvin Cobb have falsely painted them, of what the Negro is and does and thinks continue to persist, while those who represent more truly the real Negro avoid all contact with other races.

There are, however, many other ways of avoidance of proscription and prejudice. Of these one of no small importance is that popularly known as "passing," that is, those whose skin is of such color that they can pass as white may do so. This is not difficult; there are so many swarthy races represented in New York's population that even colored people who could easily be distinguished by their own race as Negroes, pass as French or Spanish or Cuban with ease. Of these there are two classes. First are those who for various reasons disappear entirely and go over the line to become white in business, social and all other relationships. The number of these is very large—much larger than is commonly suspected. To my personal knowledge one of the prominent surgeons of New York City who has an elaborately furnished suite of offices in an exclusive neighborhood, whose fees run often into four figures, who moves with his family in society of such standing that the names of its members appear frequently in the society columns of the metropolitan press, is a colored man from a Southern city. There he grew tired of the proscribed life he was forced to lead, decided to move North and forget he was a colored man. He met with success, married well and he and his wife and their children form as happy a family circle as one could hope to see. O'Neill *All God's Chillun Got Wings* to the contrary, his wife loves him but the more for his courage in telling her of his race when first they met and loved.

This doctor's case is not an exception. Colored people know many of their own who have done likewise. In New York there is at least one man high in the field of journalism, a certain famous singer, several prominent figures of the stage, in fact, in almost any field that could be mentioned there are those who are colored but who have left their race for wider opportunity and for freedom from race prejudice. Just a few days before this article is being written I received a note from a woman whose name is far from being obscure in the world of the arts. The night before, she wrote me, there had been a party at her studio. Among the guests were three Southern whites who, in a confidential mood, had told her of a plan the Ku Klux Klan was devising for capitalizing in

New York prejudice against the Negro. When I asked her why she had given me the information she told me her father, resident at the time of her birth in a Southern state, was a Negro.

The other group is made up of the many others who "pass" only occasionally. Some of these do so for business reasons, others when they go out to dine or to the theater.

If a personal reference may be forgiven, I have had the unique experience within the past seven years of investigating some thirty-seven lynchings and eight race riots by the simple method of *not* telling those whom I was investigating of the Negro blood within my veins.

Large as is the number of those who have crossed the line, they form but a small percentage of those who might follow such an example but who do not. The constant hammering of three hundred years of oppression has resulted in a race consciousness among the Negroes of the United States which is amazing to those who know how powerful it is. In America, as is well known, all persons with any discernible percentage of Negro blood are classed as Negroes, subject therefore to all of the manifestations of prejudice. They are never allowed to forget their race. By prejudice ranging from the more violent forms like lynching and other forms of physical violence down to more subtle but none the less effective methods, Negroes of the United States have been welded into a homogeneity of thought and a commonness of purpose in combating a common foe. These external and internal forces have gradually created a state of mind among Negroes which is rapidly becoming more pronounced where they realize that just so long as one Negro can be made the victim of prejudice because he *is* a Negro, no other Negro is safe from that same oppression. This applies geographically, as is seen in the support given by colored people in cities like Boston, New York and Chicago to those who oppose lynching of Negroes in the South, and it applies to that large element of colored people whose skins are lighter who realize that their cause is common with that of all Negroes regardless of color.

Unfortunately, however, color prejudice creates certain attitudes of mind on the part of some colored people which form color lines within the color line. Living in an atmosphere where swarthiness of skin brings, almost automatically, denial of opportunity, it is as inevitable as it is regrettable that there should grow up among Negroes themselves distinctions based on skin color and hair texture. There are many places where this pernicious custom is more powerful than in New York—

for example, there are cities where only mulattoes attend certain churches while those whose skins are dark brown or black attend others. Marriages between colored men and women whose skins differ markedly in color, and indeed, less intimate relations are frowned upon. Since those of lighter color could more often secure the better jobs an even wider chasm has come between them, as those with economic and cultural opportunity have progressed more rapidly than those whose skin denied them opportunity.

Thus even among intelligent Negroes there has come into being the fallacious belief that black Negroes are less able to achieve success. Naturally such a condition had led to jealousy and suspicion on the part of darker Negroes, chafing at their bonds and resentful of the patronizing attitude of those of lighter color.

In New York City this feeling between black and mulatto has been accentuated by the presence of some 40,000 Negroes from the West Indies, and particularly by the propaganda of Marcus Garvey and his Universal Negro Improvement Association. In contrast to the division between white and colored peoples in the United States, there is in the West Indies, as has been pointed out by Josiah Royce and others, a tripartite problem of race relations with whites, blacks and mulattoes. The latter mingle freely with whites in business and other relations and even socially. But neither white nor mulatto has any extensive contact on an equal plane with the blacks. It is this system which has enabled the English whites in the islands to rule and exploit though they as rulers are vastly inferior numerically to blacks and mulattoes.

The psychology thus created is visible among many of the West Indian Negroes in New York. It was the same background of the English brand of race prejudice which actuated Garvey in preaching that only those who were of unmixed Negro blood were Negroes. It is true beyond doubt that such a doctrine created for a time greater antagonisms among colored people, but an inevitable reaction has set in which, in time, will probably bring about a greater unity than before among Negroes in the United States.

We have therefore in Harlem this strange mixture of reactions not only to prejudice from without but to equally potent prejudices from within. Many are the comedies and many are the tragedies which these artificial lines of demarcation have created. Yet with all these forces and counter forces at work, there can be seen emerging some definite and hopeful signs of racial unity. Though it hearkens back to the middle ages, this is essential in the creation of a united front against that race and color prejudice with which the Negro, educated or illiterate, rich or poor, native or foreign-born, mulatto, octoroon, quadroon, or black, must strive continuously.

The Task of Negro Womanhood

Elise Johnson McDougald

Throughout the years of history, woman has been the weather-vane, the indicator, showing in which direction the wind of destiny blows. Her status and development have augured now calm and stability, now swift currents of progress. What then is to be said of the Negro woman of to-day, whose problems are of such import to her race?

A study of her contributions to any one community, throughout America, would illuminate the pathway being trod by her people. There is, however, an advantage in focusing upon the women of Harlem— modern city in the world's metropolis. Here, more than anywhere else, the Negro woman is free from the cruder handicaps of primitive household hardships and the grosser forms of sex and race subjugation. Here, she has considerable opportunity to measure her powers in the intellectual and industrial fields of the great city. The questions naturally arise: "What are her difficulties?" and, "How is she solving them?"

To answer these questions, one must have in mind not any one Negro woman, but rather a colorful pageant of individuals, each differently endowed. Like the red and yellow of the tiger-lily, the skin of one is brilliant against the star-lit darkness of a racial sister. From grace to strength, they vary in infinite degree, with traces of the race's history left in physical and mental outline on each. With a discerning mind, one catches the multiform charm, beauty and character of Negro women, and grasps the fact that their problems cannot be thought of in mass.

Because only a few have caught this vision, even in New York, the general attitude of mind causes the Negro woman serious difficulty. She is conscious that what is left of chivalry is not directed toward her. She realizes that the ideals of beauty, built up in the fine arts, have excluded her almost entirely. Instead, the grotesque Aunt Jemimas of the streetcar advertisements, proclaim only an ability to serve, without grace of loveliness. Nor does the drama catch her finest spirit. She is most often used to provoke the mirthless laugh of ridicule; or to portray feminine viciousness or vulgarity not peculiar to Negroes. This is the shadow over her. To a race naturally sunny comes the twilight of self-doubt and a sense of personal inferiority. It cannot be denied that these are potent and detrimental influences, though not generally recognized because they are in the realm of the mental and spiritual. More apparent are the economic handicaps which follow her recent entrance into industry. It is conceded that she has special difficulties because of the poor working conditions and low wages of her men. It is not surprising that only the most determined women forge ahead to results other than mere survival. To the gifted, the zest of meeting a challenge is a compensating factor which often brings success. The few who do prove their mettle, stimulate one to a closer study of how this achievement is won under contemporary conditions.

Better to visualize the Negro woman at her job, our vision of a host of individuals must once more resolve itself into groups on the basis of activity. First, comes a very small leisure group—the wives and daughters of men who are in business, in the professions and a few well-paid personal service occupations. Second, a most active and progressive group, the women in business and the professions. Third, the many women in the trades and industry. Fourth, a group weighty in numbers struggling on in domestic service, with an even less fortunate fringe of casual workers, fluctuating with the economic temper of the times.

The first is a pleasing group to see. It is picked for outward beauty by Negro men with much the same feeling as other Americans of the same economic class. Keeping their women free to preside over the family, these women are affected by the problems of every wife and mother, but touched only faintly by their race's hardships. They do share acutely in the prevailing difficulty of finding competent household help. Negro wives find Negro maids unwilling generally to work in their own neighborhoods, for various reasons. They do not wish to work where there is a possibility of acquaintances coming into contact with them while they serve and they still harbor the misconception that Negroes of any station are unable to pay as much as persons of the other race. It is in these homes of comparative ease that we find the polite activities of social exclusiveness. The luxuries of well-appointed homes, modest motors, tennis, golf and country clubs, trips to Europe and California, make for social standing. The problem confronting the refined Negro family is to know others of the same achievement. The search for kindred spirits gradually grows less difficult; in the past it led to the custom of visiting all the large cities in order to know similar groups of cultured Negro people. In recent years, the more serious minded Negro woman's visit to Europe has been extended from months to years for the purpose of study and travel. The European success which meets this type of ambition is instanced in the conferring of the doctorate in philosophy upon a Negro woman, Dr. Anna J. Cooper, at the last commencement of the Sorbonne, Paris. Similarly, a score of Negro women are sojourning abroad in various countries for the spiritual relief and cultural stimulation afforded there.

A spirit of stress and struggles characterizes the second two groups. These women of business, profession and trade are the hub of the wheel of progress. Their burden is twofold. Many are wives and mothers whose husbands are insufficiently paid, or who have succumbed to social maladjustment and have abandoned their families. An appalling number are widows. They face the great problem of leaving home each day and at the same time trying to rear children in their spare time— this, too, in neighborhoods where rents are large, standards of dress and recreation high and costly, and social danger on the increase. One cannot resist the temptation to pause for a moment and pay tribute to these Negro mothers. And to call attention to the service she is rendering to the nation, in her struggle against great odds to educate and care for one group of the country's children. If the mothers of the race should ever be honored by state or federal legislation, the artist's imagination will find a more inspiring subject in the modern Negro mother—self-directed but as loyal and tender as the much extolled, yet pitiable black mammy of slavery days.

The great commercial life of New York City is only slightly touched by the Negro woman, of our second group. Negro business men offer her most of their work, but their number is limited. Outside of this field in Negro offices, custom is once more against her, and competition is keen for all. However, Negro girls are training and some are holding exceptional jobs. One of the professors in a New York college has had a young colored woman as secretary for the past three or four years. Another holds the head clerical position in an organization where reliable handling of detail and a sense of business ethics are essential. Quietly these women prove their worth, so that when a vacancy exists and there is a call, it is difficult to find even one competent colored secretary who is not employed. As a result of the opportunity in clerical work in the educational system of New York City, a number have qualified for such positions, one having been recently appointed to the office of a high school. In other departments, the civil service in New York City is no longer free from discrimination. The casual personal interview, that tenacious and retrogressive practice introduced into the federal administration during the World War, has spread and often nullifies the Negro woman's success in written tests. The successful young woman cited above was three times "turned down" as undesirable on the basis of the personal interview. In the great mercantile houses, the many young Negro girls who might be well suited to sales positions are barred from all but menial positions. Even so, one Negro woman, beginning as a uniformed maid in the shoe department of one of the largest stores, has pulled herself up to the position of "head of stock." One of the most prosperous monthly magazines of national circulation has for the head of its news service a Negro woman who rose from the position of stenographer. Her duties involve attendance upon staff conferences, executive supervision of her staff of white office workers, broadcasting and journalism of the highest order.

Yet in spite of the claims of justice and proved efficiency, telephone and insurance companies and other corporations which receive considerable patronage from Negroes deny them proportionate employment. Fortunately this is an era of changing customs. There is hope that a less selfish racial attitude will prevail. It is a heartening fact that there is an increasing number of Americans who will lend a hand in the game fight of the worthy.

Throughout the South, where businesses for Negro patronage are under the control of Negroes to a large extent, there are already many opportunities for Negro women. But, because of the nerve strain and spiritual drain of hostile social conditions in that section, Negro women are turning away from opportunities there to find a freer and fuller life in the North.

In the less crowded professional vocations, the outlook is more cheerful. In these fields, the Negro woman is dependent largely upon herself and her own race for work. In the legal, dental and medical professions, successful women practitioners have usually worked their way through college and are "managing" on the small fees that can be received from an underpaid public.

Social conditions in America are hardest upon the Negro because he is lowest in the economic scale. The tendency to force the Negro downward, gives rise to serious social problems and to a consequent demand for trained college women in the profession of social work. The need has been met with a response from young college women, anxious to devote their education and lives toward helping the submerged classes. Much of the social work has been pioneer in nature; the pay has been small, with little possibility of advancement. For, even in work among Negroes, the better paying positions are reserved for whites. The Negro college woman is doing her bit at a sacrifice, along such lines as these: as probation officers, investigators and police women in the correctional departments of the city; as Big Sisters attached to the Children's Court; as field workers and visitors for relief organizations, missions and churches; as secretaries for traveller's aid societies; in the many organizations devoted to preventative and educational medicine; in clinics and hospitals and as boys' and girls' welfare workers in recreation and industry.

In the profession of nursing, there are over three hundred in New York City. In the dark blue linen uniform of Henry Street Visiting Nurse Service, the Negro woman can be seen hurrying earnestly from house to house on her round of free relief to the needy. Again, she is in many other branches of public health nursing, in the public schools, milk stations and diet kitchens. The Negro woman is in the wards of two of the large city hospitals and clinics. After a score of years of service in one such institution, a Negro woman became superintendent of nurses in the war emergency. Deposed after the armistice, though eminently satisfactory, she retained connection with the training school as lecturer, for the inspiration she could be to "her girls." The growing need for the executive nurse is being successfully met as instanced by the supervisors in day nurseries and private sanitariums, financed and operated in Harlem entirely by Negroes. Throughout the South there is a clear and anxious call to nurses to carry the gospel of hygiene to the rural sections and to minister to the suffering not reached by organizations already in the communities. One social worker, in New York City, though a teacher by profession, is head of an organization whose program is to raise money for the payment of nurses to do the work described above. In other centers, West and South, the professional Negro nurse is supplanting the untrained woman attendant of former years.

In New York City, nearly three hundred women share in the good conditions obtaining there in the teaching profession. They measure up to the high pedagogical requirements of the city and state law, and are increasingly leaders in the community. In a city where the schools are not segregated, she is meeting with success among white as well as colored children in positions ranging from clerk in the elementary school on up through the graded ranks of teachers in the lower grades, of special subjects in the higher grades, in the junior high schools and in the senior high schools. One Negro woman is assistant principal in an elementary school where the other assistant and the principal are white men and the majority of the teachers white. Another Negro woman serves in the capacity of visiting teacher to several schools, calling upon both white and colored families and experiencing no difficulty in making social adjustments. Still another Negro woman is a vocational counsellor under the Board of Education, in a junior high school. She is advising children of both races as to future courses of study to pursue and as to the vocations in which tests prove them to be apt. This position, the result of pioneer work by another Negro woman, is unique in the school system of New York.

In the teaching profession, too, the Negro woman finds evidence of the white worker's fear of competition. The need for teachers is still so great that little friction exists. When it does seem imminent, it is smoothed away, as it recently was at a meeting of school principals. From the floor a discussion began with: "What are we going to do about this problem of the increasing number of Negro teachers coming into our schools?" It ended promptly through the suggestion of another principal: "Send all you get and don't want over to my school. I have two now and I'll match their work with any two of the best you name." Outside of New York City, the Negro woman teacher faces problems almost as difficult as those besetting the pioneers in the field. Night riders are terrorizing the leading educators of the South, with the same tactics used years ago in the burning of buildings and in the threatening of personal injury. Negro teachers in some sections show heroism matching that of such women as Maria Becroft, Mary Wormely, Margaret Thompson, Fannie Hampton, Myrtilla Miner and others who in the early '80's faced riot and violence which closed colored schools and made educational work a hazardous vocation. Throughout the North and South, urban and rural teachers form an earnest and forward-looking group of women. They are endeavoring to hold for the future the progress that has been made in the past. The Negro woman teacher finds that, figuratively speaking, she must stand on her tip toes to do it, for educational standards are no longer what they were. Surrounded by forces which persistently work to establish the myth of his inferiority, the Negro youth must be encouraged to think vigorously and to maintain a critical attitude toward what he is taught. The Negro teacher is bending herself to the task of imparting this power to hold the spiritual and mental balance under hostile conditions. Though her salary in most places lags behind the service she is rendering (exceptions being noted where the Jeannes-Slater and Rosenwald Funds bring relief), her inspiration is the belief that the hope of the race is in the New Negro student. Of more vital import than what he is compelled to be to-day, is what he is determined to make of himself tomorrow. And, the Negro woman teacher, bringing to the class room sympathy and judgment, is a mighty force in this battle.

Comparatively new are opportunities in the field of trained library work for the Negro woman. In New York City, the Public Library system has opened its service to the employment of colored women of college grade. The vision of those in charge of their training is illuminated by fires that have somewhat of a missionary glow. There is an ever-present hope that, once trained, the Negro woman librarian will. scatter such opportunities across the country, establishing branches wherever none exist. Into such an emergency, the successful Negro woman head of the library of the Veterans' Hospital at Tuskegee, stepped from the New York Library on One Hundred and Thirty-fifth Street. Recently at this same Harlem Branch Library a Negro woman has been placed in charge of the large, permanent collection of books by or about Negroes and examples of Negro art. Another is acting head of the children's department, and several others have been assigned to branches throughout the city where there is little or no Negro patronage. They are thus rendering exceptional service, and additionally creating an impetus for the enlargement of this field for Negro women.

One might go on to such interesting and more unusual professions as bacteriology, chemistry and pharmacy, etc., and find that though the number in any one may be small, the Negro woman is creditably represented in practically every one, and according to ability, she is meeting with success. In the fields of literature and art, the Negro woman's culture has once more begun to flower. After the long quiescent period, following the harvest from the pen of Phyllis Wheatley, Negro women dramatists, poets and novelists are enjoying a vogue in print. There is every prospect that the Negro woman will enrich American literature and art with stylistic portrayal of her experience and her problems.

Closing the door on the home anxieties, the women engaged in trades and in industry faces serious difficulty in competition in the open working field. Custom is against the Negro woman in all but a few trade and industrial occupations. She has, however, been established long in the dressmaking trade as helpers and finishers, and more recently as drapers and fitters in some of the best establishments. Several Negro women are themselves proprietors of shops in the country's great fashion district. In millinery, power-sewing machine operating on cloth, straw and leather, there are few Negro women. The laissez-faire attitude of practically all trade unions has, in the past, made of the Negro woman an unwilling menace to the cause of labor. When one reviews the demands now being made by white women workers, for labor colleges, for political recognition, and for representation at world conferences, one cannot help but feel how far back on the road of labor progress is the struggling group of Negro workers. Yet, they are gradually becoming more alive to the issues involved. One Negro woman has held office and been most active in the flower and feather workers' union. Another has been a paid organizer in the garment industry for several years. Still another has co-operated as an unpaid worker, in endeavoring to prevent Negro women from breaking union strikes. Pacing with pickets, or explaining at meetings the wisdom underlying union principles, she became convinced that the problem lay as much in the short-sighted, "wait-until-a-strike-comes" policy of the labor unions themselves, as in the alienated or unintelligent attitude of the Negro worker. More sincerity and understanding was greatly needed. Within the past year, she has worked with two Negro men, a white woman and two white men, all union members, and with this committee of six has brought about a conference of accredited delegates from thirty-three unions in New York City. This is the first all-union conference held on adjusting the Negro workers' problem. As a result, a permanent organization has been formed called the Trade Union Committee for Organizing Negro Workers. Headquarters have been established and a program is well under way which includes:—organizing special industries, manned largely by Negro men and women; working to bring about changes in the constitutions of trade unions which make it impossible or difficult for Negroes to join; educating both black and white workers in union principles through conferences and speeches; making necessary adjustments among union members of the two races and taking part in righting any grievances of Negro union members.

In trade cookery, the Negro woman's talent and past experience is recognized. Her problem here is to find employers who will let her work her way to managerial positions, in tearooms, candy shops and institutions. One such employer became convinced that the managing cook, a young colored graduate of Pratt Institute, could build up a business that had been failing. He offered her a partnership. As in the cases of a number of such women, her barrier was lack of capital. No matter how highly trained, nor how much speed and business acumen has been acquired, the Negro's credit is held in doubt. An exception in this matter of capital will serve to prove the rule. Thirty years ago, a young Negro girl began learning all branches of the fur trade. She is now in business for herself, employing three women of her race and one Jewish man. She has made fur experts of still another half-dozen colored girls. Such instances as these justify the prediction that the foothold which is being gained in the trade world will, year by year, become more secure.

Because of the limited fields for this group, many of the unsuccessful drift into the fourth social grade—the domestic and casual workers. These drifters increase the difficulties of the Negro women suited to housework. New standards of household management are forming and the problem of the Negro woman is to meet these new businesslike ideals. The constant influx of workers unfamiliar with household conditions in New York keeps the situation one of turmoil. The Negro woman, moreover, is revolting against residential domestic service. It is a last stand in her fight to maintain a semblance of family life. For this reason, principally, the number of day or casual workers is on the increase. Happiness is almost impossible under the strain of these conditions. Health and morale suffer, but how else can her children, loose all afternoon, be gathered together at nightfall? Through it all she manages to give satisfactory service and the Negro woman is sought after for this unpopular work, largely because her honesty, loyalty and cleanliness have stood the test of time. Through her drudgery, the women of other groups find leisure time for progress. This is one of her contributions to America.

It is apparent from what has been said that even in New York City, Negro women are of a race which is free neither economically, socially nor spiritually. Like women in general, but more particularly like those of other oppressed minorities, the Negro woman has been forced to submit to overpowering conditions. Pressure has been exerted upon her, both from without and within her group. Her emotional and sex life is a reflex of her economic station. The women of the working class will react, emotionally and sexually, similarly to the working-class woman of other races. The Negro woman does not maintain any moral standard which may be assigned chiefly to qualities of race, any more than a white woman does. Yet she has been singled out and advertised as having lower sex standards. Superficial critics who have had contact only with the lower grades of Negro women, claim that they are more immoral than other groups of women. This I deny. This is the sort of criticism which predicates of one race, to its detriment, that which is common to all races. Sex irregularities are not a matter of race, but socio-economic conditions. Research shows that most of the African tribes from which the Negro sprang have strict codes for sex relations. There is no proof of inherent weakness in the ethnic group.

Gradually overcoming the habitual limits imposed upon her by slave masters, she increasingly seeks legal sanction for the consummation and dissolution of sex contracts. Contrary to popular belief, illegitimacy among Negroes is cause for shame and grief. When economic, social and biological forces combined bring about unwed motherhood, the reaction is much the same as in families in other racial groups. Secrecy is maintained if possible. Generally the married aunt or even the girl's mother claims the illegitimate child as her own. The foundling asylum is seldom sought. Schooled in this kind of suffering in the days of slavery, the Negro woman often tempers scorn with sympathy for weakness. Stigma does fall upon the unmarried mother, but perhaps in this matter the Negro's attitude is nearer the modern enlightened ideal for the social treatment of the unfortunate. May not this, too, be considered another contribution to America?

With all these forces at work, true sex equality has not been approximated. The ratio of opportunity in the sex, social, economic and political spheres is about that which exists between white men and women. In the large, I would say that the Negro woman is the cultural equal of her man because she is generally kept in school longer. Negro boys, like white boys, are usually put to work to subsidize the family income. The growing economic independence of Negro working women is causing her to rebel against the domineering family attitude of the cruder working-class husband. The masses of Negro men are engaged in menial occupations throughout the working day. Their baffled and suppressed desires to determine their economic life are manifested in overbearing domination at home. Working mothers are unable to instill different ideals in the sons. Conditions change slowly. Nevertheless, education and opportunity are modifying the spirit of the younger Negro men. Trained in modern schools of thought, they begin to show a wholesome attitude of fellowship and freedom for their women. The challenge to young Negro womanhood is to see clearly this trend and grasp the proffered comradeship with sincerity. In this matter of sex equality, Negro women have contributed few outstanding militants, a notable instance being the historic Sojourner Truth. On the whole the Negro woman's feminist efforts are directed chiefly toward the realization of the equality of the races, the sex struggle assuming the subordinate place.

Obsessed with difficulties which might well compel individualism, the Negro woman has engaged in a considerable amount of organized action to meet group needs. She has evolved a federation of her clubs, embracing between eight and ten thousand women in New York state alone. The state federation is a part of the National Association of Colored Women, which, calling together the women from all parts of the country, engages itself in enterprises of general race interest. The national organization of colored women is now firmly established, and under the presidency of Mrs. Bethune is about to strive for conspicuous goals.

In New York City, many associations exist for social betterment, financed and operated by Negro women. One makes child welfare its name and special concern. Others, like the Utility Club, Utopia Neighborhood, Debutantes' League, Sempre Fidelius, etc., raise funds for old folks' homes, a shelter for delinquent girls and fresh-air camps for children. The Colored Women's Branch of the Y. W. C. A. and the women's organizations in the many churches as well as the beneficial lodges and associations, care for the needs of their members.

On the other hand, the educational welfare of the coming generation has become the chief concern of the national sororities of Negro college women. The first to be organized in the country, the *Alpha Kappa Alpha*, has a systematized, a continuous program of educational and vocational guidance for students of the high schools and colleges. The work of Lambda Chapter, which covers New York City and its suburbs, has been most effective in carrying out the national program. Each year, it gathers together between one and two hundred such students and gives the girls a chance to hear the life stories of Negro women, successful in various fields of endeavor. Recently a trained nurse told how, starting in the same schools as they, she had risen to the executive position in the Harlem Health Information Bureau. A commercial artist showed how real talent had overcome the color line. The graduate physician was a living example of the modern opportunities in the newer fields of medicine open to women. The vocations, as outlets for the creative instinct, became attractive under the persuasion of the musician, the dressmaker and the decorator. A recent graduate outlined her plans for meeting the many difficulties encountered in establishing a dental office and in building up a practice. A journalist spun the fascinating tale of her years of experience. The *Delta Sigma Theta* Sorority (national in scope) works along similar lines. Alpha Beta Chapter of New York City, during the current year, presented a young art student with a scholarship of $1,000 for study abroad. In such ways as these are the progressive and privileged groups of Negro women expressing their community and race consciousness.

We find the Negro woman, figuratively struck in the face daily by contempt from the world about her. Within her soul, she knows little of peace and happiness. But through it all, she is courageously standing erect, developing within herself the moral strength to rise above and conquer false attitudes. She is maintaining her natural beauty and charm and improving her mind and opportunity. She is measuring up to the needs of her family, community and race, and radiating a hope throughout the land.

The wind of the race's destiny stirs more briskly because of her striving.

WORLDS OF COLOR

The Negro Mind Reaches Out[1]

W. E. B. DuBois

O nce upon a time in my younger years and in the dawn of this century I wrote: "The problem of the twentieth century is the problem of the color line." It was a pert and singing phrase which I then liked and which since I have often rehearsed to my soul and asked:— how far is this prophecy or speculation? To-day in the last years of the century's first quarter, let us examine the matter again, especially in the memory of that great event of these great years, the World War. Fruit of the bitter rivalries of economic imperialism, the roots of that catastrophe were in Africa, deeply entwined at bottom with the problems of the color line. And of the legacy left, the problems the world inherits hold the same fatal seed; world dissension and catastrophe still lurk in the unsolved problems of race relations. What then is the world view that the consideration of this question offers?

Most men would agree that our present problem of problems was not the Color Problem, but what we call Labor, the problem of allocating work and income in the tremendous and increasingly intricate world-embracing industrial machine that our civilization has built. But despite our concern and good will, is it not possible that in its consideration our research is not directed to the vital spots geographically? Our good will is too often confined to that labor which we see and feel and exercise around us, rather than directed to the periphery of the vast circle, where unseen and inarticulate, the determining factors are at work. And may not the continual baffling of our effort and failure of our formula be due to just such mistakes? Modern imperialism and modern industrialism are one and the same system; root and branch of the same tree. The race problem is the other side of the labor problem; and the black man's burden is the white man's burden. At least it will be of absorbing interest, to step within these distant world shadows, and, looking backward, to view the European and white American labor problem from this wide perspective, remembering always that empire is the heavy hand of capital abroad.

---

1. Reprinted, with revisions by the author, from *Foreign Affairs*, an American Quarterly Review, New York, Vol. III, No. 3.

With nearly every great European empire to-day walks its dark colonial shadow, while over all Europe there stretches the yellow shadow of Asia that lies across the world. One might indeed read the riddle of Europe by making its present plight a matter of colonial shadows, speculating on what might happen if Europe became suddenly shadowless—if Asia and Africa and the islands were cut permanently away. At any rate here is a field of inquiry, of likening and contrasting each land and its far-off shadow.

The Shadow of Portugal

I was attending the Third Pan-African Congress and I walked to the Palacio dos Cortes with Magellan. It was in December, 1923, and in Lisbon. I was rather proud. You see Magalhaes (to give him the Portuguese spelling) is a mulatto—small light-brown and his hands quick with gestures. Dr. José de Magalhaes is a busy man: a practising specialist; professor in the School of Tropical Medicine whose new buildings are rising; and above all, deputy in the Portuguese Parliament from Sao Thomé, Africa. Thus this Angolese African, educated in Lisbon and Paris, is one of the nine colored members of European Parliaments. Portugal has had colored ministers and now has three colored deputies and a senator. I saw two Portuguese in succession kissing one colored member on the floor of the house. Or was he but a dark native? There is so much ancient black blood in this peninsula.

Between the Portuguese and the African and near African there is naturally no "racial" antipathy—no accumulated historical hatreds, dislikes, despisings. Not that you would likely find a black man married to a Portuguese of family and wealth, but on the other hand it seemed quite natural for Portugal to make all the blacks of her African empire citizens of Portugal with the rights of the European born.

Magalhaes and another represent Sao Thomé. They are elected by black folk independent of party. Again and again I meet black folk from Sao Thomé—young students, well-dressed, well-bred, evidently sons of well-to-do if not wealthy parents, studying in Portugal, which harbors annually a hundred such black students.

Sao Thomé illustrates some phases of European imperialism in Africa. This industrial rule involves cheap land and labor in Africa and large manufacturing capital in Europe, with a resultant opportunity for the exercise of pressure from home investors and the press. Once in a while—not often—a feud between the capitalists and the manufacturers at home throws sudden light on Africa. For instance, in the Boer War the "Cocoa Press" backed by the anti-war Liberals attacked the Unionists and exposed labor conditions in South Africa. In retaliation, after the war and when the Liberals were in power, the Unionists attacked labor conditions in the Portuguese cocoa colonies.

When I heard that an English Lieutenant-Colonel was lecturing in Lisbon, on this very island and its cocoa, I hastened to listen. As he talked, I remembered. He was soothing the Portuguese.

The Colonel was an avowal reactionary, a hater of the "Aborigines Protection Society," Nevinson, Morel and all their ilk, and his explanations were most illuminating. It would seem that "little Englanders" backed by the Cadbury "Cocoa" press of "pacifist" leanings, made a severe attack on the Unionists during the Boer War and particularly attacked labor conditions on the Rand; besides opposing Chamberlain, "Empire preference" and protection. When the Liberals came into power in 1906 the Unionists in retaliation began to attack labor conditions in Portuguese Sao Thomé, where Cadbury and others got their cocoa and made the profits out of which they supported the "Daily Mail." The Colonel declared that labor conditions in Sao Thomé were quite ideal, whereas Nevinson and others had declared that they constituted black slavery. The point that interests us, however, is that the English cocoa manufacturers were forced by frantic efforts to justify themselves and deny all responsibility. They therefore proceeded to say that it wasn't true and if it was, the Portuguese were responsible. Under cover of this bitter controversy an extraordinary industrial revolution took place: a boycott was placed on Portuguese cocoa the world over, and under the mists of recrimination the center of the cocoa-raising industry was transferred from Portuguese to English soil—from Sao Thomé and Principé to British Nigeria and the Gold Coast. Before 1900 less than one thousand tons of cocoa had been raised in British West Africa annually; by 1920 this had risen to one hundred and seventy thousand tons.

Of the real facts behind this rush of smoke I only know: that in the end two new groups of black folk appeared above the horizon—the black proprietors in Sao Thomé who still raise the best cocoa in the world and who, freed of the over lordship of English capital have achieved a certain political independence in the Portuguese empire; and the black peasant proprietors of the cocoa farms of Nigeria who have performed one of the industrial miracles of a century and become the center of a world industry. In this development note if you please the characteristic of all color-line fights—the tearing across of all rational division of opinion: here is Liberalism, anti-slavery and cocoa capitalism fighting Toryism, free Negro proprietors and economic independence. Thus with a democratic face at home, modern imperialism turns a visage of stern and unyielding autocracy toward its darker colonies. This double-faced attitude is difficult to maintain and puts hard strain on the national soul that tries it.

Thus in this part of Portuguese Africa the worst aspects of slavery melted away and colonial proprietors with smaller holdings could afford to compete with the great planters; wherefore democracy, both industrially and politically, took new life in black Portugal. Intelligent black deputies appeared in the Portuguese parliaments, a hundred black students studied in the Portuguese universities and a new colonial code made black men citizens of Portugal with full rights. But in Portugal, alas! no adequate democratic control has been established, nor can be with an illiteracy of seventy-five percent; so that while the colonial code is liberally worded, and economic power has brought some freedom in Sao Thomé, unrestrained Portuguese and English capital still rules in parts of Angola and in Portuguese East Africa, where no resisting public opinion in England has yet been aroused. This shadow hangs heavily over Portugal.

The African shadows of Spain and Italy are but drafts on some imperial future not yet realized, and touch home industry and democracy only through the war budget. But Spain is pouring treasure into a future Spanish Morocco, and Italy has already poured out fabulous sums in the attempt to annex north and northeast Africa, especially Abyssinia. The prince who is to-day visiting Europe is the first adult successor of that black Menelik who humbled Italy to the dust at Adowa in 1896. Insurgent Morocco, independent Abyssinia and Liberia are, as it were, shadows of Europe on Africa unattached, and as such they curiously threaten the whole imperial program. On the one hand, they arouse democratic sympathy in homeland which makes it difficult to submerge them; and again, they are temptations to agitation for freedom and autonomy on the part of other black and subject populations. What prophet can tell what world-tempest lurks in these cloud-like shadows? Then, there is Belgium.

The Shadow of Belgium

THERE IS A LITTLE BLACK man in Belgium, whose name is Mfumu Paul Panda. He is filled with a certain resentment against me and American Negroes. He writes me now and then, but fairly spits his letters at me,—and they are always filled with some defense of Belgium in Africa, or rather with some accusation against England, France and Portugal there. I do not blame Panda, although I do not agree with his reasoning. Unwittingly summer before last I tore his soul in two. His reason knows that I am right, but his heart denies his reason. He was nephew and therefore by African custom heir of a great chief who for thirty years, back to the time of Stanley, has co-operated with white Belgium. As a child of five, young Panda was brought home from the Belgian Congo by a Belgian official and given to his maiden sister. This sister reared the little black boy as her own, nursed him, dressed him, schooled him and defended against the criticism of her friends his right to university training. She was his mother, his friend. He loved her and revered her. She guided and loved him. When the second Pan-African Congress came to Brussels it found Panda leader of the small black colony there and spokesman for black Belgium. He had revisited the Congo and was full of plans for reform. And he thought of the uplift of his black compatriots in terms of reform. All this the Pan-African Congress changed. First it brought on his head a storm of unmerited abuse from the industrial press: we were enemies of Belgium; we were pensioners of the Bolshevists; we were partisans of England. Panda hotly defended us until he heard our speeches and read our resolutions.

The Pan-African Congress revealed itself to him with a new and unexplicable program. It talked of Africans as intelligent, thinking, self-directing and voting men. It envisaged an Africa for the Africans and governed by and for Africans, and it arraigned white Europe, including Belgium, for nameless and deliberate wrong in Africa. Panda was perplexed and astonished; and then his white friends and white mother rushed to the defense of Belgium and blamed him for consorting with persons with ideas so dangerous and unfair to Belgium. He turned upon us black folk in complaining wrath. He felt in a sense deceived and betrayed. He considered us foolishly radical. Belgium was not perfect, but was far less blood guilty than other European powers. Panda continues to send me clippings and facts to prove this.

In this last matter he is in a sense right. England and France and Germany deliberately laid their shadow across Africa. Belgium had Africa thrust upon her. Bismarck intended the Congo Free State for Germany and he cynically made vain and foolish Leopold temporary custodian; and even after Bismarck's fall, Germany dreamed of an Africa which should include Congo, half the Portuguese territory and all the French, making Germany the great and dominant African power. For this she fought the Great War.

Meantime, and slowly, Belgium became dazzled by the dream of empire. Africa is but a small part of Britain; Africa is but a half of larger France. But the Congo is eighty-two times the size of little Belgium, and at Tervuren, wily Leopold laid a magic mirror—an intriguing flash of light, a museum set in rare beauty and approached by magnificent vistas—a flash of revealing knowledge such as no other modern land possesses of its colonial possessions. The rank and file of the Belgians were impressed. They dreamed of wealth and glory. They received the Congo from Leopold as a royal gift—shyly, but with secret pride. What nation of the world had so wonderful a colony! and Belgium started to plan its development.

Meantime the same power that exploited the Congo and made red rubber under Leopold—these same great merchants and bankers—still ruled and guided the vast territory. Moreover, Belgium, impoverished by war and conquest, needed revenue as never before. The only difference then between the new Congo and the old was that a Belgian liberal public opinion had a right to ask questions and must be informed. Propaganda intimating that this criticism of Belgium was mainly international jealousy and that the exploitation of black Belgium would eventually lower taxes for the whites,—this was nearly enough to leave the old taskmasters and methods in control in spite of wide plans for eventual education and reform.

I remember my interview with the socialist Minister for Colonies. He hesitated to talk with me. He knew what socialism had promised the worker and what it was unable to do for the African worker, but he told me his plans for education and uplift. They were fine plans, but they remain plans even to-day, and the Belgian Congo is still a land of silence and ignorance, with few schools, with forced industry, with all the land and natural resources taken from the people and handed over to the State, and the State, so far as Congo is concerned, ruled well-nigh absolutely by profitable industry. Thus the African shadow of Belgium gravely and dangerously overshadows that little land.

The Shadow of France

I KNOW TWO BLACK MEN in France. One is Candace, black West Indian deputy, an out-and-out defender of the nation and more French than the French. The other is René Maran, black Goncourt prize-man and author of *Batouala*. Maran's attack on France and on the black French deputy from Senegal has gone into the courts and marks an era. Never before have Negroes criticized the work of the French in Africa.

France's attitude toward black and colored folk is peculiar. England knows Negroes chiefly as colonial "natives" or as occasional curiosities on London streets. America knows Negroes mainly as freedmen and servants. But for nearly two centuries France has known educated and well-bred persons of Negro descent; they filtered in from the French West Indies, sons and relatives of French families and recognized as such under the Code Napoleon, while under English law similar folk were but nameless bastards. All the great French schools have had black students here and there; the professions have known many and the fine arts a few scattered over decades; but all this was enough to make it impossible to say in France as elsewhere that Negroes cannot be educated. That is an absurd statement to a Frenchman. It was not that the French loved or hated Negroes as such; they simply grew to regard them as men with the possibilities and shortcomings of men, added to an unusual natural personal appearance.

Then came the war and France needed black men. She recruited them by every method, by appeal, by deceit, by half-concealed force. She threw them ruthlessly into horrible slaughter. She made them "shock" troops. They walked from the tall palms of Guinea and looked into the mouths of Krupp guns without hesitation, with scarcely a tremor. France watched them offer the blood sacrifice for their adopted motherland with splendid *sang-froid*, often with utter abandon.

But for Black Africa, Germany would have overwhelmed France before American help was in sight. A tremendous wave of sentiment toward black folk welled up in the French heart. And back of this sentiment came fear for the future, not simply fear of Germany reborn but fear of changing English interests, fear of unstable America. What Africa did for France in military protection she could easily repeat on a vaster scale; wherefore France proposes to protect herself in future from military aggression by using half a million or more of trained troops from yellow, brown and black Africa. France has 40,000,000 Frenchmen and 60,000,000 Colonials. Of these Colonials, 845,000 served in France during the war, of whom 535,000 were soldiers and 310,000 in labor contingents. Of the soldiers, 440,000 came from North and West Africa. The peace footing of the French army is now 660,000, to whom must be added 189,000 Colonial troops. With three years' service and seven years' reserve, France hopes in ten years' time to have 400,000 trained Colonial troops and 450,000 more ready to be trained. These Colonial troops will serve part of their time in France.

This program brings France face to face with the problem of democratic rule in her colonies. French industry has had wide experience in the manipulation of democracy at home, but her colonial experience is negligible. Legally, of course, the colonies are part of France. Theoretically colonials are French citizens and already the blacks of the French West Indies and the yellows and browns of North Africa are so recognized and represented in Parliament. Four towns of Senegal have similar representation; but beyond this matters hesitate.

All this brings, however, both political and economic difficulties. Diagne, black deputy from Senegal, was expelled from the Socialist party because he had made no attempt to organize a branch of the party in his district. And the whole colonial bloc stand outside the interests of home political parties, while these parties know little of the particular local demands of colonies. As this situation develops there will come the question of the practicality of ruling a world nation with one law-making body. And if devolution of power takes place what will be the relation of self-governing colonies to the mother country?

But beyond this more or less nebulous theory looms the immediately practical problem of French industry. The French nation and French private industry have invested huge sums in African colonies, considering black Africa alone. Dakar is a modern city superimposed on a native market place. Its public buildings, its vast harbor, its traffic are imposing. Conakry has miles of warehouses beneath its beautiful palms. No European country is so rapidly extending its African railways—one may ride from St. Louis over halfway to Timbuktu and from Dakar 1,500 miles to the Gulf of Guinea.

The question is, then, will France be able to make her colonies paying industrial investments and at the same time centers for such a new birth

ALAIN LOCKE

of Negro civilization and freedom as will attach to France the mass of black folk in unswerving loyalty and will to sacrifice. Such a double possibility is to-day by no means clear. French industry is fighting to-day a terrific battle in Europe for the hegemony of reborn Central Europe. The present probabilities are that the future spread of the industrial imperialism of the West will be largely under French leadership. French and Latin imperialism in industry will depend on alliance with western Asia, northern and central Africa, with the Congo rather than the Mediterranean as the southern boundary. Suppose that this new Latin imperialism emerging from the Great War developed a new antithesis to English imperialism where blacks and browns and yellows, subdued, cajoled and governed by white men, form a laboring proletariat subject to a European white democracy which industry controls; suppose that, contrary to this, Latin Europe should evolve political control with black men and the Asiatics having a real voice in Colonial government, while both at home and in the colonies democracy in industry continued to progress; what would this cost? It would mean, of course, nothing less than the giving up of the idea of an exclusive White Man's World. It would be a revolt and a tremendous revolt against the solidarity of the West in opposition to the South and East. France moving along this line would perforce carry Italy, Portugal and Spain with it, and it is the fear of such a possible idea that explains the deep-seated resentment against France on the part of England and America. It is not so much the attitude of France toward Germany that frightens white Europe, as her apparent flaunting of the white fetish. The plans of those who would build a world of white men have always assumed the ultimate acquiescence of the colored world in the face of their military power and industrial efficiency, because of the darker world's lack of unity and babel of tongues and wide cleft of religious differences. If now one part of the white world bids for dark support by gifts of at least partial manhood rights, the remainder of the white world scents treason and remains grim and unyielding in its heart. But is it certain that France is going to follow this program?

I walked through the native market at St. Louis in French Senegal—a busy, colorful scene. There was wonderful work in gold filigree and in leather, all kinds of beads and bracelets and fish and foods. Mohammedans salaamed at sunset, black-veiled Moorish women glided like somber ghosts with living eyes; mighty black men in pale burnooses strode by,—it was all curious, exotic, alluring. And yet I could not see quite the new thing that I was looking for. There was no color line particularly visible and yet there was all the raw material for it. Most of the white people were in command holding government office and getting large incomes. Most of the colored and black folk were laborers with small incomes. In the fashionable cafés you seldom saw colored folk, but you did see them now and then and no one seemed to object. There were schools, good schools, but they fell short of anything like universal education for the natives. White and colored school children ran and played together, but the great mass of children were not in school.

As I looked more narrowly, what seemed to be happening was this: the white Frenchmen were exploiting black Africans in practically the same way as white Englishmen, but they had not yet erected or tried to erect caste lines. Consequently, into the ranks of the exploiters there arose continually black men and mulattoes, but these dark men were also exploiters. They had the psychology of the exploiters. They looked upon the mass of people as means of wealth. The mass therefore had no leadership. There was no one in the colony except the unrisen and undeveloped blacks who thought of the colony as developing and being developed for its own sake and for the sake of the mass of the people there. Everyone of intelligence thought that Senegal was being developed for the sake of France and inevitably they tended to measure its development by the amount of profit.

If this sort of thing goes on will not France find herself in the same profit-taking colonial industry as England? Indeed, unless she follows English methods in African colonies can she compete with England in the amount of profit made, and if she does not make profit out of her colonies how long will her industrial masters submit without tremendous industrial returns? Or if these industrial returns come, what will be the plight of black French Africa? *Batouala* voices it. In the depths of the French Congo one finds the same exploitation of black folk as in the Belgian Congo or British West Africa. The only mitigation is that here and there in the Civil Service are black Frenchmen like René Maran who can speak out; but they seldom do.

For the most part, as I have said, in French Africa, educated Africans are Europeans. But if education goes far and develops in Africa a change in this respect must come. For this, France has a complete theoretical system of education beginning with the African village and going up to the colleges and technical schools at Goree. But at present it is, of course, only a plan and the merest skeleton of accomplishment. On the picturesque island of Goree whose ancient ramparts face modern and commercial Dakar I saw two or three hundred fine black boys of high school rank gathered in from all Senegal by competitive tests and taught thoroughly by excellent French teachers in accordance with a curriculum which, as far as it went, was equal to that of any European school; its graduates could enter the higher schools of France. A few hundred students out of a black population of nineteen millions is certainly but a start. This development will call for money and trained guidance and will interfere with industry. It is not likely that the path will be followed and followed fast unless black French leaders encourage and push France, unless they see the pitfalls of American and English race leadership and bring the black apostle to devote himself to race uplift not by the compulsion of outer hate but by the lure of inner vision.

As yet I see few signs of this. I have walked in Paris with Diagne who represents Senegal—all Senegal, white and black,—in the French parliament. But Diagne is a Frenchman who is accidentally black. I suspect Diagne rather despises his own black Wolofs. I have talked with Candace, black deputy of Guadaloupe. Candace is virulently French. He has no conception of Negro uplift, as apart from French development. One black deputy alone, Boisneuf of Martinique, has the vision. His voice rings in parliament. He made the American soldiers keep their hands off the Senegalese. He made the governor of Congo apologize and explain; he made Poincaré issue that extraordinary warning against American prejudice. Is Boisneuf an exception or a prophecy?

One looks on present France and her African shadow, then, as standing at the parting of tremendous ways; one way leads toward democracy for black as well as white—a thorny way made more difficult by the organized greed of the imperial profit-takers within and without the nation; the other road is the way of the white world, and of its contradictions and dangers, English colonies may tell.

The Shadow of England

I LANDED IN SIERRA LEONE last January. The great Mountain of the Lion crouched above us, its green sides trimmed with the pretty white villas of the whites, while black town sweltered below. Despite my diplomatic status I was haled before the police and in the same room where criminals were examined I was put through the sharpest grilling I ever met in a presumably civilized land. Why? I was a black American and the English fear black folk who have even tasted freedom. Everything that America has done crudely and shamelessly to suppress the Negro, England in Sierra Leone has done legally and suavely so that the Negroes themselves sometimes doubt the evidence of their own senses: segregation, disfranchisement, trial without jury, over-taxation, "Jim Crow" cars, neglect of education, economic serfdom. Yet all this can be and is technically denied. Segregation? "Oh no," says the colonial official, "anyone can live where he will—only that beautiful and cool side of the mountain with fine roads, golf and tennis and bungalows is assigned to government officials." Are there black officials? "Oh yes, and they can be assigned residences there, too." But they never have been. The Negroes vote and hold office in Freetown—I met the comely black and cultured mayor—but Freetown has almost no revenues and its powers have been gradually absorbed by the autocratic white colonial government which has five million dollars a year to spend. Any government prosecutor can abolish trial by jury in any case with the consent of the judge, and all judges are white. White officials ride in special railway carriages and I am morally certain—I cannot prove it—that more is spent by the government on tennis and golf in the colony than on popular education.

These things, and powerful efforts of English industry to reap every penny of profit for England in colonial trade, leaving the black inhabitants in helpless serfdom, have aroused West Africa, and aroused it at this time because of two things—the war, and cocoa in Nigeria. The burden of war fell hard on black and British West Africa. Their troops conquered German Africa for England and France at bitter cost and helped hold back the Turk. Yet there was not a single black officer in the British army or a single real reward save citations and new and drastic taxation even on exports.

But British West Africa had certain advantages. After the decline of the slave trade and before the discovery that slavery and serfdom in Africa could be made to pay more than the removal of the laboring forces to other parts of the world, there was a disposition to give over to the natives the black colonies on the fever coast and the British Government announced the intention of gradually preparing West Africans for self-government. Missionary education and the sending of black students to England raised a small Negro intelligentsia which long struggled to place itself at the head of affairs. It had some success but lacked an economic foundation. When the new industrial imperialism swept Africa, with England in the lead, the presence of these educated black leaders was a thorn in the flesh of the new English industrialists. Their method was to crowd these leaders aside into narrower and narrower confines as we have seen in Sierre Leone. But the Negroes in the older colonies retained possession of their land and, suddenly, when the cocoa industry was transferred from Portuguese Africa, they gained in one or two colonies a new and undreamed of economic foundation. Instead of following the large plantation industry, cocoa became the product of the small individual native farm. In 1891 a native sold eighty pounds of the first cocoa raised on the Gold Coast. By 1911 this had increased to 45,000 tons and in 1916 to 72,000 tons. In Nigeria there has also been a large increase, making these colonies to-day the greatest cocoa producing countries in the world.

Moreover, this progress showed again the new democratic problems of colonization, since it began and was fostered by a certain type of white colonial official who was interested in the black man and wanted him to develop. But this official was interested in the primitive black and not in the educated black. He feared and despised the educated West African and did not believe him capable of leading his primitive brother. He sowed seeds of dissension between the two. On the other hand, the educated West African hated the white colonial leader as a supplanter and deceiver whose ultimate aims must be selfish and wrong; and as ever, between these two, the English exploiting company worked gradually its perfect will.

Determined effort was thus made by the English, both merchants and philanthropists, to cut the natives off from any union of forces or of interests with the educated West Africans. "Protectorates" under autocratic white rule were attached to the colonies and the natives in the protectorates were threatened with loss of land, given almost no education and left to the mercy of a white colonial staff whose chief duty gradually came to be the encouragement of profitable industry for the great companies. These companies were represented in the governing councils, they influenced appointments at home and especially they spread in England a carefully prepared propaganda which represented the educated "nigger" as a bumptious, unreasoning fool in a silk hat, while the untutored and unspoiled native under white control was nature's original nobleman. Also they suggested that this "white" control must not admit too many visionaries and idealists.

This policy has not been altogether successful, for the educated Negro is appealing to English democracy and the native is beginning to seek educated black leadership. After many vicissitudes, in 1920 a Congress of West Africa was assembled on the Gold Coast, and from this a delegation was sent to London "to lay before His Majesty the King in Council through the colonial ministry certain grievances." This was an epoch-making effort and, as was natural, the Colonial Office, where imperial industry is entrenched, refused to recognize the delegation, claiming that they did not really represent black West Africa. Nevertheless, through the League of Nations Union and the public press this delegation succeeded in putting its case before the world. They described themselves as "of that particular class of peaceful citizens who, apprehensive of the culminating danger resulting from the present political unrest in West Africa—an unrest which is silently moving throughout the length and breadth of that continent—and also appreciating the fact that the present system of administration will inevitably lead to a serious deadlock between the 'Government and the Governed,' decided to set themselves to the task of ameliorating this pending disaster by putting forward constitutionally a program, the carrying of which into operation will alleviate all pains and misgivings."

The final resolutions of the Congress said, "that in the opinion of this Conference the time has arrived for a change in the Constitution of several British West African colonies, so as to give the people an effective voice in their affairs both in the Legislative and Municipal Governments, and that the Conference pledges itself to submit proposals for such reforms."

The reasons for this demand are thus described:

"In the demand for the franchise by the people of British West Africa, it is not to be supposed that they are asking to be allowed to copy a foreign institution. On the contrary, it is important to notice that the principle of electing representatives to local councils and bodies is inherent in all the systems of British West Africa. . . From the foregoing it is obvious that a system by which the Governor of a Crown Colony nominates whom he thinks proper to represent the people is considered by them as a great anomaly and constitutes a grievance and a disability which they now request should be remedied."

Never before has black Britain spoken so clearly or so cogently. For the most part the African population of the empire has been silent.

Since the war not only has West Africa thus spoken but the colored

West Indies have complained. They want Home Rule and they are demanding it. They asked after the war: Why was it that no black man sat in the Imperial Conference? Why is it that one of the oldest parts of the empire lingers in political serfdom to England and industrial bondage to America? Why is there not a great British West Indian Federation, stretching from Bermuda to Honduras and Guiana, and ranking with the free dominions? The answer was clear and concise—Color.

In 1916 a new agitation for representative government began in Granada. The fire spread to all the West Indies and in 1921 a delegation was received by the Colonial Office in London at the same time that the Second Pan-African Congress was in session.

Here were unusual appeals to English democracy—appeals that not even commercial propaganda could wholly hush. But there was a force that curiously counteracted them. Liberal England, wanting world peace and fearing French militarism, backed by the English thrift that is interested in the restored economic equilibrium, found as one of its most prominent spokesmen Jan Smuts of South Africa, and Jan Smuts stands for the suppression of the blacks.

Jan Smuts is to-day, in his world aspects, the greatest protagonist of the white race. He is fighting to take control of Laurenço Marques from a nation that recognizes, even though it does not realize, the equality of black folk; he is fighting to keep India from political and social equality in the empire; he is fighting to insure the continued and eternal subordination of black to white in Africa; and he is fighting for peace and good will in a white Europe which can by union present a united front to the yellow, brown and black worlds. In all this he expresses bluntly, and yet not without finesse, what a powerful host of white folk believe but do not plainly say in Melbourne, New Orleans, San Francisco, Hongkong, Berlin, and London.

The words of Smuts in the recent Imperial Conference were transcribed as follows: "The tendencies in South Africa, just as elsewhere, were all democratic. If there was to be equal manhood suffrage over the Union, the whites would be swamped by the blacks. A distinction could not be made between Indians and Africans. They would be impelled by the inevitable force of logic to go the whole hog, and the result would be that not only would the whites be swamped in Natal by the Indians but the whites would be swamped all over South Africa by the blacks and the whole position for which the whites had striven for two hundred years or more now would be given up. So far as South Africa was concerned, therefore, it was a question of impossibility. For white South Africa it was not a question of dignity but a question of existence."

Back of all these attitudes is Fear. Back of the whole British Imperial Conference was fear. The worlds of color to-day are curiously and nicely balanced—a little push here, a little yielding there and the end of the vast resulting movements may be anything. The dominating thing in that Conference was the fear of the colored world.

This almost naïve setting of the darker races beyond the pale of democracy and of modern humanity was listened to with sympathetic attention in England. It is without doubt to-day the dominant policy of the British Empire. Can this policy be carried out? It involves two things—acquiescence of the darker peoples and agreement between capital and labor in white democracies.

This agreement between capital and labor in regard to colored folk cannot be depended on. First of all, no sooner is colored labor duly subordinate, voiceless in government, efficient for the purpose and cheap, than the division of the resultant profit is a matter of dispute. This is the case even in South Africa and it came as a singular answer to Smuts. In South Africa white labor is highly paid, can vote, and by a system of black helpers occupies an easy and powerful position. It can only retain this position by vigorously excluding blacks from certain occupations and by beating their wages down to the lowest point even when as helpers they are really doing the prohibited work. It is to the manifest interest of capitalists and investors to breach if not overthrow this caste wall and thus secure higher profits by cheaper and more pliable labor. Already South African courts are slowly moving toward mitigating the law of labor caste and in retaliation the white labor unions have joined Smuts' political enemies, the English-hating Boer party of independence, and have overthrown the great premier.

But how curious are these bedfellows—English capital and African black labor against Dutch home-rulers and the trades unions. The combinations are as illogical as they are thought-producing, for after all if South Africa is really bent on independence she must make economic and political peace with the blacks; and if she hates Negroes more than she hates low wages she must submit even more than now to English rule.

Now what is English rule over colored folk destined to be? Here comes the second puzzling result of the Smuts philosophy. I was in

London on the night of the Guild Hall banquet when the Prime Minister spoke on "Empire Policy and World Peace" and gave a sort of summing up of the work of the Imperial Conference. It was significant that in the forefront of his words, cheek by jowl with Imperial "foreign policy," stood the "intensity of feeling in India on the question of the status of British Indians in the Empire." What indeed could be more fundamental than this in the building of world peace? Are the brown Indians to share equally in the ruling of the British Empire or are they an inferior race? And curiously enough, the battle on this point is impending not simply in the unchecked movement toward "swaraj" in India but in Africa—in the Union of South Africa and in Kenya.

In South Africa, despite all Imperial explanations and attempts to smooth things out, Smuts and the Boers have taken firm ground: Indians are to be classed with Negroes in their social and political exclusion. South Africa is to be ruled by its minority of whites. But if this is blunt and unswerving, how much more startling is Kenya. Kenya is the British East Africa of pre-war days and extends from the Indian Ocean to the Victoria Nyanza and from German East Africa to Ethiopia. It is that great roof of the African world where, beneath the silver heads of the Mountains of the Moon, came down in ancient days those waters and races which founded Egypt. The descendant races still live there with fine physique and noble heads—the Masai warriors whom Schweinfurth heralded, the Dinka, the Galla, and Nile Negroes—the herdsmen and primitive artisans of the beautiful highlands. Here was a land largely untainted by the fevers of the tropics and here England proposed to send her sick and impoverished soldiers of the war. Following the lead of South Africa, she took over five million acres of the best lands from the 3,000,000 natives, herded them gradually toward the swamps and gave them, even there, no sure title; then by taxation she forced sixty per cent of the black adults into working for the ten thousand white owners for the lowest wage. Here was opportunity not simply for the great landholder and slave-driver but also for the small trader, and twenty-four thousand Indians came. These Indians claimed the rights of free subjects of the empire—a right to buy land, a right to exploit labor, a right to a voice in the government now confined to the handful of whites.

Suddenly a great race conflict swept East Africa—orient and occident, white, brown and black, landlord, trader and landless serf. When the Indians asked rights, the whites replied that this would injure the rights of the natives. Immediately the natives began to awake. Few of them were educated but they began to form societies and formulate grievances. A black political consciousness arose for the first time in Kenya. Immediately the Indians made a bid for the support of this new force and asked rights and privileges for all British subjects—white, brown and black. As the Indian pressed his case, white South Africa rose in alarm. If the Indian became a recognized man, landholder and voter in Kenya, what of Natal?

The British Government speculated and procrastinated and then announced its decision: East Africa was primarily a "trusteeship" for the Africans and not for the Indians. The Indians, then, must be satisfied with limited industrial and political rights, while for the black native— the white Englishman spoke! A conservative Indian leader, speaking in England after this decision, said that if the Indian problem in South Africa were allowed to fester much longer it would pass beyond the bounds of domestic issue and would become a question of foreign policy upon which the unity of the Empire might founder irretrievably. The Empire could never keep its colored races within it by force, he said, but only by preserving and safeguarding their sentiments.

Perhaps this shrewd Kenya decision was too shrewd. It preserved white control of Kenya but it said in effect: "Africa for the Africans!" What then about Uganda and the Sudan, where a black leadership exists under ancient forms; and, above all, what about the educated black leadership in the West Indies and West Africa? Why should black West Africa with its industrial triumphs like Nigeria be content forever with a Crown Government, if Africa is for the Africans?

The result has been a yielding by England to the darker world— not a yielding of much, but yielding. India is to have a revision of the impossible "diarachy"; all West Africa is to have a small elective element in its governing councils; and even the far West Indies have been visited by a colonial undersecretary and parliamentary committee, the first of its kind in the long history of the islands. Their report is worth quoting in part: "Several reasons combine to make it likely that the common demand for a measure of representative government will in the long run prove irresistible. The wave of democratic sentiment has been powerfully stimulated by the war. Education is rapidly spreading and tending to produce a colored and black intelligentsia of which the members are quick to absorb elements of knowledge requisite for entry into learned professions and return from travel abroad with minds emancipated and enlarged, ready to devote time and energy to propaganda among their own people."

Egypt too is Africa and the Bilad-es-Sudan, Land of the Blacks, has in its eastern reaches belonged to Egypt ever since Egypt belonged to the Sudan—ever since the Pharaohs bowed to the Lords of Meroe. Fifty times England has promised freedom and independence to Egypt and to-day she keeps her word by seizing the Sudan with a million square miles, six million black folk and twenty million dollars of annual revenue. But Egypt without the Sudan can never be free and independent and this England well knows, but she will hold the Sudan against Egypt as "trustee" for the blacks. That was a fateful step that the new Conservatives took after the Sirdar was murdered by hot revolutionists. Its echo will long haunt the world.

If now England is literally forced to yield some measure of self-government to her darker colonies; if France remains steadfast in the way in which her feet seem to be tending; if Asia arises from the dead and can no longer be rendered impotent by the opium of international finance, what will happen to imperialistic world industry as exemplified in the great expansion of the nineteenth and early twentieth centuries?

Labor in the Shadows

THIS IS THE QUESTION THAT faces the new labor parties of the world—the new political organizations which are determined to force a larger measure of democracy in industry than now obtains. The trade union labor movement dominant in Australia, South Africa and the United States has been hitherto autocratic and at heart capitalistic, believing in profit-making industry and wishing only to secure a larger share of profits for particular guilds. But the larger labor movement following the war envisages through democratic political action real democratic power of the mass of workers in industry and commerce. Two questions here arise: Will the new labor parties welcome the darker race to this industrial democracy? And, if they do, how will this affect industry?

The attitude of the white laborer toward colored folk is largely a matter of long continued propaganda and gossip. The white laborers can read and write, but beyond this their education and experience are limited and they live in a world of color prejudice. The curious, most childish propaganda dominates us, by which good, earnest, even intelligent men have come by millions to believe almost religiously that white folk are a peculiar and chosen people whose one great accomplishment is civilization and that civilization must be protected from the rest of the world by cheating, stealing, lying, and murder. The propaganda, the terrible, ceaseless propaganda that buttresses this belief day by day—the propaganda of poet and novelist, the uncanny welter of romance, the half knowledge of scientists, the pseudo-science of statesmen—all these, united in the myth of mass inferiority of most men, have built a wall which many centuries will not break down. Born into such a spiritual world, the average white worker is absolutely at the mercy of its beliefs and prejudices. Color hate easily assumes the form of a religion and the laborer becomes the blind executive of the decrees of the masters of the white world; he votes armies and navies for "punitive" expeditions; he sends his sons as soldiers and sailors; he composes the Negro-hating mob, demands Japanese exclusion and lynches untried prisoners. What hope is there that such a mass of dimly thinking and misled men will ever demand universal democracy for all men?

The chief hope lies in the gradual but inevitable spread of the knowledge that the denial of democracy in Asia and Africa hinders its complete realization in Europe. It is this that makes the Color Problem and the Labor Problem to so great an extent two sides of the same human tangle. How far does white labor see this? Not far, as yet. Its attitude toward colored labor varies from the Russian extreme to the extreme in South Africa and Australia. Russia has been seeking a *rapprochement* with colored labor. She is making her peace with China and Japan. Her leaders have come in close touch with the leaders of India. Claude McKay, an American Negro poet travelling in Russia, declares: "Lenin himself grappled with the question of the American Negroes and spoke on the subject before the Second Congress of the Third International. He consulted with John Reed, the American journalist, and dwelt on the urgent necessity of propaganda and organization work among the Negroes of the South."

Between these extremes waver the white workers of the rest of the world. On the whole they still lean rather toward the attitude of South Africa than that of Russia. They exclude colored labor from empty Australia. They sit in armed truce against them in America where the Negroes are forcing their way into ranks of union labor by breaking strikes and underbidding them in wage.

It is precisely by these tactics, however, and by hindering the natural flow of labor toward the highest wage and the best conditions in the world that white labor is segregating colored labor in just those parts of the world where it can be most easily exploited by white capital and thus giving white capital the power to rule all labor, white and black, in the rest of the world. White labor is beginning dimly to see this. Colored labor knows it, and as colored labor becomes more organized and more intelligent it is going to spread this grievance through the white world.

The Shadow of Shadows

How much intelligent organization is there for this purpose on the part of the colored world? So far there is very little. For while the colored people of to-day are common victims of white culture, there is a vast gulf between the red-black South and the yellow-brown East. In the East long since, centuries ago, there were mastered a technique and philosophy which still stand among the greatest the world has known; and the black and African South, beginning in the dim dawn of time when beginnings were everything, have evolved a physique and an art, a will to be and to enjoy, which the world has never done without and never can. But these cultures have little in common, either to-day or yesterday, and are being pounded together artificially and not attracting each other naturally. And yet quickened India, the South and West African Congresses, the Pan-African movement, the National Association for the advancement of Colored People in America, together with rising China and risen Japan—all these at no distant day may come to common consciousness of aim and be able to give to the labor parties of the world a message that they will understand.

After all, the darker world realizes the industrial triumphs of white Europe—its labor-saving devices, its harnessing of vast radical forces, its conquest of time and space by goods-production, railway, telephone, telegraph and flying machine, it sees how the world might enjoy these things and how it does not, how it is enslaved by its own ingenuity, mechanized by its own machinery. It sees Western civilization spiritually bankrupt and unhappy.

Africa is happy. The masses of its black folk are calmly contented, save where what is called "European" civilization has touched and uprooted them. They have a philosophy of life logical and realizable.

Their children are carefully educated for the life they are to lead. There are no prostitutes, there is no poverty. In Asia too (although here I speak by hearsay, knowing Asiatics but not Asia) there is, over vast spiritual areas, peace and self-realization; a certain completeness of individual life; a worship of beauty even among the masses; adequate handling of matter for certain personal ends and satisfactions, and a religious spirit which is neither hypocritical nor unbelieving. On the other hand Africa and Asia have no command of technique or mastery of physical force that can compare with that of the West; they know practically nothing of mass-time production and their knowledge of the facts of the universe is far behind modern knowledge.

That comfort is necessary to complete human happiness, who can for a moment doubt? But what shall the world pay for this completeness— what is it paying now? First of all, it has in the heyday of its triumph been able or willing to supply comfort but to a minority of its own population. The majority of the whole people of Europe have poor food, inadequate clothing, bad shelter, inadequate amusement and misleading education. They are more comfortable than the African savages only in their water supply, their foods and their opportunity to look at brilliantly lighted streets.

To save then this efficient organization of work, this synchronization of human industrial effort the like of which the world never before saw—to save this, and led by the idea that at all hazards it must be saved, white Western Europe has long been united in a determination to make the colored worlds contribute to its comfort, subordinate themselves to its interests, become part of its machine. It argues that on this path alone lies salvation for the lazy South and the sleepy East; that upon them lies the salvation of the world; and they ignore with perfect ignorance the possibility that lazy enjoyment and silent contemplation of life, without a surplus or even a sufficiency of modern comfort may for a moment be held an end and ideal of existence; or that the efficient West and North can learn of the lazy South and sleepy East.

If now the world, and particularly the laboring world, should come to realize that industrial efficiency as measured by the amount of goods made and the size of the private profit derived therefrom is not the greatest thing in the world; and that by exchanging European efficiency for African leisure and Asiatic contemplation they might gain tremendously in happiness, the world might be less afraid to give up economic imperialism. Moreover, future economic imperialism can only be held together by militarism. Militarism is costly and to increasing masses of men since the Great War, hateful; more than this—the darker world is held in subjection to Europe by its own darker soldiers. Africa is owned and held almost entirely by Europe; but at the same time Africa is held and kept in subjection to Europe by black troops; black troops in the Sudan, black troops in French Africa, black troops in British West Africa, black troops in Belgian Congo, black troops in Italian Africa, black troops in Kenya, in Uganda, and in former German Africa. Mutual jealousies, widespread ignorance, tribal hatreds and red uniforms make this to-day a most effective method of military control. But for how many years can this be depended upon? Indian soldiers hold India in subjection to England and France. They cannot always be expected to do this. Some day they are bound to awake.

Above all this rises the shadow of two international groups—the Jews and the modern Negroes. The Jews are, in blood, Spanish, German, French, Arabian and American. Their ancient unity of religious faith is crumbling, but out of it all has come a spiritual unity born of suffering, prejudice and industrial power which can be used and is being used to spread an international consciousness. Where this spirit encounters a rampant new nationalism as in Poland or bitter memories of national loss as in Germany, or racial bigotry as in America, it stirs an Anti-Semitism as cruel as it is indefinite and armed in fact not against an abused race but against any spirit that works or seems to work for the union of human kind.

And toward this same great end a new group of groups is setting its face. Pan-Africanism as a living movement, a tangible accomplishment, is a little and negligible thing. But there are twenty-three millions of Negroes in British West Africa, eighteen millions in French Africa, eleven millions and more in the United States; between eight and nine millions each in the Belgian Congo and Portuguese Africa; and a dozen other lands in Africa and America have groups ranging from two to five millions. This hundred and fifty millions of people are gaining slowly an intelligent thoughtful leadership. The main seat of their leadership is to-day the United States.

In the United States there are certain unheralded indications of development in the Negro problem. One is the fact that for the first time in America, the American Negro is to-day universally recognized as capable of speaking for himself. To realize the significance of this one has but to remember that less than twenty-five years ago a conference of friends of the Negro could meet at Lake Mohonk to discuss his problems without a single Negro present. And even later than that, great magazines could publish symposiums on the "Negro" problem without thinking of inviting a single Negro to participate. Again, a revolution is happening under our eyes with regard to lynching. For forty years, not less than a Negro a week and sometimes as many as five a week have been lynched in order to enforce race inferiority by terrorism. Suddenly this number in 1923 was cut in half and it looks as though the record of 1924 was going to be not more than one Negro lynched each month and all this was due primarily to the tremendous onslaught of the National Association for the Advancement of Colored People against lynching and their broad-casting of the facts.

Finally and just as important is the new national policy as to immigration, born of war. This policy is seemingly a tremendous triumph of the "Nordics" and not only cuts down the foreign immigration to the United States from 1,000,000 a year to 160,000, but also seeks to exclude the Latins and Jews and openly to insult Asiatics. Now despite the inhumanity of this, American Negroes are silently elated at this policy. As long as the northern lords of industry could import cheap, white labor from Europe they could encourage the color line in industry and leave the Negroes as peons and serfs at the mercy of the white South. But to-day with the cutting down of foreign immigration the Negro becomes the best source of cheap labor for the industries of the white land. The bidding for his services gives him a tremendous sword to wield against the Bourbon South and by means of wholesale migration he is wielding it. But note again the extraordinary bed fellows involved in this paradox; Negro laborers, white capitalists and "Nordic" fanatics against Latin Europe, Southern task masters, labor unions, the Jews and Japanese!

Led by American Negroes, the Negroes of the world are reaching out hands toward each other to know, to sympathize, to inquire. There are few countries without their few Negroes, few great cities without its groups, and thus with this great human force, spread out as it is in all lands and languages, the world must one day reckon. We face, then, in the modern black American, the black West Indian, the black Frenchman, the black Portuguese, the black Spaniard and the black African a man gaining in knowledge and power and in the definite aim to end color slavery and give black folk a knowledge of modern culture.

There are those who see in the movement only danger—only the silly agitation of would-be fomenters of trouble. They discount it, laugh at it and secretly and openly obstruct it. When the Pan-African Congress planned to meet in Brussels all the industrial exploiters of the Belgian Congo united to misrepresent its objects, distort its actions and punish its local supporters. When the same Congress met in France strong pressure was exerted to keep it from any interference with the investments of French capital in Africa. When the Congress met in England it was dubbed "French" in sympathy and anarchistic in tendency. And yet slowly but surely the movement grows and the day faintly dawns when the new force for international understanding and racial readjustment will and must be felt.

To some persons—to more human beings than ever before at one time in the world's history, there came during the Great War, during those terrible years of 1917 and 1918, a vision of the Glory of Sacrifice, a dream of a world greater, sweeter, more beautiful and more honest than ever before; a world without war, without poverty and without hate.

I am glad it came. Even though it was a mirage it was eternally true. To-day some faint shadow of it comes to me again.

My ship seeks Africa. Ten days we crept across the Atlantic; five days we sail to the Canaries. And then turning we sought the curve of that mighty and fateful shoulder of gigantic Africa. Slowly, slowly we creep down the coast in a little German cargo boat. Yonder behind the horizon is Cape Bojador whence in 1441 came the brown Moors and black Moors who through the slave trade built America and modern commerce and let loose the furies of the world. Another day afar we glide past Dakar, city and center of French Senegal. Thereupon we fall down, down to the burning equator past the Guinea and Gambia, to where the Lion mountain glares, toward the vast gulf whose sides are lined with Silver and Gold and Ivory. And now we stand before Liberia; Liberia that is a little thing set upon a Hill;—thirty or forty thousand square miles and two million folk; but it represents to me the world. Here political power has tried to resist the power of modern capital. It has not yet succeeded, but its partial failure is not because the republic is black, but because the world has failed in this same battle; because organized industry owns and rules England, France, Germany, America and Heaven. And can Liberia escape the power that rules the world? I do not know; but I do know unless the world escapes, the world as well as Liberia will die; and if Liberia lives it will be because the World is reborn as in that vision splendid of 1918.

And thus again in 1924 as in 1899 I seem to see the problem of the 20th century as the Problem of the Color Line.

WHO'S WHO OF THE CONTRIBUTORS

LOCKE, ALAIN: editor and contributor, *The New Negro, Negro Youth Speaks, The Negro Spirituals, The Legacy of the Ancestral Arts;* born Philadelphia, Pa., September 13, 1886; educated at Philadelphia public schools; Harvard College, A.B., 1907; graduate study, Oxford University (Rhodes Scholar from Pennsylvania), 1907–10; University of Berlin, 1910–11; Harvard University, Ph.D., 1918; Assistant Professor and Professor of Philosophy, Howard University, Washington, D. C., 1912–25. Author: *Race Contacts and Interracial Relations,* 1916, and numerous articles on social problems and belles lettres. Editor, Harlem Number, *Survey Graphic,* March, 1925.

BARNES, ALBERT C.: *Negro Art and America;* born Philadelphia, Pa.; educated at Central High School, Philadelphia, the University of Pennsylvania, and University of Heidelberg, M.D., University of Pennsylvania, 1892, art collector and connoisseur, and founder of the Barnes Foundation, Merion, Pa. Editor of the *Journal of the Barnes Foundation,* co-editor of *Les Arts a Paris,* and author of the *Art of Painting,* Barnes Foundation Press, 1924.

BRAITHWAITE, WILLIAM STANLEY: *The Negro in American Literature;* born Boston, 1878; educated at public schools of Boston and Newport; poet, journalist, editor, and pioneer anthologist of contemporary American poetry. Author: *Lyrics of Life, The House of Falling Leaves, The Poetic Year, The Story of the Great War.* Compiler of *The Book of Elizabethan Verse, The Book of Georgian Verse, The Book of Restoration Verse.* Contributing editor, the *Boston Transcript;* Spingarn Medallist, 1918.

FISHER, RUDOLPH: *The City of Refuge* and *Vestiges;* born Washington, D. C., 1897; educated at public schools of New York and Providence, R. I., Brown University, A.B. and A.M., 1920 (Phi Beta Kappa, Delta Sigma Rho, and Sigma XI); Howard University Medical School, M.D., 1924. Has published short stories in the *Atlantic Monthly, Survey Graphic,* and *The Crisis.* First story prize winner in the Amy Spingarn Prize Contest for 1925.

TOOMER, JEAN: *Carma-Fern,* from *"Cane";* born Washington, D. C., 1894; educated at public schools and Dunbar High, Washington; after a varied experience of travel, taught four months at Sparta,

Ga.; since then has lived in New York. Frequent contributor to *The Little Review, Secession, The Double Dealer, Broom, Opportunity,* and *The Crisis.* Author: *"Cane,"* a novel, 1923.

MATHEUS, JOHN F.: *Fog;* born Keyser, W. Va.; educated at the public schools, Steubenville, O., Western Reserve University, A.B., 1910, Columbia University, A.M., 1921; teacher of languages, Florida A. & M. College, Tallahassie, 1910–22, since 1922 Professor of Romance Languages, West Virginia Collegiate Institute.

HURSTON, ZORA NEALE: *Spunk;* born Jacksonville, Fla.; educated at Baltimore, Md., Morgan Preparatory, and Howard University; journalism and writing in New York. *Spunk* was the second prize story in the 1925 *Opportunity* Literary Contest.

WALROND, ERIC D.: *The Palm Porch;* born British Guiana, 1898; educated at St. Stephen's Boys' School, Black Rock, Barbadoes, later Canal Zone public schools, and three years, 1913–16, under private tutors in Colon; employed Health Department, Cristobal, and as reporter of the *Star* and *Herald,* 1916–18; came to New York in 1918; spent three years at the College of the City of New York and one year as special student at Columbia University; has served variously as stenographer in the British Recruiting Mission. Associate Editor, the *Brooklyn and Long Island Informer* and later *The Negro World,* and is now Business Manager of *Opportunity.* Contributor of reviews, stories and articles, *Vanity Fair, The New Republic, The Smart Set, the Saturday Review of Literature, Current History, The Independent, Opportunity,* etc.

NUGENT, BRUCE: *Sahdji;* born Washington,. D. C., 1905; educated at public schools and high school, Washington; art student.

CULLEN, COUNTÉE P.: *Selected Poems* and *Heritage;* born New York City, 1903; educated at New York public schools; De Witt Clinton High, New York University, A.B., 1925 (Phi Beta Kappa); student of English and journalism; winner of numerous poetry prize contests; has contributed verse to *Harper's, The Nation, The American Mercury, Scribner's, Survey Graphic, The Crisis, Opportunity, Folio,* etc. Author: *Color,* Harper & Brothers, 1925.

MCKAY, CLAUDE: *Selected Poems;* born Jamaica, 1889, early education there; served in the Kingston Constabulary; came to United States in 1912; two years student of agriculture at Kansas State University; since then has followed journalism and writing; visited Russia in 1921; and has since lived abroad in Germany and France;

formerly associate editor, *The Liberator* and *The Masses;* contributor to these, *The Seven Arts, The Crisis,* etc. Author: *Songs of Jamaica, Spring in New Hampshire* (London), *Harlem Shadows,* Harcourt, Brace and Howe, 1922.

GRIMKE, ANGELINA W.: *The Black Finger;* born Boston, Mass., 1880; educated in private academies and Boston Latin and Normal School, since 1916; teacher of English, Dunbar High School, Washington, D. C. Contributor of verse and essays to numerous magazines. Author of *Rachel,* Cornhill Co., 1920.

SPENCER, ANNE: *Selected Poems;* born Bramwell, W. Va., 1882; educated at Virginia Seminary, Lynchburg, Va., where she now resides; engaged in writing and social work.

JOHNSON, GEORGIA DOUGLAS: *Selected Poems;* born Atlanta, Ga., 1886; educated at Atlanta High School and Oberlin College; frequent verse contributor to *Liberator, The Worker's Monthly, The Crisis,* and *Opportunity.* Author: *The Heart of a Woman and Other Poems,* 1918, *Bronze, a Book of Verse,* Brimmer, 1922.

ALEXANDER, LEWIS: *Enchantment;* born Washington, D. C., 1898; educated at public schools and Dunbar High; has spent two years at Howard University; acted in the Ethiopian Art Theatre Company; member of the Playwriters' Circle and the Ira Aldridge Players.

HUGHES, LANGSTON: *Selected Poems* and *Jazzonia;* born Joplin, Mo., 1902; educated at Lawrence, Kansas and Cleveland High School, Ohio; spent one year at Columbia University; since then has travelled extensively in Africa and Europe "on his own and for the sake of experience"; now living in Washington, D. C. Contributor, *The Crisis, The Worker's Monthly, Vanity Fair, Opportunity.* Author: *The Weary Blues,* a volume of verse. Alfred Knopf, 1925.

GREGORY, MONTGOMERY: *The Drama of Negro Life;* born Washington, D. C., 1888; educated at Harvard College, A.B., 1910; Instructor, Assistant Professor and Professor of English, Howard University, 1911–24; Organizer and Director of the Howard Players, 1919–24, now supervisor of Negro schools, Atlantic City, N. J. Contributor of articles on the drama in various magazines.

FAUSET, JESSIE REDMON: *The Gift of Laughter;* born at Philadelphia, Pa.; educated in the Philadelphia public schools, Cornell University, A.B., special courses at the University of Pennsylvania and the Sorbonne; teacher of French and Latin, Dunbar High

School, Washington; since 1920, Literary Editor of *The Crisis*. Author of numerous magazine articles, verse and stories; also *There is Confusion*, a novel, Boni & Liveright, 1924.

RICHARDSON, WILLIS: *Compromise;* born Wilmington, N. C., 1889; educated at public schools and Dunbar High School, Washington, D. C.; now engaged in the government clerical service; since 1917 has written numerous one act and larger plays, of which the following have been produced: *The Deacon's Awakening*, St. Paul, 1921; *The Chip Woman's Fortune*, by the Chicago Folk Theatre, 1923; *Mortgaged*, by the Howard Players, 1924, and *The Broken Banjo*, the Amy Spingarn Prize Play in New York, 1925. Has contributed articles on Negro Drama to *Opportunity* and *The Crisis*.

ROGERS, JAMES A.: *Jazz at Home;* journalist and correspondent, on staff of *The Messenger* and *The Amsterdam News*, New York. Author: numerous articles and *From Superman to Man*, Chicago, 1917.

SCHOMBURG, ARTHUR A.: *The Negro Digs Up His Past;* born San Juan, Porto Rico; educated public and private schools, and St. Thomas College; came to the United States in 1891, and has since been engaged as law clerk and in business. Author and book collector; president of the American Negro Academy; co-founder of the Negro Society for Historical Research. Author: *Phyllis Wheatley*, a critical edition, Fred Heartman, New York, 1916; *A Check List of American Negro Poetry*, New York, 1916, and numerous historical pamphlets and reprints.

FAUSET, ARTHUR HUFF: *American Negro Folk Lore;* born Flemington, N. J., 1899; educated at Philadelphia public schools, the Central High School and the Philadelphia School of Pedagogy, A.B., University of Pennsylvania, 1921, A.M., *ibid.*, 1924; has taught since 1918 in the Philadelphia public schools, and has specialized in the study of folk lore, making a research of Nova Scotia folk lore under the auspices of the American Folk Lore Society, 1923, and one in the lower South, especially the Mississippi Delta Region, in the summer of 1925.

Part II

KELLOGG, PAUL UNDERWOOD: *The Negro Pioneers;* born Kalamazoo, Mich., 1879; graduate Kalamazoo High School; special courses Columbia University, 1901–06; Hon. A.M. Amherst, 1911; city editor Kalamazoo *Daily Telegraph*, 1898–1901; on staff *The Survey* since 1902; since 1912 editor *The Survey* and the *Survey Graphic;* director *The Pittsburgh Survey*, 1907–08. Editor, *Pittsburgh Survey*. Joint author with Arthur Gleason, *British Labor and the War*, 1918.

JOHNSON, CHARLES S.: *The New Frontage on American Life;* born Bristol, Va.; 1893; A.B. Virginia Union University, 1916; Ph.B. University of Chicago, 1917, graduate study in social science in Chicago while research investigator of the Chicago Urban League, Associate Executive Secretary of the Chicago Race Relations Commission, compiled material and wrote sections of their report, "The Negro in Chicago," 1921, since 1921, director of Research and Publicity, National Urban League, and editor of *Opportunity; a Journal of Negro Life*.

JOHNSON, JAMES WELDON: *The Creation—a Negro Sermon,* and *Harlem, the Culture Capital;* born Jacksonville, Fla., 1872; educated at public schools of Jacksonville, at Atlanta University and at Columbia University, Hon.D.Litt., Atlanta University, Howard University, 1923; taught school in Jacksonville; came to New York and was engaged with J. Rosamund Johnson and others in libretto and song writing for the musical comedy stage; seven years United States Consul in Venezuela and Nicaragua; journalist and publicist; Executive Secretary, The National Association for the Advancement of Colored People, New York City; Spingarn Medallist, 1925. Author: *The Autobiography of an Ex-Colored Man, The English Libretto of Goyescas*, 1915; *Fifty Years and Other Poems*, Cornhill Co., 1917. Editor, *The Book of America Negro Poetry*, Harcourt, Brace & Howe, 1922, and *The Book of American Negro Spirituals*, Viking Press, 1925.

MILLER, KELLY: *Howard; the National Negro University;* born Winnsboro, S. C., 1863; educated at Howard University, A.B., 1886; post graduate study Howard and Johns Hopkins University; since 1890 Professor of Mathematics, and later Professor of Sociology, Howard University and Dean of the College of Arts and Sciences, subsequently the Junior College; author, sociologist, publicist. Author: *Race Adjustment*, 1909; *The Appeal to Conscience,* 1918; *The Everlasting Stain*, 1924, and numerous monographs, articles and pamphlets on education and race questions.

MOTON, ROBERT RUSSA: *Hampton-Tuskegee—Missioners of the Masses;* born Amelia County, Va., 1867; educated at Hampton Institute;

graduated 1890; officer and later Commandant Hampton, 1890–1915; since 1916 Principal of Tuskegee Institute; President Negro Business League since 1919; educator and publicist, member numerous inter-racial committees and foundations; Hon. LL.D., Va. Union and Wilberforce, A.M., Williams, 1923. Author: *Racial Good Will*, 1916; *Finding a Way Out,* an autobiography, 1920, and numerous public addresses and publications.

FRAZIER, E. FRANKLIN: *Durham—Capital of the Black Middle Class;* born Baltimore, September 24, 1894; educated at public schools, Baltimore, Howard University, A.B., 1916; taught Tuskegee, Lawrenceville and Baltimore High School, A.M., Clark University, 1920; Research Fellow, New York School of Social Work, 1920–21; American Scandinavian Foundation Fellow, 1921–22; studied the Co-operative Movement and People's High Schools in Denmark, Professor of Social Science, Morehouse College, 1922–24; since then Director of the Atlanta School of Social Work. Contributor of articles on social problems: *The Crisis, Opportunity, Southern Workman, Howard Review,* and *Journal of Social Forces*.

DOMINGO, W. A.: *The Gift of the Black Tropics;* born Kingston, Jamaica, 1889; educated at public schools and the Board School, Kingston; came to the United States in 1910, and has since been engaged in business and journalism. Editor, *The Emancipator* (1920–21), contributor to *The Messenger, The Crusader, The Negro World, Survey Graphic,* etc.

HERSKOVITS, MELVILLE J.: *The Negro's Americanism;* born Bellefontaine, Ohio; educated at public schools; Ph.B, 1920, the University of Chicago; A.M., 1921, and Ph.D., 1922, Columbia University; Fellow in Anthropology, Board of Fellowships in the Biological Sciences, National Research Council, working on the problem of variability under Racial Crossing with special reference to Negro-White Crossing 1923 to date; Lecturer in Anthropology at Howard University, 1925; and at Columbia University, 1925–26; scientific papers in anthropological and sociological journals and contributor to the *Nation, American Mercury, Survey,* etc.

WHITE, WALTER F.: *The Paradox of Color;* born Atlanta Georgia; educated at public schools and Atlanta University, A.B., 1916; has lived in New York since 1918 as Assistant Executive Secretary of the National Association for the Advancement of Colored People. Has travelled extensively as special investigator for this Association, making reports on numerous lynchings, race riots and other social studies. Contributor to the *Nation, Century, Forum, Freeman, Survey, Liberator, The Outlook, New Republic, The Crisis, Bookman*. Author: *Fire in the Flint*, a novel, Knopf, 1925, and *Flight*, Knopf (in press).

McDougald, Elsie J.: *The Task of Negro Womanhood;* born and educated in New York City, varied experience as teacher, social investigator and vocational guidance expert, the New York Urban League, the Manhattan Trade School, the Henry Street Settlement, the New York branch United States Department of Labor, the New York School system, and now vice-principal of Public School 89. Supervisor of the Women's Trade Union League and Y. W. C. A. Survey, published 1919 as *A New Day for the Colored Woman Worker*. Contributor of articles on welfare and social service work to educational journals, *The Crisis, Opportunity,* and *Survey Graphic*.

Du Bois, W. E. Burghardt: *Worlds of Color;* born at Great Barrington, Mass., 1868; educated at Fisk University, A.B., 1888, Harvard University, 1893, A.B. University of Berlin, graduate study in History and Sociology, Ph.D. (Harvard), 1895; professor of Economics and History at Atlanta University, 1896–1910. Editor, *The Atlanta Studies,* till 1911; since 1910 Director of Publicity, the National Association for the Advancement of Colored People, and Editor of *The Crisis;* author and publicist; founder of the Pan-African Congresses. Author: *The Suppression of the Slave Trade* (Harvard Historical Studies, Vol. I), *The Philadelphia Negro, The Souls of Black Folk, John Brown, a Biography, The Quest of the Silver Fleece, Star of Ethiopia,* a Pageant, 1914; *Darkwater,* 1920; *The Negro,* 1915; *The Gift of Black Folk,* 1924.

A Note About the Author

Alain Locke (1885–1954) was an African American philosopher, scholar, educator, and patron of the arts. Born in Philadelphia, Locke was raised the only child of Pliny Ishmael and Mary Locke. His father was the first Black employee of the United States Postal Service, and his mother was a teacher. He excelled at Central High School before enrolling at Harvard University in 1907, where he was made a member of the Phi Beta Kappa Society, was awarded the Bowdoin prize, and became the first African American recipient of the prestigious Rhodes Scholarship. He attended Hertford College at Oxford, overcoming several rejections from other schools attached to the university to study literature, philosophy, Greek, and Latin. After four years as an assistant professor at Howard University, Locke returned to Harvard to complete his doctoral dissertation on the nature of social values. Back at Howard, he worked as the chair of the philosophy department and advocated for equal pay for Black and white faculty, which ultimately led to his dismissal in 1925. That same year, he expanded an issue of *Survey Graphic*, a sociopolitical magazine, into *The New Negro*, a groundbreaking anthology of writing from Countee Cullen, Langston Hughes, Zora Neale Hurston, Jean Toomer, and himself. *The New Negro* would become a foundational text of the Harlem Renaissance, establishing Locke's reputation as a leading voice on African American arts and culture and a figurehead of the movement. He regained his position at Howard University in 1928, teaching generations of philosophy students until his retirement in 1953. Due to his race and homosexuality, Locke has been long overlooked by scholars and the public at large.

A Note from the Publisher

Spanning many genres, from non-fiction essays to literature classics to children's books and lyric poetry, Mint Edition books showcase the master works of our time in a modern new package. The text is freshly typeset, is clean and easy to read, and features a new note about the author in each volume. Many books also include exclusive new introductory material. Every book boasts a striking new cover, which makes it as appropriate for collecting as it is for gift giving. Mint Edition books are only printed when a reader orders them, so natural resources are not wasted. We're proud that our books are never manufactured in excess and exist only in the exact quantity they need to be read and enjoyed.

Discover more of your favorite classics with Bookfinity™.

- Track your reading with custom book lists.
- Get great book recommendations for your personalized Reader Type.
- Add reviews for your favorite books.
- AND MUCH MORE!

Visit **bookfinity.com** and take the fun Reader Type quiz to get started.

Enjoy our classic and modern companion pairings!